S

THE
POISONED TREE

Kevin Taylor with Keith Mumby

SIDGWICK & JACKSON
LONDON

Acknowledgements

I want to say thank you to all the people who have helped me and my family to survive the bleak years covered in this story. Whether it was a policeman's cheery 'Hello' or a gift of money, the warmth and support received from the people of Manchester has been most moving and welcome. I'd like to list individual names but it would need another book to do so. There is also the possibility that someone may be victimized for their generosity. So, rather than mention only some, and appear to overlook others, I thought it best to keep this a general acknowledgement. Please, all of you, accept my heart-felt thanks and gratitude.

Unquestionably, to my wife, Beryl, I owe an enormous debt for her loyalty and courage throughout the difficult years. I cannot thank her enough, or my daughters, for their love and devotion. It has been a great comfort to have a close-knit family.

I would also like to thank my friend, Dr Keith Mumby, whose considerable writing skills have allowed me to tell this story in an exciting and dramatic way.

Kevin Taylor

Publishers' Note
The publishers wish to acknowledge the contribution of Nick Treeby to the publication of this book.

First published in Great Britain in 1990 by
Sidgwick & Jackson Ltd
1 Tavistock Chambers, Bloomsbury Way
London WC1A 2SG

Copyright © 1990 by Kevin Taylor and Keith Mumby

ISBN 0-283-06056-6

Photoset by Rowland Phototypesetting Ltd
Bury St Edmunds, Suffolk
Printed in Great Britain by
Butler and Tanner Ltd, Frome, Somerset

Contents

Rankings

Reference to the rank of police officers occurs many times in this text. For convenience, abbreviations are used where rank is referred to. A table, in ascending order, of these abbreviations and their meaning is given here to assist the reader:

DC	Detective Constable
D Sgt	Detective Sergeant
DI	Detective Inspector
DCI	Detective Chief Inspector
DS	Detective Superintendent
DCS	Detective Chief Superintendent
ACC	Assistant Chief Constable
DCC	Deputy Chief Constable
CC	Chief Constable

1
Arrest

On 30 September 1987, I rose as usual around 7.30 am. It was to be a day I will never forget. It started quietly, as usual. I had a swim with my wife, Beryl, in our indoor pool. The house had been converted from a sixteenth-century East Lancashire stone mill by the banks of the River Irwell. In earlier times, Wood Mill, as it was called, had made blankets for soldiers in the Napoleonic Wars but finally succumbed during the slump in the textile trade in the 1950s. We had brought it to life again, as a family home. The design, reworking most of the original stone materials, was largely my own and incorporated all the features we wanted.

Although I had my thoughts on other more pressing matters that day, it would have been a good time to reflect on the satisfaction of owning such a house. It was certainly a long way from my origins in the back streets of Salford and, of all the trappings of success, acquired through many years of patient hard work, this one gave my wife and me the most satisfaction.

As well as a pool and jacuzzi there were two substantial lounges. The smaller of the two had heated Italian marble floors and a genuine Adam fireplace, retrieved from the demolition of a country house. The other was fifty feet long, and nearly as wide, with a small cocktail bar at one end. We used it mainly for entertaining. It had a giant back projector for the TV, so that it could be seen across such a large room. On the wall was a mounted bluefish, caught and given to me by Angelo Dundee, the American boxing promoter and manager of Mohammed Ali. Throughout the other rooms, bedrooms and hallways, we displayed our curios and other memorabilia of numerous trips across the world. One of the outstanding features of the house was the beautiful stained-glass windows, made by my uncle, Joseph Ivison, his last work before he died. I suppose it would be right to call it a special house. It had actually been used as a TV film set intended to give the impression of luxury and grandeur; to us it was home. We were comfortable and assured.

In happier days we had held many exciting parties here, attended by people representing all walks of life, from members of parliament and cabinet ministers to out-of-work labourers. Celebrities, especially stars of Manchester's long running soap, *Coronation Street*, were often present on these occasions. Children of the guests were always welcome, and would romp in the pool and jacuzzi while the adults talked and drank. If it was summertime, the party-goers would spill outside onto the lawns, for champagne and canapés, or a buffet overlooking the wooded hills of Summerseat, not far from Bury. The wine-cellar was usually very well stocked and we rarely felt like stinting when we wanted to celebrate. One of my favourite party tricks was to challenge guests to tell the difference between my Margaux, at £40 a bottle, and a Marks and Spencer's Rioja, at £4. The Rioja usually won, and everybody enjoyed the joke at the expense of wine poseurs. These were good times and it once seemed that they would last for ever.

But on this day breakfast was a subdued affair. We ate alone. Our daughters, Kate aged eighteen and Emma aged fifteen, were absent. It was a fortunate coincidence.

The meal was soon over. I got up from the table feeling a great sense of foreboding. Even before I had put on my coat, my wife Beryl, noted for her poise and fortitude, was in tears. The reason for the gloom and despondency was that I was going to work that day, to be arrested for something we both knew I hadn't done.

I held her and comforted her. 'Cheer up,' I said. 'At least now it's out in the open and we know where we stand. We can start fighting and I believe that, in the end, we'll win. We'll beat them.'

And with that, I drove to work, facing a nightmare come true.

At the office, I met Derek Britton, my fifty-four-year-old accountant. He too was to be arrested on the same charge. Yet Britton was one of the most straightforward men I have ever met and incapable of anything dishonest or devious. It was unreal.

Like me, Britton had a lot to lose and not just in the professional sense. After a disastrous first marriage, now in middle age, he had recently re-married. At a time when his peers were going to seed, pottering about the garden in wellingtons at week-ends and reminiscing in pubs about women they'd known, Britton had been given a second chance and seized it. Alma, his pretty young wife, had given birth to a beautiful baby girl, Samantha. Until the present difficulties, happiness and wealth had seemed just around the corner for him. We had been increasingly successful in our property deals and Britton's share would have been enough to retire on comfortably, if he had wished.

Now this.

The arrangement made with the police, through our lawyer, Ian Burton, was that the two of us would meet up and walk over to Bootle Street Police Station, where the formal charging would take place at 10.30 am. Instead, so typical of the numerous petty indignities and deceits that had characterized the investigation since it began, the police violated this agreement, turned up at the office at 10.00 and made a peremptory arrest. Far from being spared any embarrassment, we were to be led humiliatingly across Deansgate, the main street of the city where we were so well known, in custody.

Several policemen were present at the arrest, under the command of Detective Inspector Anthony Stephenson, who had been leading the enquiry into my commercial affairs. By a coincidence, one of the other inspectors assigned to this arrest had been a social friend of mine, probably unknown to his seniors. He looked very uncomfortable but managed a friendly smile in my direction when he thought nobody was looking. Stone-faced, Stephenson informed Britton and me that the Director of Public Prosecutions had decided we should be charged with attempting to defraud the Co-op Bank of £240,000 and he cautioned us that we were not obliged to say anything, but that anything we did say would be written down and could be used in evidence. We both chose to remain silent.

What the majority of officers in the room didn't know was that Sir Thomas Hetherington, the Director of Public Prosecutions, had resisted police pressure to bring these charges for fifteen months. Why, if he considered that there was insufficient evidence to show there was a case to answer, were charges being brought now? Was it any coincidence that our arrest came exactly on the day Hetherington retired from office and could no longer oppose the action?

Stephenson took my safe keys and we were led away, surrounded by policemen. The number of arresting officers was an obvious attempt to make the gravity of the supposed crime seem greater than it was. Given that we had already agreed to present ourselves personally at the police station, with our lawyer, a show of strength was not needed. It was self-evident we were not going to run away; we had had two years since the start of investigations in which to do so if we had wished.

Bootle Street Police Station was a dispiriting place, Dickensian, dingy and intimidating, even to anyone not in custody. Fingerprints

3

and photographs were taken for CID records and afterwards we were given a dirty scrap of rag to wipe the ink from our fingers. It was apparently all that was available. Just another petty detail to undermine the dignity of men who knew they were being wrongfully charged.

Several of the uniformed officers looked distinctly embarrassed at what they were being asked to do. Why should this be so, if it was just a routine case? Throughout the whole four-year phoney investigation into my affairs, only one thing helped me retain even a shred of faith in the police: that was the way the average uniformed officers so clearly showed their disagreement at the injustice of what was being done by a handful of their senior colleagues in the CID.

Until the events that were now overtaking me, I had always held firmly to the Conservative Party line and believed implicitly in the rightness of the police, notwithstanding the fact that one of my acquaintances, an ex-detective, made no secret of the fact that there were men in jail who he had put there by making a perjured statement in court. The justification was always, 'They were crooks anyway, so they deserved what they got.' What was needed to clean up society was 'more law and order'. After all, wasn't that the Gospel emanating from Downing Street?

Now I knew differently. Accusations of police vendettas, corruption and violence no longer appeared simply as left-wing propaganda intended to smear the Establishment and undermine democracy. These were now suddenly a living, frightening reality. One thought kept crossing my mind: if this can happen to me, a pillar of the community, chairman of the Conservative Association and with the wealth to pay for the best lawyers in town, what chance have the poor Asian and black kids in the poverty areas got? The answer, of course, was none.

The echoes of the same shocking truth came home to me again later in the holding cells at the Manchester City Magistrates' Court. I overheard several youths talking among themselves. It wasn't that they were discussing being beaten by the police and showing each other bruises that was disturbing. It was the total lack of surprise or outrage on the part of these youngsters and the fact that they seemed to accept such acts of violence as a normal tenet of life that was so difficult to reconcile with the 'few rotten apples' explanation for police brutality.

Shortly before noon, Britton and I appeared in court before the stipendiary magistrate, Mr Derek Fairclough. We were remanded to appear before a magistrate for a committal hearing at a future date, to be decided. The barrister representing the Crown Prosecution Service was insistent on bail surety, presumably to enhance the illusion that I was a major crook. She mentioned that over £1 million was involved in the fraud, which was never true at any stage. Fortunately, the magistrate appeared sympathetic to our troubles, pointing out we were well-known businessmen, each with a family, and hardly likely to try and solve our problems by absconding. No bail was set and no restrictions on travel imposed. We were free, at least for the time being.

Of course, the arrest was not a total surprise. We knew the investigation into my affairs had been taking place since mid-1985. Indeed, lawyers had been battling with the police over this issue since that date. At first the motive for the enquiry had seemed completely baffling until, in May 1986, it became my absolute certain belief that the police campaign to persecute me stemmed entirely from events that had taken place across the Irish Sea. I am referring to the controversy surrounding the Deputy Chief Constable of Manchester John Stalker's removal from the sensitive enquiry into alleged murders by RUC officers in Northern Ireland.

Stalker was poking his nose into areas where, it seemed, his bosses didn't want him to go, beavering away to get at 'The Truth' and threatening to cause a great deal of embarrassment to the security forces. The justifications for his sacking from the investigation were trivial and vague. Only one charge came anywhere near sufficient weight to excuse such a dramatic and startling action and that was associating with known criminals. Time and again, my name came up in this connection. But I had no criminal history and had never been accused of any wrong-doing in my life. It was well known that I played cards with anyone willing to join me in a hand and that on occasion this sometimes brought me into contact with shady characters. But that didn't make me a crook.

Two months of investigation of Stalker by dozens of detectives from the West Yorkshire Constabulary, at a cost reputed to be in the region of £250,000, failed to find any significant misdemeanour. The police were under pressure to come up with something concrete; otherwise there was going to be egg on some very important chins. It seemed that the only thing to do was to fix me up with a criminal history. So 'Get Stalker' in effect became 'Fit up Taylor'. And that's exactly what happened. Coldly and cynically, a group of police officers within the Greater Manchester Police force set about the task of making me into a criminal, fabricating the charges and concocting evidence.

5

Outrageous? Of course. Incredible? Well it's hardly believable. But it is chillingly true, as you will read in this book.

But there is more to it than police abuses within the GMP. The breathtaking scale of the operation, the profligate expenditures and the cavalier ride through the safeguards of the statutes enshrined in our laws bear all the hallmarks of a higher authority. Nothing on this scale had ever been attempted in the UK before and such a massive high-pressure campaign could not possibly be countenanced, never mind executed, without full planning and co-ordination at the Joint Intelligence Committee level and, yes, that of the Cabinet itself. The implications should cause the reader to shudder.

This is a story of the determined and corrupt abuse of power against the ordinary citizen, frighteningly like the early days of the Third Reich in Germany, when the due processes of law and order were misused for the purpose of destroying or removing imagined enemies of the state. Hitler could not have risen to power without his bully boys, who were supposedly operating within the legal system, at least to begin with. Eventually, as we all know, justice was abandoned totally, in favour of summary imprisonments and executions.

Think about that when you read this narrative. It may be more than an exposé of how certain crooked public officials destroyed one of Britain's top cops by persecuting his close friend. You may be looking at the start of a police state in Britain.

In the end, they failed, and so I am free to tell the tale. But it was a close thing, because of the massive and plausible edifice of lies and false evidence that had been fabricated. It was only because my barrister was able to force into the open real proof of what had been done that I escaped being sent to jail. The most obvious question to the reader will be: how on earth did they ever expect to get away with it? Were these police officers so contemptuous of the judicial system they were supposed to uphold that it meant nothing to them? Or were their bosses higher up so arrogant and cocksure in the belief that everyone in public service can be bought, at a price, and that nowhere along the line there would be an honest judge or official to say 'Enough is enough'? Actually, it may have been neither of these possibilities.

The truth is, the police conspirators expected little trouble in reaching their objective and securing a successful conviction. After all, most businessmen have skeletons in the closet, don't they? Little grey areas? I had a reputation for being a big spender. I was, if I say so myself, known for having a wide circle of friends and I liked to see people happy and didn't mind what it cost. It was assumed I therefore probably had some sort of hidden income, right? It should have been easy to find a crime.

But it wasn't. To their obvious surprise and consternation, the massive (and costly) trawl found nothing of consequence. Not many businessmen in Manchester could survive a detailed scrutiny by over a dozen detectives over a period of three years and come out smelling sweet. The fact that I did, and that the charges when finally brought were so pitifully weak, with such threadbare and contrived evidence, is probably the most eloquent evidence possible that I was essentially clean. If I had been mixed up in drugs, extortion, handling stolen goods or any other organized criminal racket, it would have been discovered within weeks or months at the outside.

Therein lies my chief complaint against my persecutors: they did not give up when it was obvious that I had nothing to hide. Instead, they continued to press for a conviction by underhanded means, solely to justify what had been done to Stalker. In any civilized country, such a blatant attack on an ordinary citizen in pursuit of even a legitimate goal must be anathema and any government which supports such activities is not fit to call itself democratic. What is even more shocking is that, as the reader will learn, the chief perpetrators of this conspiracy tried to obscure their involvement in what was done by using the screen of 'national interest' as a cover.

The joke is that, as my wife was often to say, if I had really committed a crime and been sent to jail, I would have been out again in less time than it took to bring me to trial and I would not have had to suffer the five years of harrowing persecution that were to follow.

Conspiracy to defraud the Co-op Bank? It is crucial to this case that the bank did not make a complaint. Why should it? The bank didn't lose money, it made money from my companies. At all times it was secured in its loans to me by mortgages over property well in excess of the loan. If that were not enough, I gave cross-guarantees on all my companies and unlimited personal guarantees, including a second mortgage on my home. Does that sound like an attempt to swindle the bank? In fact, after the police enquiry started, there was a further offer of a loan. Why would a bank want to give me more money if it thought it was being robbed? One of the important questions in this case is and remains: *when and where was this alleged crime first reported to the police?* The truth is, it never was, but rather the police went out looking for one and that fact alone argues strongly in favour of corrupt intentions on behalf of the police.

One of the biggest difficulties with the prosecution case was that the Co-op Bank had happily lent me money. I had a £2 million facility by 1984 and, as one director testified in court, I was considered a good customer. To plug this breech in their allegation of fraud, the police also charged one of the bank's managers and turned it into a conspiracy case. I had recruited Terence Bowley, the corporate business manager, it was argued, and in 1984 we had hatched between us a plot to defraud the bank of £240,000. To call this accusation far-fetched would be to do those who propounded it a service. It was the hysterical fantasy of desperate and despicable men who would stop at nothing. Consider that Bowley was in sole charge of the Corporate Lending Department, bringing in nearly £70 million of new business a year and handling some very large accounts: why would a man in his position, a high-flier with a glittering career in front of him, stoop to a part-share from swindling a mere £240,000? To him, I was peanuts: Bowley was among the big boys. If he had wanted to defraud the bank – jeopardize his career and his entire future on one twirl of the dice – why would he have settled for such a tiny sum of money when he could have swindled millions of pounds? It wasn't logical.

Even more absurdly, the police were unable to provide a single shred of evidence that Bowley received any financial reward whatever from this so-called conspiracy. Also, I had only met Bowley half a dozen times; the rest of my affairs were conducted by one of his deputies.

But don't think the stupidity of this assertion stopped the prosecution going ahead; on 15 September 1987 Bowley, too, was arrested and charged.

A fourth man was eventually drawn into the web. Vincent McCann, a quantity surveyor, business associate and friend of mine, was arrested and charged with being part of the same conspiracy on 5 October 1987. McCann was so peripheral to my affairs with the bank, the story began to take on a surrealistic aspect. But those who understood the significance of his inclusion realized the cunning of this manoeuvre. There was no question but that McCann would have made a star witness for the defence, and so to silence his potential as such, he was joined to the prosecution. Ultimately, McCann was to spend nearly £40,000 of his own moneey on defending himself, before he was finally ruined and allowed Legal Aid – a very considerable fine for an innocent man. No evidence was brought up in the trial that would justify charging him. But unfortunately, in Britain today, justice is so costly it is beyond the financial means of the average individual. Only the wealthy or the poor can afford it. Once implicated, McCann too was on the road to destitution.

Ultimately, dozens of lives were to be wrecked or damaged by the sprawling tentacles of the Stalker Affair. Men who helped the defence, by lending money and other support, were themselves investigated by the police, who visited their bankers and clients until they could no longer function viably. Even my lawyers were investigated and attacked for trying to help me. Ironically, many of those harmed had never met Stalker but they certainly felt the shock-wave of his professional demise.

After the arrest, months dragged by. In fact, the investigation was still going on intensively over a year later, with more and more requests for adjournment of the committal hearing, as police still tried to cobble together enough evidence to make the prosecution seem credible.

Ultimately, they were still carrying out enquiries and interviewing potential witnesses during the actual trial, in January 1990. I was even being followed right up to the evening before the trial collapsed.

Extraordinary delays seemed to be a feature of everything surrounding the case against me. Ostensibly the enquiry had been going on since 1985 (we reveal that it began in 1984, in fact, as soon as Stalker crossed swords with RUC chiefs), with over a dozen detectives involved at different levels, including the personal intervention of the head of CID, a massive concentration of fire-power when it is seen against the background knowledge that a major international multi-million pound fraud would have been completed in less time and with a fraction of the personnel. As Stalker says in his book (1988), 'In the three years that investigators say they have been looking into [Taylor's] business, his bank accounts and his life, international terrorists and mass murderers have been investigated, tried, convicted and imprisoned.'

Could it be that the CID were afraid to bring their case before the scrutiny of even a magistrate, never mind twelve just men and true? Or was it that they were waging a war of attrition against me to destroy my business and financial resources, so that I was a spent force and couldn't fight back against my oppressors?

What the police hadn't reckoned with is that I would counter-attack. In fact I did so, and I hit hard. In late 1986, we brought a prosecution against three senior police officers for 'conspiring to pervert the course of justice' and only a judgement against us saved the police from catastrophe. So there was an important motive for crippling my resources and we will bring evidence that this is exactly what the police set out to do. Some aspects of the so-called 'investigation' are

9

hard to interpret in any other way than a deliberate act of sabotage. With a sort of *déjà vu*, it calls to mind the police acting as judge, jury and executioner with their shoot-to-kill policy in Ulster, which is where it all began.

This audacity in striking out at my oppressors had the unfortunate effect of unleashing the whole fury of the Establishment against me. Stalker had made them look fools and had earned the full force of their retribution. Now I had done the same thing. Panic set in. Special Branch men were assigned to the case. We can trace over twenty-five man-years of police officers' time spent exclusively on the pursuit of the case against myself. And that makes no allowance for the surveillance squads, accountants' time looking into my companies and lawyers' acting on behalf of the Crown; a total probably in the region of fifty years. Various people involved in the case have estimated the cost to the tax-payer of this prosecution to be, conservatively, in the region of £10,000,000. One legal expert reckoned twice that figure would not be out of reckoning. It would simply not be possible to mount an operation of this kind without the full consent of the government and there can be no doubt of involvement at the highest levels in the crimes exposed in the following pages. Horrified? You should be. We are talking about the squandering of the state exchequer in a dedicated onslaught against one tiny individual, for the sole purpose of protecting the power-mongers who strut in corridors of Whitehall from damaging and inconvenient revelations.

As one lawyer on the case has said: 'I know of no case since the War and in living memory where such an unmerited set of proceedings has been infused with such extravagance and expense.' So much were the costs within the Greater Manchester Police, that we can reveal that funds were diverted from other resources to hide what was really happening. This too argues strongly in favour of a corrupt enquiry. Why should it be necessary to hide costs, if the case truly warrants investigation?

Unquestionably, with such a mountainous investment, the police were committed to keep pushing onward no matter what. They *must* get a conviction of some kind, to avoid humiliation or, even worse, exposure. This stick-at-nothing desperation alarmed me. My worry was that since so much money had been spent on investigating me, the unit involved would do anything in their powers, including planting drugs or false evidence, to justify their actions and avoid being caught out in the folly and wrongness of their attempts to target me. Most inner-city dwellers know of stories of these kind of 'fit-ups' by the police and have a very real dread of being targeted for such actions.

In fact, I lived for over two years with the fear that I would be found conveniently dead in the swimming pool at home having 'committed suicide', because (supposedly) I couldn't stand the ignominy and strain of the criminal investigations, victim of yet another Special Branch take-out. And often, when I passed a window, I found myself thinking, 'Will it be now?' Try to imagine the stress of that.

In theory, at the committal, if the police failed to show sufficient evidence to justify a trial, the case would be thrown out by the magistrate. However, there was no realistic expectation of winning the fight or being exonerated at this stage; it was merely a flexing of muscles. The police had a chance to parade their strength and go for a 'dummy run'. The defence, on the other hand, had resolved to keep most of its best cards close to its chest. There was no point in letting the opposition know how strong our hand was.

Even despite this restraint by my legal team, it was almost a rout for the Greater Manchester Police, as witness after witness shot holes in the fabric of the prosecution case; remember, these were people supposedly testifying for the Crown.

Sinister questions emerged. Why was it that there were remarkable discrepancies between what a witness was supposed to have said in a statement to the police and what that individual came to say on oath in court? Some witnesses, we learned, had been asked to make a second statement, to 'strengthen' their testimony. These second statements were remarkably similar to each other, in some cases almost verbatim. Strange, if the witnesses were speaking spontaneously and without coercion. Also, it was uncovered that many key police witnesses had been shown only selective parts of the documentation and asked to pass an opinion which was adverse to myself and the other defendants. Even more alarmingly, DI Anthony Stephenson, the detective in charge of the case, admitted deliberately withholding from the DPP an important valuation on one of my properties which would have done much to weaken the police allegation of over-valuing land and yet had produced an 'expert witness' to pass an opinion without the benefit of seeing this vital document.

Thus the police case, weak as it was, seemed even more insubstantial under cross-examination. Four defence lawyers, experienced legal men, all with a good 'working relationship' with the police, shared the view that in their combined years of court-room experience they had never seen a case with more pathetic evidence or such a blatant attempt to force the point that someone was guilty when clearly they were not.

Inevitably, the magistrate, Mr David Loy, announced that all defendants were to go forward on all charges, unconditionally. He had apparently been fully satisfied of the need to try the case against myself, Britton and McCann but was concerned about the inclusion of Bowley. Leading counsel for the prosecution added his weight by giving legal authority to the magistrate, pointing out that, even if there was no financial motive, trying to further his career or merely wishing to arrogate a decision to himself to which he was not entitled would be sufficient grounds for there to have been an offence. I found this extraordinary, since no evidence for either of these two subsidiary motives had been produced either. However, Mr Loy concurred with the prosecution and Bowley, too, went forward. Without him, it needs hardly be said, the prosecution case would be worthless.

Conspiracy? Yes, there was a conspiracy all right. An official plot to hound me to destruction. We know the men involved. We can say how they did it. It can all be tied in decisively to John Stalker and it is possible to follow the determined thread of attack against him, going back two years before his removal, and, even more startlingly, we can reveal that it was still going on over seven months after his re-instatement and final resignation. Why? To save some important hides, without doubt.

So secret was this other plot that it acted as a force within a force, a Mafia-style gang of policemen without proper restraint and not answerable to the law. These men met in secret locations (including deserted police stations), ruthlessly suppressed normal communications, by-passed command channels on the orders of the Chief Constable, violated procedures which exist to safeguard individuals and generally behaved like criminals themselves. We know this from our own documentary evidence and it is backed up by information passed to us by ordinary bobbies, who hated what was happening within their profession. Things became so bad, the atmosphere so dark and murky at police headquarters in Chester House, that the morale within the GMP eventually suffered badly as a result. One senior detective describes what he called a 'web of deceit'.

This book gives the whole story and we go far beyond the Stalker Affair. Our version of events is backed up by thousands of pages of documentation, hours of interviews and much foot-slogging in pursuit of the truth. What you will read here are facts that show judicial corruption on a scale that will make you cringe if you were proud of what was once British justice. The Irish people are now rightly alarmed and suspicious of it, if indeed it exists any longer. We have recently felt the shock waves of the scandal of the wrongful jailing of the so-called 'Guildford Four'. Certain members of the police force, it seems, are willing to take it upon themselves to decide who they want to jail and then systematically set about fabricating a case to obtain a successful conviction. 'The police don't know any other way,' says one former prosecuting barrister in Manchester. That's how much cynicism exists today in the legal profession regarding police activities.

The scale of the Guildford Four incident, disgraceful as it is, is nevertheless small, when compared to the magnitude, length and depth of the iniquities that went into the machinations against Stalker and myself. This is not about the bent methods of one or two policemen in trying to pin down the IRA. We are talking now about dozens of detectives, working crookedly for years, in conjunction with Crown Prosecution Service members and senior lawyers, even the involvement of several government departments, to bring about a wholly outrageous abuse of the process of law. In fact, the Stalker Affair, in full, is probably the most heinous misfeasance ever perpetrated by public officials in Britain and one which has irretrievably damaged our image as a nation of civilized and just people, both at home and abroad. Unfortunately, we have a closed secretive government in Whitehall, one too arrogant and elitist to answer to its people, and so some aspects of the story may remain beyond view. The arch-villains will hide behind the net of bureaucracy and the Official Secrets Act and may never be made to answer for their actions.

Of course there will be denials. That's only to be expected. But we have the witnesses ready to speak and thousands of pages of documented evidence. These will be unfolded as the narrative proceeds. But in the meantime, to give the reader a taste of what is to come and to counter any early disbelief, because of the sweeping breadth of these accusations against the government and police force, here are some tantalizing questions that have come to light so far:

> Why was it that after I had tried for months to co-operate with the police, offering myself unreservedly for interview, that search warrants were finally issued by which the police could force entry into places where they had already been offered access?
> Why did police officers, ostensibly involved in a drugs search, not bring sniffer dogs, not lift any floorboards, take merely one hour and remove only photographs showing John Stalker at a party with petty criminals present? Also how did they know exactly where to look in the house for what they wanted, if they had never visited the premises before?

Why was it that head of V Division, C S Topping, was personally involved in such a petty fraud case, to the extent of compromising himself at the Co-op Bank? Normally the head of CID in a force of several thousand men wouldn't even get involved in a multi-million pound fraud, never mind a case this insignificant.

Why were police officers, under the direction of the Chief Constable, involved in entering my bank to gather illegal information several months before obtaining the requisite authority to do so from a judge? Can a senior detective expect us to believe 'nothing was said' during seventeen hours of improper visiting time spent at the bank (stated on oath in court)?

Why did the detective in charge of the case swear false evidence in front of a judge? Why did the judge ask for it to be sealed in an envelope and never opened, except on his direct order?

What was the sinister purpose of the Drugs Intelligence Unit, operating within the GMP? It lasted for three years, cost over one million pounds and never charged anyone, but existed solely to investigate myself and my connections with Stalker (note that a police lawyer, in court, admitted that I was *not* suspected of drugs trafficking).

Why did Chief Constable Jim Anderton forbid Stalker to see the Taylor file when he was reinstated to office? What had he to hide if it was a bona fide enquiry?

Why was information from a well-known informant taken up concerning me, which did not implicate me in any known crime, when the same document gave full details of crimes committed by other Manchester businessmen who were never even interviewed, much less charged?

Why did a man with a Belfast accent put a gun to my head and threaten me but not pull the trigger? Three policemen were in the room at the time and did nothing. Afterwards there were no questions asked. Was this arranged deliberately, to frighten me?

Why were the only police witnesses at my trial non-Masons and was it a coincidence that the senior officers, who *were* Masons, were not asked to appear, even though they had been on the case the longest?

If this was a bona fide case which supposedly had nothing to do with Stalker, why did a junior policeman assigned to my case say in court he had 'never been involved in investigating a Deputy Chief Constable before'? And why did detectives on my case make a number of visits to a night watchman who thought he had seen John Stalker near a property site belonging to one of my companies?

If a real crime was being prosecuted, with evidence of such, why was it necessary to intimidate witnesses and, as emerged in court, threaten several bank witnesses with being charged themselves unless they co-operated? One securities clerk stated he had been forced under duress to sign a statement that he knew contained serious inaccuracies.

Why, if this came out in court, did the prosecution not withdraw their case at once, as would be normal when such gross irregularities came to light?

If there was no conspiracy, how come there was so much support for the rough deal that I received from so many prominent lawyers and why were so many top people in the legal profession (including judges) upset if it wasn't that they saw justice being abused?

Why was John Thorburn [Stalker's Number Two] ordered not to inform John Stalker of events proceeding in Manchester concerning myself and why was his three-point memorandum to Anderton in protest completely ignored, contrary to proper police procedure?

If it was a straightforward case of fraud, why were prisoners in jail offered freedom if they would put something on paper to implicate Stalker and me in crime?

There is more. Much more. We have the full story, at last. Small sections are missing, and indeed may never be known, unless justice is done and the men concerned are brought to trial. In that event, we shall have access to all the appropriate papers. But there is enough of the jig-saw to discern the whole sorry picture.

The fact that the story can be told, in the fullness that has been achieved, is largely a tribute to the courage and tenacity of two men, helped surreptitiously by police officers who knew what was going on and hated it sufficiently to want to provide valuable information to the defence.

The first of these two remarkable individuals is a bankrupt solicitor unable to practise until discharged (now fully re-instated, as of 1 January 1990). He was to spend three years investigating the police investigating me, with an expertise that few detectives could hold a candle to, tearing down the barriers to truth with bulldog-like ferocity. The other is a brilliant young barrister, not even a QC, but a courageous advocate who spent thousands of hours wading through the mountains of paper that the police threw at the case, picking at the lies, half-truths and inconsistencies until he knew every twist and turn, every nuance of the evidence, and was able to demolish the credibility of policemen testifying at the trial and expose their lies. Indeed, this is as much their story as mine. The scale and depths of what they eventually uncovered and told here could not have been guessed at in the summer of 1986, when the Stalker Affair rocked the media.

We have chosen to tell it here in a format similar to that of a thriller. That is, the events have been unfolded as they appeared to the participants and not necessarily in chronological order. Unravelling the mystery has been described stage by stage, exactly as would be done in a detective novel, the final resolution only coming together at the end, simply because this is the way it happened in real life. It makes a gripping narrative and one that lacks nothing of drama, bearing in mind this is a true story and the stresses and strains of the principal actors in it have been experienced and suffered to the full.

For the readers properly to appreciate the story and its revelations, it is necessary to set the stage, complete with a backscene. First comes a re-telling of the main points of the Stalker Affair with a few of my own emphases. Then a brief gallop through my own history, detailing how I rose to be a well-known figure in Manchester, how I became involved with Stalker and why I would be the almost inevitable choice for a plot against him. Then finally, we come to the main events of this book and the majority of chapters are given over to relating the facts in full and disturbing detail.

2
The Stalking of Stalker

John Stalker was one of Britain's top cops. His career, until the Affair broke, was illustrious and unblemished. He had climbed rapidly through the ranks. At thirty-eight years of age, with the rank of Detective Chief Superintendent, he was head of Warwickshire CID, the youngest in the country. He had worked for Special Branch and gained valuable experience. In 1974, when the IRA waged a bombing campaign in Manchester, Stalker's special knowledge had helped a great deal in tracking down the culprits.

In 1979 Stalker was positively vetted by government agencies, again in 1980, and in 1982 given clearance for access to 'highest-security classified material'. In 1983, he was specially selected to attend a year-long course at the Royal College of Defence Studies, a prestigious posting given to only two policemen each year. The studies, which were shared with top military brains from the UK, the Commonwealth and NATO, are all about defence and policing issues that affect Western democracy. The signs were, Stalker was being groomed for higher things.

On 24 May 1984, some two months after his appointment as Deputy Chief Constable of the Greater Manchester Police and in the year after the Royal College of Defence Studies course, Stalker was appointed to head up an enquiry into six controversial deaths in Northern Ireland.

All six deaths had taken place in late 1982, within a few weeks of a notorious murder in which three RUC officers had been blown up by a landmine hidden in a culvert along the Kinnego embankment just outside Lurgan. All the victims were suspected IRA terrorists though it subsequently became evident that one of them, seventeen-year-old Michael Tighe, had no paramilitary connections. They were all gunned down by police hit squads working under Special Branch instructions – 'terminated with extreme prejudice', as MI5 jargon has

17

it. None of the men was armed at the time and the incidents had all the hallmarks of revenge killings. On the face of it, the police had taken it upon themselves to eliminate men they believed were responsible for the landmine attack, without proof and without the benefit of a trial. This was the so-called 'shoot-to-kill' policy.

But in a community torn by strife, many killings were on a tit-for-tat basis. As one member of the DUP interviewed about these killings on the BBC programme, *Panorama*, said, 'My reaction I believe was that of most law-abiding citizens in Northern Ireland, that the police had at last done what people wanted them to do and that was to take effective action against the IRA to eliminate these terrorists who had been butchering the people of Northern Ireland.'

There the incidents would probably have rested, were it not for the fact that in a subsequent trial of the police officers (who were all incidently acquitted of murder), it emerged that those officers making their reports had falsified their statements because they had been ordered by their senior officers to do so. In each incident, the men had rapidly been removed from the scene by Special Branch men, told what to say when questioned by the CID, and told it was all covered by the Official Secrets Act (which was not the case).

The real public outrage came from this elaborate cover-up operation. There may or may not have been a 'shoot-to-kill' policy, but the blatant perversion of fundamental police methods and the discovery that certain 'high-ups' within the RUC were apparently telling their junior officers to lie and falsify evidence in order to obstruct the course of justice was disturbing news and wholly unacceptable to the British public and even the majority of Ulster Loyalists, quite apart from the predictable gnashing of teeth in the Republican camp.

It was this cover-up operation, as much as the murders themselves, that Stalker was sent to investigate. The originator of the request was Sir John Hermon, Chief Constable of the RUC. Philip Myers (later Sir Philip Myers) was HM Inspector of Constabulary at the time and he was Stalker's immediate senior, though it turned out that Myers had little power or effectiveness when the going got tough. The many battles with bureaucracy that Stalker had, and the apparent obstruction to the progress of his enquiries, are well told in Stalker's own book and need not delay the current text.

The three main points to note are that Hermon seemed fanatically reluctant to allow any documentation of the enquiry to go forward before the Director of Public Prosecutions in Northern Ireland (Sir Barry Shaw). He also appeared very obstructive in the matter of access to a tape-recording of the shooting of Michael Tighe in a hayshed, obtained fortuitously because of an MI5 electronic surveillance 'bug'. This tape, or a transcript of it, was expected to reveal whether or not the police had given reasonable warning before opening fire on Tighe and McCauley and was therefore crucial to what may well have become a murder enquiry. Thirdly, when it came to suspending two senior officers on Stalker's recommendation, Hermon refused this request as well.

In view of the obvious unwillingness on Hermon's part to co-operate with Stalker, one can't help wondering why he called him in in the first place. Presumably he was pressured to do so, to get rid of some of the public stink. The question of relevance here was whether Sir John Hermon, having called him in, was ultimately part of the plot to get rid of Stalker, perhaps because 'Honest John' hadn't understood the full potential of the situation and was finding out more than he should. Hermon always maintained he was not a participant in the decision to remove Stalker, but we shall make a surprising revelation later, indicating a strong suspicion that he was very much involved.

Shortly before taking up his Northern Ireland appointment, Stalker and his wife Stella were our guests at Wood Mill. After a pleasant meal and a swim John and I sat in the jacuzzi, where a lot of conversation among family and friends customarily took place, talking about the implications of his new role. I urged Stalker not to take on the job.

'Nothing is more certain than that you are ear-marked for the top, John,' I said. 'If you take on this job, it could destroy you.' Little did I think, when I spoke those words, that it would ultimately destroy me instead.

'What makes you say that?'

'For one thing you'll be a Catholic in a predominantly Protestant area. It's a virtual war out there, you won't get anybody's support. Both sides will be your enemy. It's a no-win situation,' I told him.

But Stalker, as we know, didn't listen to my importuning. He took the assignment.

Early in 1985, I had a chance to press my point again. Stalker was finding it difficult to finish his enquiry. Most of the work had been completed and the only item outstanding was gaining access to the transcript of the tape of the hayshed killing. After months of conflict with Hermon and growing tired of the ducking and weaving aimed at frustrating the conclusion of his enquiry, Stalker had decided to visit the Home Secretary for guidance (not mentioned in Stalker's book).

I asked if the Home Secretary had offered any helpful advice and Stalker replied that he hadn't.

'What do you intend to do?' I asked him.

'I'm going to go back and just do my job, as a copper.'

'Can't you see they are leaving you out on a limb? You're not indispensable; you can be sacrificed if it suits their purpose,' I warned.

'What do you suggest?'

'Resign,' I urged. 'Get out now and concentrate on your career.'

It was tempting, as Stalker relates in his book. Such a prominent walk-out would have attracted massive media coverage and perhaps overcome the apparent inertia over the release of the tape. But Stalker again ignored my warnings and so, for a second time, missed the chance to avoid the tide of misfortune that was to engulf him. Instead he did not resign but pressed on trying to get at the contents of that crucial tape. The rest is history.

On 29 May 1986, just three days before he was due to go to Belfast to be given the vital transcript and interview Sir John Hermon, possibly under caution, Stalker was taken off the case. Two days later, with an announcement by Norman Briggs, chairman of the Police Authority, that Stalker was on 'extended leave' pending the investigation of certain disciplinary complaints, there was furore in the media. Nobody supposed for a minute that it was a mere coincidence that Stalker was removed from his enquiry at this critical stage, just before he was due to be given access to what could be highly sensitive evidence that might implicate RUC chiefs – or even worse, the government in Downing Street – in non-democratic policing methods. It was a 'fix', and Stalker was 'stitched up', was the tenor of headlines, and speculation, accusation and counter-accusation went rolling on for weeks – all that summer in fact.

Nobody knew for sure what Stalker was supposed to be guilty of, but certain rumours were persistent. One was that he had been improperly associating with the criminal fraternity around Manchester, and the name Kevin Taylor kept coming up. Yet I had never even been charged with any criminal activity, let alone been found guilty. I was at that time a successful property developer, chairman of the Manchester Conservative Association, involved with several charities, in other words, a successful and upright citizen.

True, I was a man who enjoyed gambling. I spent some time in casinos; I played cards or backgammon. That meant I rubbed shoulders with a few doubtful characters. But the fact that I sometimes played cards with undesirables didn't make me a crook. The police investigating Stalker were later to try to blacken my character extensively using these social connections, but I would like to point out that casinos and bookmakers are happy to entertain criminals, current or reformed, and take their money. Nobody censures them for it nor is it illegal. Why is it morally different for an individual to do the same thing?

More serious was my alleged involvement with the so-called 'Quality Street Gang'. There was never any such gang, but several Manchester characters had styled themselves that way as a joke, in commemoration of a Quality Street TV advertisement of the 1960s, depicting rather suave, debonair crooks. In fact, they worked hard almost every day on their car sales pitch, in all weathers, which is hardly to be expected if they were indeed criminals. None had any serious convictions, though it was an obsession of certain senior police officers within the Greater Manchester Police force to try to tie them in with serious organized crime. True, they did have brushes with the police, but there was never anything serious. The official argument was that they were guilty but simply had avoided prosecution. It was more likely that they were a convenient peg on which to hang unsolved crimes.

I had maintained a friendly relationship with at least two of the 'gang'. They had been commercial neighbours when I was in business selling vans in the early 1970s and it was always a personal principle that, just because I had found a little success, I did not intend to get rid of all my earlier acquaintances. It didn't make me a crook to know members of the QSG on first-name terms. More importantly, knowing me didn't make Stalker a disciplinary case.

The second rumour was that Stalker had accepted free hospitality from me, the implication being that Stalker was somehow compromised and was likely to return unusual 'police favours'. The accusation concerned a trip on my yacht, *Diogenes*, starting from Miami in December 1981. Stalker and I both denied there had been a 'freebie' or anything improper about the holiday together, although friends recognized that it would be rather out of character for me to allow *anyone* else to pay when I was host, never mind a close friend. The fact is that, as Stalker tells in his own book, he paid his share in cash. At the time there was no thought of the possibility he would be asked to prove his contribution.

What was missed in the ensuing lengthy speculations in the media about the boat was the irony that Stalker spent the entire nine days violently ill with nausea and vomiting. 'I brought up curry I had eaten ten years before,' he was later to joke during after-dinner speeches. What with that, and on one occasion lying ill in the bottom of the boat while I broke out the guns to scare off possible pirates in the vicinity, Assistant Chief Constable John Stalker did not have a good trip. Finally, when I scalded myself so badly I couldn't handle the boat, the holiday was aborted and we flew home early. In view of our denials, this second reason for suspension also appeared invalid.

It is worth pointing out that Stalker was vetted by the government agencies and given his highest security classification *after* the Miami trip. It would hardly do justice to MI5 to suppose that clearance would be given to a bent copper 'on a pension' to a crafty property developer. It was simply that, until this moment, no one saw any slight taint to two friends on holiday together, and that someone was now trying to re-write history for some sinister and hidden purpose.

A conspiracy to get Stalker off the enquiry in Northern Ireland seemed the only logical explanation. It was a matter of finding him guilty first, then looking for the evidence. Nor was the theory rendered less plausible by the refusal of the Home Office or Downing Street to comment on what had taken place. The official silence in fact lent weight to the supposition that Stalker's removal had been sanctioned at government level, and was not just a disciplinary matter within the GMP.

In an attempt to allay any further suspicions of foul play, an enquiry was set up to investigate the allegations against Stalker. It was headed by Colin Sampson, the Chief Constable of West Yorkshire Police. After weeks of enquiries, at enormous cost, the investigation was completed and a report was submitted, including 146 documents, 169 statements and 50 other exhibits. The police authority sat on 22 August 1986 to decide on its recommendations. Stalker had been found guilty, the report said, on eight counts of misusing police vehicles, one of showing political bias, and one of associating with persons likely to bring disrepute on the police. The charge of accepting a free holiday with me was unproven, though in the style of true bureaucratic finger-poking, the report sought to criticize Stalker for not having paid for his air ticket to Miami with a credit card.

The police authority, by a majority vote, roundly rejected Sampson's recommendation for a disciplinary tribunal and Stalker was reinstated, though this was not unanimous.

He returned to work the next day, 23 August. The enormous ineptitude of it all left the public gasping with astonishment. Clearly, the Sampson enquiry had been an attempt to depose Stalker and it had failed signally.

Inevitably, the Sampson Report was eventually leaked to the Press. Clearly, someone on the inside didn't like what had been done to Stalker. The newspapers had a field day. Several senior journalists,

such as David Leigh and Paul Lashmar of *The Observer* and Peter
Murtagh of the *Guardian*, re-interviewed many of the witnesses quoted
in the Report and obtained from them very different stories to what had
been reputedly said. Thus, evidence for any possible misdemeanours,
badly investigated and presented as it was, began to look even more
suspect. It seemed there were no solid grounds on which to take such
precipitate and drastic action against Stalker. The charges of misusing
police cars were derisory. Eight journeys were catalogued, totalling
less than one hundred miles in all. In fact, Stalker's record in this
respect was better than that of his own Chief Constable, Jim Anderton.
The latter was well-known for having a police car to transport him to
and from the numerous social functions he attended, usually leaving
his chauffeur standing outside for hours in what could be seen as a
shocking waste of man-hours. It was not that anyone minded that, in
principle. Arguably it was one of the perks of the Chief Constable's
job. It was the hypocrisy of wanting to criticize Stalker and his trivial
use of official vehicles that affronted common sense and decency. Even
more so considering that Stalker claims that he used cars for safety
reasons, in view of IRA threats against his life. Sampson's team hadn't
even bothered to check whether this assertion of Stalker's was true.
They were too busy, it seemed, trying to find out whether he danced
with men in bars or had free sausage rolls at football club socials.

The accusation of showing political bias by attending the Tory
Association Ball was as laughable as it was vague. In any case, Stalker
had received permission from Jim Anderton to attend this function.

Only the charge that he had been seen at parties and other social
occasions in the presence of criminals seemed to bear any weight. The
criminals were all said to be friends of mine and most had no serious
convictions. One individual reported as having a criminal record had
been prosecuted for stealing potatoes in 1944 at the age of ten years –
Stalker would only have been four years old at the time. The absurdity
of this criticism of Stalker is in the fact that most people do not go
round at parties asking guests whether they have a criminal record or
not before chatting to them. Perhaps we have all, at some time or
other, spoken to people with a criminal background. How would we
know?

In fact, Stalker was only once physically present in a room with a
member of the Quality Street Gang and that was with over a hundred
people at my fiftieth birthday party in 1982, also before Stalker
was given access to highest-rated classified material. This man had
gate-crashed since he was not one of the fraternity to whom I was
disposed to be friendly and none of us could remember inviting him.

A photograph came to light showing Stella Stalker talking to this man.

The aim of the Sampson Report seemed to be more a question of blacking by association. I knew the Quality Street Gang and I knew Stalker – therefore Stalker was mixed up with the Quality Street Gang. Infantile logic, only worrying because CID officers took it seriously. The nation winced and the image of our detectives as sleuths took a considerable battering that summer. In fact, the whole episode did immense damage to the image of the police.

Stalker was never to return to the RUC enquiry. Many people asked: why not, if he had been exonerated of serious misconduct? The inference seemed all too obvious. There was an official cover-up into the RUC's activities, after all. Stalker doesn't mention in his book whether there really was a shoot-to-kill policy. James Prior, Secretary of State at the time of the shootings, remains adamant that there wasn't any such official policy but that doesn't mean one didn't exist at grass-roots' level. Why did Stalker remain silent? I believe he was afraid of what he had found out.

The one aspect of the whole Affair which no one seems to have considered very much is the irony that it may have been very necessary to get Stalker off the case. All that was wrong perhaps, in terms of justice and decency, was the crass, underhanded and farcical way it was done. Stalker was pushing further and further into areas that were dangerous, not so much to people's reputations, which is widely supposed to be the main issue, but to the viability of the secret service operations in Ulster. Indeed, arguably, he may have put lives at risk, had he continued the way he was going, because he did not fully understand the issues involved.

It is now believed that Stalker had stumbled onto the existence of cross-border liaison operations between MI5 and the *garda síochána* (the Irish police force). Reputedly, the *garda* had actually been penetrated by an MI5 'mole' known as The Badger, who was not high-ranking but was in a very influential position. He was leaking intelligence information gathered south of the border to MI5, who were then able to use it with devastating effect against terrorists. Furthermore, there were rumours that some of the British special hit squads actually operated south of the border, in the territory of another sovereign state. This isn't to say that it wasn't all done with the complete collusion of the Irish government. It certainly must have been, and The Badger was knowingly left in place for years. But the facts are told here to explain what the extremely sensitive issues were that John Stalker may have put at risk with his dogged determination to get at 'The Truth'.

The truth was, of course, that undercover operations are necessary and dangerous; some part, at least, of the organization must be kept secret and, yes, sanction must come from high up in the political tree. This is not meant, in any way, to condone a shoot-to-kill policy or that the deaths should not have been properly investigated and put before the DPP. Stalker was right in trying to avoid a whitewash. But we are talking now of a very real and bloody battle for democracy and the need for decent right-minded governments to unite against a common enemy. In any war there has to be a fifth column and not even someone as self-assured as John Stalker would be right to try to compromise it. Make no mistake, the government in Dublin wants to see the IRA put out of action just as much as Whitehall and to embarrass them would be foolish in the extreme. They are our friends and allies. It's just that they can't be seen to be too overt, without antagonizing certain of their own people. All the puffing and trumpeting in the media about what the Brits are up to is just a front and the hostility is far less real than apparent.

Why else would there be virtual silence from Dublin on the Stalker issue? The fact is that 'Honest John' was doing the politicians there little good and potentially undermining Anglo-Irish relations. It is useful, once again, to look at chronological details. Stalker's interim report, which showed how his enquiry was going and was unreservedly critical of the RUC and Special Branch in Northern Ireland, was submitted on 18 September 1985. The Anglo-Irish Agreement was signed at Hillsborough Castle, Belfast, on 15 November. A full revelation of an RUC scandal, with damaging trials and possible convictions, was the last thing that either side wanted. It could only help the IRA cause and that was bad news for both countries.

All this persuades me that there was a lot to what Stella Stalker said at a secret meeting with Beryl and me, while the Sampson enquiry was at its height. She asked to speak with us urgently and a meeting took place in a car park of the Swan Hotel, near Knutsford. Her main concern was that I should not say or do anything which might compromise or embarrass her husband. However, she made a strange remark: 'This isn't just to do with six deaths in Northern Ireland, you know, it's more like six hundred. The Irish and American government are in on it and what was done to John.' The implications are provocative, to say the least.

*

Re-instated and back at work as Deputy Chief Constable of the Greater Manchester Police, Stalker's problems were far from over. Life under Jim Anderton – who had made it abundantly plain that he had wanted Stalker out, and who had made no secret of his resentment of Stalker's return – was not easy.

The official noises were friendly and reassuring enough. 'Anderton Welcomes Stalker' and 'Police Chief Welcome for Stalker after Fears of Rift' were typical headlines. In a carefully worded statement, Anderton said to the Press, 'John Stalker and I have always worked very well together in the public interest and for the good of the force and there is no reason why we cannot do so again. A police force without a Deputy Chief Constable is certainly not fully effective and I am glad to have John Stalker back on duty again.'

The reality was different from the oozing cant. The Chief Constable displayed a high-handed contempt for Stalker that manifested itself in many petty, small-minded acts of attrition. Most serious among these was Anderton's attempt to block financial aid for Stalker's legal bill. Altogether he was in debt to the sum of over £21,000 in trying to defend himself against the spurious charges that had been brought, a hefty fine for a man who had been found guilty of no serious offence other than perhaps of being too much of a conscientious copper. The Police Committee would have paid, even if Stalker had been guilty, once matters had gone to the tribunal stage, but in the circumstances refused.

Public donations towards Stalker's bill started to pour in, but Anderton made it a personal campaign to get the donations stopped, and only the Home Secretary got it unblocked, subject to the ultimate approval of the Police Committee. They referred it in turn to the Association of Chief Police Officers, the president of which was, guess who? – Jim Anderton. The ACPO objected, but were happily not able ultimately to stop the tide of donations reaching Stalker.

There were numerous other minor acts that revealed the small-mindedness of Manchester's Chief Constable and showed him in very poor light, such as not allowing Stalker to park his car in a nearby police station while he was attending a Police Authority meeting, an act of 'supreme pettiness'. Anderton failed to telephone Stalker on his first four days back at work (Anderton was on holiday in the Lake District), an omission which Stalker describes rightly as 'a childish discourtesy'. He was also not above leaving his office locked and no message for Stalker.

Always publicity conscious (in fact many would say it was his single biggest aberration), Anderton seems to have pointedly issued press releases without informing Stalker beforehand. One of these earned the derisory headline 'I'm in charge', in which Anderton tried to make an issue of his rank and authority over Stalker. On a number of occasions he disappeared for days on end without telling Stalker where he was going, despite the fact that Stalker was his deputy. This was not just bad manners, but downright unprofessional.

But it was the blatant failure to inform Stalker of the decision, in December 1986, to re-open the Moor's murder searches that was the last straw. It was a deliberate affront to Stalker's position and authority as Deputy Chief Constable to keep him in the dark over a matter of such local and national importance. Stalker tells in his book how four hundred constables drafted in for the search and most media men in the country heard about it before he did. Yet he was the only senior officer remaining within GMP who had been involved in the original enquiry in 1967.

What Stalker probably did not know, but this book will reveal when the story is welded to the Stalker narrative, is that the whole charade was probably no more than a PR exercise. It was designed to divert attention from the fact that, on the recommendation of senior counsel, certain senior police officers, including James Anderton and Peter Topping, head of CID, had been summonsed with a conspiracy to pervert the course of justice and these men were running scared. Just how scared will be revealed when we come to this in detail. As an antidote, they wanted a show to recover some of their sagging omnipotence, and this was the means they chose. It was a completely pointless exercise and had no worthwhile policing motives.

For Stalker, the writing was on the wall. He decided to quit while ahead and resigned on 18 December 1986. After working three months' notice, he finally left the police force on 13 March 1987, ironically a Friday. It was notable that Anderton did not even bother to say goodbye or wish his former colleague well.

Far from being at a loss, Stalker walked straight into a plum job as general manager of Brookside Productions Ltd, responsible for the successful Channel 4 soap *Brookside*. Since then he has written his own bestselling account of the affair so firmly attached to his name. It is a disappointing document, considering that the events of summer 1986 were of such momentous public interest: squeaky clean and laundered of all the real issues, apparently on the advice of his publisher's legal department and partly because he was trying to write the story without all the facts that we now have available.

He is now also a regular broadcaster and a renowned after-dinner speaker. In fact, he is now well-off and for him and his family, the end of the matter is basically a happy one.

Sadly this is not the case for me and my family. By the time the furore had died down for Stalker, and he was fully embarked on his new life, I was destitute. Things had gone so wrong that my companies were in liquidation, the money gone. No bank would allow me even an ordinary current account, never mind trading facilities. Yet still I hadn't been charged with anything. I had been tried, sentenced and hanged without the chance to defend myself. The police, as we shall reveal, had undertaken an orchestrated campaign of financial harassment against me, far beyond the needs of a legitimate investigation. I was trying to fight back through the courts, using what rights I could to defend myself, and at each stage losing. It is proverbially difficult to fight the Establishment: such laws as there are don't seem to apply to them and their procedures, only to the common man. Nevertheless, my actions were sufficiently frightening to my oppressors that they wanted me financially castrated.

It was only a matter of time before we lost the house. By October 1987, I was on the dole; all the fair-weather friends had gone when the money ran out; the humiliation and devastation were complete. Once formally charged, all matters relating to the case became *sub judice*. I could no longer argue my troubles in the public arena. In effect I was silenced. Yet it was to be a further two years before the case came to trial and I was able, at last, to defend myself against the charges brought and clear my name. Two further years of poverty and stress.

To preserve his own position, Stalker, in his book, wants us to believe that his troubles came about because of me. Facts say otherwise. As you will discover in these pages, I was attacked solely as a means of getting at Stalker.

3
Let the Good Times Roll

To understand this story in full and to understand how I came to be at the centre of the storm surrounding Stalker, it is necessary to know something of my past. An individual is the product of his environment and events never happen in isolation or without reference to earlier history. As the saying goes, 'No man is an island.'

I was born in 1932 and raised in Salford, a city whose deprivation in those years was portrayed so faithfully and movingly by Walter Greenwood in *Love on the Dole*. Life for the majority of families was basically about getting enough to eat and keeping warm. These were the main necessities and anything beyond that was an extra. The desire of working-class people was to be, above all else, 'respectable'. Folk may have been poor but they had fierce self-respect and took pride in achievements that did not cost money, such as hard work, honesty and cleanliness. So ingrained were these attitudes to life that for the average housewife they became almost an obsession that would drive her to wash and scrub until late at night and donkey-stone the front door-steps until they gleamed.

My father left home while we were very young and my mother was left to struggle to bring up my sister and me in an age when there was no automatic support for a single-parent family. The poverty trap and the ensuing problems keeping up with the rent meant moving home constantly. I had to learn to re-adjust to new social contacts each time and possibly this early experience helped to give me a facility for making friends and taught me to enjoy a gregarious life-style, for which I became noted in later years.

For countless people in downtrodden Salford, life revolved around the ubiquitous pawn shops. On pay-day, Friday, there would be queues at the brokers to redeem the family's best clothes for the weekend. Everyone wanted to look their finest for the Saturday night

29

dance and church on Sunday. Then on Monday, the bubble would burst, as the harsh reality of poverty reasserted itself. Best suits and dresses would have to go back to the pawn shop, the few resulting meagre pennies being used to buy food for the coming week.

Families were so preoccupied with the drudgery of this day-to-day survival that there was little time for the real education of children. Life had to be learned the hard way and the lessons were sometimes tough and unjust. However, there was one positive side to this, which is that it gave a powerful incentive to a youngster to better himself and tended to breed kids who would grow up hungry for money and success. I'm sure it had that effect on me.

My first job came when I was twelve: delivering furniture on a tricycle. It was hard work but I earned, with tips, an average of £1 each Saturday. It was a welcome addition to the family coffers and my first taste of relative wealth. But every mother's dream was for her son to learn a trade. So when I left school at fourteen, I duly signed on as an apprentice pattern maker. The pay was eight shillings and sixpence a week; after deducting food and tram fares, there was not enough left for someone with ambitions.

Consequently, when I heard at sixteen years of age that if a lad joined the railways as a cleaner, within weeks he could pass a simple test to become a spare fireman, I had no hesitation. Firing work was paid at the full man's rate – at that time, five pounds three shillings a week. A fortune!

So I went to work on the railways and learned how to stoke locomotives (yes, there is a technique to shovelling coal). Because there was such a shortage of firemen just after the war, I would end up firing most days, and was soon working in excess of eighty hours a week. This meant virtually no social life but the money was excellent and very much needed at home.

Being a fireman was a hard, unglamorous occupation, varying between being frozen stiff and burning hot, soaked to the skin or covered in ashes. But I had the satisfaction of being occasionally allowed a turn at driving a locomotive, unofficially, of course. So at the age of seventeen, I became a sometime train driver, an achievement that most lads dreamt about but never attained.

Then came the army, two years obligatory National Service. The basic training took place at Catterick Camp with the 17th/21st Lancers who had fought so illustriously at the Charge of the Light Brigade. Now they had traded horses for tanks. I learned to be a wireless operator and a gunner.

Subsequently, I joined the 5th Royal Inniskillen Dragoon Guards (the 'Fifth Skins') and was posted to Paderborn, in Germany. At this time a medical orderly was needed. I applied on the strength of very limited first aid training while with the railways, and got the job. I had a natural aptitude and interest in matters medical and within a few months I was running the garrison clinic.

One of my many recollections is of delivering the wife of one of the soldiers as she gave birth in the ambulance on the way to hospital. Not many eighteen-year-old youths can boast such an experience. It almost put me off sex!

Then came Korea. My National Service term was due to expire within months, a factor which disqualified me for service there. So in order to go I signed on for a further three years, a classic case of youthful idealism and the fatuous optimism of 'It can't happen to me', I suppose. Without it how would the army ever get recruits?

The brutal reality of war in that theatre of horrors is well recorded elsewhere and need not delay us here, except to comment that the great obscenity of such carnage and killing is that it is always young men, with so much to look forward to, who die like cattle for a cause they often do not even understand. I was in no way different from hundreds of thousands of other youths swept up in the tide of slaughter and, like all of them, I had to learn to come to terms with it, cheerfully or otherwise. There was no choice but to get on with the job, day by day, and just hope that you lived till the next sunrise.

As a medical orderly, I was continually exposed to the grimness of death and mutilation. It was a stern awakening for a lad still in his teens. Only a soldier's mysterious sense of 'duty' could have made anything positive out of the sad and wasteful destruction of life.

A much happier side of my service in Korea was two-way trading with the American and Canadian forces. Because of the nature of my post I was able to travel to and from camp freely, in a way that no other troops were. It didn't take me long to realize that there was a useful role to be played, exchanging goods between allied armies. For example, the British lads were well supplied with beer and liquor; the Yanks were not. On the other hand, American food supplies were far superior to our meagre rations. I found I could get up to $50 for a bottle of good Scotch, and that beer could be traded for linen, razor blades, toilet paper, chocolate bars, butter and delicious coffee. A case of gin would buy a jeep and all the subalterns in my regiment soon had one each.

Nor were all the acquisitions confined to fair trading. On one occasion, a few of us went over to the American lines, which had been temporarily abandoned while under shelling, and retrieved a broken-down half-track vehicle from the Imjim river. We towed it back to British lines. With an engine overhaul it was soon made serviceable, the US army signs were painted out and the engineers put wooden racks in the rear, suitable for holding stretchers. It did sterling service as an ambulance before the end of my tour of duty.

Unofficial medical work included treating American soldiers for what were, in those days, considered unmentionable diseases. Fraternizing with Korean women was expressly forbidden and anyone found to have a 'dose' was usually given an extra twelve months in the front line. This amounted to a virtual death-sentence, so men were reluctant to go to their own medics. Instead, word got around about the Limey orderly who would give penicillin shots and sulphatriad tablets. There were daily queues outside my tent.

By a curious coincidence, one of my barristers on the fraud case was introduced to an officer, now a general, who remembered me from these years and spoke jocularly of my 'entrepreneurial activities'.

Eventually, my tour in Korea came to an end and, after a brief spell in the Middle East, I was demobbed and found myself once more a civilian. I have no regrets about the years I spent in uniform. In fact, I've a lot to thank the army for. It was the first thing to get me out of the streets of Salford and show me that there was a lot more to life and a big wide world out there.

It seemed natural to resume a career on the railways. I signed on once again and reported for duty. But on my first shift there was a letter from the regional manager telling me that, because of the time spent in the army, I couldn't start at my old grade. I would have to begin again at the bottom. This was too much for me. I quit.

A succession of jobs followed, including work in a battery factory, as a stevedore and labouring on a building site. I was still searching for what I wanted to do in life.

About this time, I fell in love with Hilda Mattiussi, a girl from one of the wealthy Manchester Italian ice-cream families. The romance was obviously doomed from the start because of the great social distance betwen us. It was my first affair and so the parting was particularly painful. I never saw her again, until a chance meeting thirty years later. She was in a wheelchair, suffering from multiple sclerosis but looking as beautiful as ever.

It was in selling that I discovered my real talents. First came sewing machines. I was given a basic sales training course and sent to Liverpool.

This city has long been known as the salesman's graveyard but it held no terrors for me. In my first week I broke the company's national record and that first pay packet (commission only) was over £128. I remember showing my step-father, who had always tried to persuade me that going 'down the pit' was the only worthwhile job for a man (he worked an eighteen-inch seam all his life and died very young, covered in scars). Nor was this first success a fluke; it was repeated week after week after week. I was on my way to freedom and success.

The sales training changed me a great deal. It brought improvements to my life in general; not just an increased ability to part someone from their money but it taught me how to get on well with others. Up to that time, I'd had almost no personal life and consequently had learned little in the way of social skills. The course instructor had drummed into us the necessity of smiling at the customer and being pleasant. He probably meant it as no more than a trick, something to put the customer off his or her guard, but I saw no reason not to be sincere about it. It worked just as well and I had the satisfaction of knowing that the smiles I got back were equally genuine. 'Be friendly and people will be friendly back to you', that was the motto. I virtually based my life on his words and it has had far-reaching consequences.

Once a salesman, you can sell anything. My next scheme was marketing shop refrigerators and food stocks to complement them. This was in the days long before the emergence of supermarkets and the idea was completely revolutionary at the time. My partner and I made a big success of it but that folded when the refrigerator supplier went bankrupt, due to earlier business indiscretions catching up with him.

Taking a completely different direction, I was involved in setting up the first casino in Birmingham. New and liberal gaming laws had been enacted in 1961 and it was a free-for-all for anyone with an entrepreneurial frame of mind. But I wasn't happy and sold out in 1962.

Instead, it was as a player that I made my mark in the gaming world. By the early 1960s, I had become a good player at kalooki, a kind of thirteen-card rummy. On the face of it, it is a game that is easy to learn but real skill only comes after years of experience. Also there is an in-built stamina factor and often the man who stays fresh and alert longest is the one who wins. I seemed to have a natural aptitude for it. I became very sharp indeed and won good money consistently.

Inevitably the craze reached London, as part of the gambling boom that swept the country in the early 1960s. So, as an established expert, I decided to try my luck in the capital and set out one grey morning,

Dick Whittington-style, to make my fortune as a card professional.

I arrived with very little money and booked into the Devere Hotel in Kensington. That same afternoon I joined the Victoria Sporting Club in Bayswater and went straight to the huge kalooki room (in those days there was no forty-eight-hour rule). I asked boldly for the biggest game in the house and found myself seated with some very wealthy people. I started winning and for four years never stopped.

My reputation as a kalooki player began spreading and players would seek me out to challenge my supremacy, much as gunmen did who fought duels in the Wild West. Few people got the better of me in these shoot-outs. These were times of riches and plenty. Yet I never entirely lost sight of my Northern attitudes to money and wealth. One very rich female patron of Crockford's was tipping the croupier £100 each time she won. 'They do work so hard,' she told me, confidingly. 'There are men lifting dustbins who break their backs for a fraction of that money,' I snapped at her, angrily. She refused to speak to me again.

Eventually I got into the very exclusive Nightingale Club in Berkeley Square and was soon playing cards with bankers, stockbrokers and captains of industry. It became my little kingdom and I remained there for about two and a half years. These were the heady days when casinos were the great social meeting places of the rich and famous and I met, dined with or played cards with virtually anyone who was anybody in London at that time, including most of the film and TV celebrities in town.

I was able to move into luxurious quarters in New Cavendish Street and lived a high lifestyle of champagne, oysters and caviar that seemed as far away from my Salford roots as it was possible for a young man to be. The winnings were considerable but I must admit I spent as if there was no tomorrow. Supremely confident of my ability always to earn more, there seemed no incentive to put money aside for a rainy day. After all, I could win a year's average salary in one night.

I recall one occasion in the Olympic Club, which had a very wealthy Greek clientele. I'd just won at chemin-de-fer and at the end of the shoe I asked to join the biggest table, in the *salle privée*, but for once the manager, Manny Lewis, whom I had known since my Manchester days, said 'It's not for you Kevin,' which in gambling parlance means 'It would be wise for you not to play.' It later turned out that on that night several tankers and other ships had changed hands.

My first brush with underworld characters also came at this time. I was playing kalooki one evening and suddenly became conscious of being watched. I turned round and standing behind me were a group of very shady characters, people who at that time were 'household names'. They studied my play for some time and the boss, one of London's best-known gangsters, leaned over and said, 'Good luck to you, son. Get plenty!' as they left.

Several weeks later, I got a telephone call, asking me to go to the Grosvenor House Hotel and play poker for these men.

'It's not my game,' I argued.

'You can play it, can't you?'

'Of course I can.'

'Well, just play it as you know how.'

'What about a float?' I asked.

'You'll be met.'

And sure enough, I was. A pudgy envelope containing £20,000 was handed to me on arrival. That night I won £180,000. The croupier was magic. I couldn't see what he was doing. All I know was that every time I got a good hand, somebody had a hand nearly as good. My wages for the work was £27,000, a huge sum of money for the year 1963. But it was never to be repeated.

Not long afterwards, on a visit home to Manchester, I met Beryl Rooney. I fell in love with her and married her in 1965. Although I didn't realize it at the time, she was to become the most important influence on my whole life.

She was probably more prudent with money than me, though we never argued about the spending excesses. 'We weren't squandering income, just living,' she insists pragmatically. 'I didn't worry because I always knew he could earn more.'

I was so certain of her caution with money that I once gave her £500 to go shopping in Bond Street and had a £2,000 bet with one of my gambling friends that she wouldn't spend any of it. A few hours later, unaware that to buy a dress would have cost me over £2,000, Beryl returned with all the cash and I collected my winnings.

'I wouldn't do it again,' she says, with a heavy sarcasm.

At first, I think my life-style fascinated her. I kept nothing from her; she knew exactly what I did for a living. But eventually, the glamour and excitement began to pall. For Beryl it was essentially a lonely life, since I was out working every night until dawn and sleeping most of the day. The opportunities to enjoy married life together were very few. Her unhappiness grew and I sensed it. Partly because of this and partly because Beryl had become pregnant, I made the momentous decision to abandon the gambling life and return to Manchester. Beryl gave me no ultimatum. It was my own decision.

*

The first serious business venture was Vanland, a second-hand commercial vehicle sales pitch in Ancoats, close to the heart of Manchester. I began in 1966 by purchasing an old van for £15 which I renovated and sold for £80. I gave Beryl £40 for housekeeping, bought another van, then another, then two, until I had sufficient stock to rent a plot of land and hang out a sign. I used to repair and paint the vehicles myself, working in all weathers without any protective clothing. The result was two bouts of pneumonia and a collapsed lung. It was certainly no easy way to riches.

The episode would hardly be worth a mention, except for the fact that it was at this time that I first made contact with some of the men later to become known as the 'Quality Street Gang'. Some of the 'members' sold used cars from the pitch next door to me. They helped me out in lots of ways and even lent me money without quibbling. I knew about their reputation but to me they were just good neighbours. Nothing was too much trouble for them if you asked. I dismiss the idea they were organized big-time crooks and I'd far rather spend the time of day with the likes of them than many of the people I met when I later went into politics.

By coincidence, another fateful encounter took place at this time. Beryl was out in a rainstorm when an unknown woman dashed up and asked to share her umbrella. She introduced herself as Stella Stalker. I met John shortly afterwards and we soon became firm friends. My two girls attended the same convent school as Stalker's daughters and John and I became involved together in fund-raising events for the Parent Teachers Association.

It was Stalker who first warned me to keep my business neighbours at arm's length, probably concerned that I might be associating with petty criminals. Also, as he advanced in rank and his role as a policeman took on more and more responsibility, Stalker saw fit to point out to me several times that there were to be no police 'favours'. Based on that understanding and a firm mutual respect, our friendship grew as we each prospered in our own way, and was to last until the shocking events of 1986.

In 1972, I switched to property developing, and so started on the road that was to lead me to become a millionaire. I started out by leasing a plot of land a few hundred yards from Strangeways Prison, with only a three-year lease. The site was due to be redeveloped as a roundabout marking the end of the M602 Eccles Motorway. It was a huge gamble, but then I was nothing if not a gambler, and saw possibilities that nobody else did. Ultimately I was proved right.

Salford City Council decided against the motorway scheme and deliberately built a council estate right across the path of the proposed
carriageway, which put paid to the roundabout for ever.

Even so, on such a short lease, it made no sense to build to the tune
of £120,000, which is what I did. Not surprisingly, no finance houses
would entertain it, but I was so determined I wouldn't let that stop
me. Instead I financed the deal by taking advance premiums from
prospective tenants, and using that to pay for the construction work.
This was at the time when there was an influx of Asian immigrants
from Amin's troubled Uganda, and these refugees, noted for their
industriousness, were keen to get started on business in the northwest.
For me it was the classic good luck story of being in the right place at
the right time.

'I remember men arriving at the door with carrier bags full of pound
notes,' recalls Beryl. 'Looking back, I think it is miraculous that they
were willing to part with all that money for leases on buildings that
hadn't even been started.'

Their trust in me was fully justified, however, and the job did get
done to everyone's satisfaction. I hired workmen and became a building contractor. I would usually don a hard hat and wellingtons, work
on-site in the mornings and then get washed and changed for meetings
with bankers and other professionals over lunch, to get the resources
that I needed. Rents soon started to pour in. Ultimately, I put up over
eighty warehouses in the vicinity, acquiring more and more plots of
land.

The units were leased at a substantial rent, proving the demand
was there and my judgement was sound. The nice thing about getting
good rents is that the little jobs that need constantly attending to can
be done for no charge and sometimes there were a few little extra
favours thrown in. It made for excellent relations with the tenants.

In 1974, I was joined by Derek Britton, an accountant. I needed
help by this time. Like many small businessmen, I had started out
with an idea and was able to put it into practice but without any
administrative know-how to back up what I was doing. Between us,
we put together a credible business plan. Barclay's liked the scheme,
once they were convinced the future of the site was secure, and agreed
to back it. With major institutional money available to finance the
proper purchase of further plots and buildings, expansion was rela-
tively straightforward. Rapid growth was assured and the good times
began to roll.

Not that it was all plain sailing. There were numerous battles
with the planning department. 'The trouble is that people in local

37

government prefer to say no rather than yes,' says Britton. 'They are more concerned about their jobs than the community and don't like to take controversial decisions.' The planners really wanted small factory units on the site, not warehousing or cash-and-carry units. As Britton says: 'They thought they would be creating jobs. All they would have created, naturally, was empty factory units, if nobody had any use for them.'

As it was, the city planners could have little objection to clothing or wholesale in this area, since it was well known for this kind of commerce. What they got was a booming market, one of the largest in Europe and which today is the thriving hub of Manchester's Asian community. The self-evident prosperity of the Moulton Street Precinct, as it became known, is my personal contribution to community relations in Manchester.

In the mid 1970s I tried my hand at making money overseas. On a trip to Malawi I met an Asian businessman and together we tried to set up a business supplying second-hand earth-moving equipment to Zambia. There were orders to the tune of £11 million, but only weeks before invoices and letters of credit had been successfully processed, Frelimo guerillas closed the Mozambique border and locked out hard currency from Zambia.

Not long afterwards, I was back in Africa, this time in Sudan. I planned to tender for the first black-topped road from Port Sudan to Khartoum, a $600 million project financed by the World Bank, but that contract, too, never materialized and to this day the road remains unbuilt, thanks to the machinations of the Crown agents. True, these are dreams. But it only needs one of them to succeed and you're very, very rich.

Besides, there was a positive side to these failures. I had met and stayed with a number of Asian businessmen on my travels in Africa and enjoyed their company, as I think they did mine. Once home in Manchester it seemed most Asian families now knew who I was, where I'd been and what I'd done. People I had never heard of would call and say: 'You stayed with an uncle (cousin, brother-in-law, etc.) of mine in Africa. He said you were a good man, and I would like to do business with you.' Word had got around that I was non-racist and could be trusted. All of a sudden the Precinct, which up to then had not been anywhere near at capacity, was fully let. Income soared and, of course, I was delighted.

*

By the early 1980s, there was a large annual income to be disposed of. I bought a Rolls-Royce; one of the toys one has to have when one is newly rich. I also bought an ocean-going yacht, the *Diogenes*, for £85,000 in February 1981. It was possibly the single worst mistake I ever made and was to have far-reaching repercussions in years to come.

Among the many people who enjoyed hospitality on board while the boat was based in Miami were members of the so-called Quality Street Gang, briefly in March 1981 and again, in June 1981. These were no more than social visits and I was happy to entertain the boys by way of a thank you for the help they had given me in the Vanland days, when I was often struggling to make ends meet. Stalker himself was to make the fateful trip with me in December of the same year, which was cut short when I scalded myself badly and we had to fly home.

In 1982, I had the *Diogenes* moved to the Mediterranean base of Puerto Banus, outside Marbella. She came first to Salford docks for a refit. Once in Spain, apart from occasional day cruises, *Diogenes* remained moored in the harbour as little more than a floating caravan. It was only when she came to be used by a man who was probably a drug-runner that she would feature again so ingloriously in this narrative.

These were the years when Beryl and I made frequent trips to America and met with the big stars. I had struck up a special friendship with Angelo Dundee, world-famous boxing promoter and former manager of Mohammed Ali. Beryl and I stayed with him and his wife on several occasions. Dundee and I went fishing together in the Gulf and he presented me with a prize bluefish he'd caught and had mounted, which, as I've mentioned, hung on my wall until the day we lost our home. Through Angelo and his many acquaintances, we had some wonderful days in Las Vegas where we met a number of celebrities. Best of all, from my wife's point of view, was dinner at Frank Sinatra's table. But there were others, such as Vic Damone, Paul Anka and Mohammed Ali himself, who can probably still remember the Limey from Lancashire with his off-beat and pungent jokes.

Then there were the parties. These are still talked about today: like the New Year's Eve party at the New Orleans restaurant on Princess Street, Manchester, when the decorations caught fire and the flames were put out by using bottles of Dom Perignon champagne as extinguishers.

Most of our celebrations were less exclusive occasions, however. A favourite venue was the Film Exchange Club, where I had a special table. People would gather until the numbers had grown to party proportions. I would often invite strangers over to join us, just because I thought they looked interesting and enjoyed hearing about other people's triumphs and vicissitudes. I found my own little mixture of orange liqueur and brandy was particularly good at breaking down inhibitions and making new friends. These were great days. Sometimes the gatherings would last until the small hours and gradually the numbers would whittle down, until by breakfast time it was just myself plus a few exhausted retainers anxious to cry for quarter. This is where my stamina training in kalooki served me well. I kept bright and fresh while others wilted.

'How do you manage to keep going?' I was often asked.

'Practice!' was my reply.

In 1979, I got bitten by the bug of politics. It was inevitable that anyone with money and an expensive car sooner or later comes to the notice of the Conservative Party and its money-making machine. At first I was invited to be patron of the Tory Association Ball. In fact, I took this assignment for two years running, a rare breed of masochism. I'd been warned it would cost me a lot of money, and it did, but I wasn't deterred.

From there I got drawn in gradually, deeper and deeper. I was persuaded to stand as the municipal candidate for Cheetham Ward. I knew I had no chance of winning in such a Labour stronghold but I was not going to be defeated without putting up a good fight. I canvassed very determinedly and, as a result, I increased the Labour vote by 50 per cent!

It was not an experience I wished to repeat. Instead, I concentrated on other areas and my fund-raising abilities carried me rapidly up through the wards until, in 1983, I became chairman of the Manchester Conservative Association.

It meant a great deal of time spent with key political figures of the day, including Cabinet Ministers such as Kenneth Clarke and Linda Chalker, some of whom visited me for a meal at Wood Mill. Often these visits were connected with money-raising events and the house itself was used on a number of occasions for these Tory rah-rahs.

Social contact with Cabinet figures and other Conservative Party high-ups raises an interesting point. What about security vetting? Obviously it isn't necessary to investigate everyone who meets a minister, but here was someone close in, moving up the scale very fast, with a high public profile. It seems inconceivable to me that I had not been checked out by MI5 and rated OK. Yet it didn't stop them blacking my name and discarding me like a used boot when it suited their shabby tactics. Nice people to work with.

One of my friends blames my involvement in politics for much of the trouble that was to befall me later. He could be right. Some people didn't like my colourful life-style and gambling. They thought it would get the party a bad name. Things came to a head with a scheme I proposed for using pretty girls to raise funds from the Tory faithful. There was a move to unseat me, but it failed. Most of the party members could see the sense of what I was trying to do and stuck by me.

People tell me there were rumours of a knighthood at this time. It would not be unreasonable to suppose this may have occurred. The job that I was doing for the Conservative Party in Manchester usually received a knighthood, by tradition. The loss of that magic tap on the shoulder is one of the many disbenefits to befall me in the Stalker scandal. It could never happen now, despite being the Party's most successful fund-raiser ever in this city; I have dared to challenge the Establishment – and I have won.

That being the case, possibly my highest political honour was dinner with Margaret Thatcher in 1983, not much in return for all those years of service. In the walkabout before dinner, I did get a chance to button-hole her and talk about the textile industry. It seemed to me that many northern mills had been closed down, even while viable, and investment diverted to create more profit from overseas goods. I blamed Tory policies and union-bashing. I tried to explain to her that even a modest subsidy might keep the mills going and save enormous sums that would have to be expended if the workforces were put on the dole. But as soon as she heard the word 'subsidy' I could see the curtain come down in her eyes. She didn't listen.

As chairman of the Conservative Association, I retained the re-sponsibility for organizing the annual ball. These were grand affairs costing £50 a ticket, though some companies paid several thousands for a table. It was attending one of these balls in November 1985 that got John Stalker into trouble the following year.

A long shadow fell with the arrival of one Victor Roberts in the late 1970s. I found him work as a gesture, to help him out. He had been seriously injured in a motoring accident and I felt sorry for him. Several friends warned me not to trust him but, unfortunately, I didn't listen.

Roberts enjoyed my unreserved hospitality for several years. He was taken on free trips to America and given endless favours. When

41

he came to marry, I actually bought the engagement ring, financed his wedding (even down to the photographs), paid for the honeymoon and put a deposit on the house for the newly-weds. These unusual acts of generosity I mention solely because Roberts was a man who was later at the head of the queue when it came to dishing the dirt on me. According to one police officer on the case, Roberts needed no prompting; he was happy to put the boot in against me. Roberts even features in the Sampson Report, saying my business reputation was 'less than respectable'. Such is the blackness of human ingratitude.

The split, when it finally came, was in relation to a shady deal Roberts proposed. He wanted to use his connection with a man who at that time worked in the City Estates and Valuations Office of Manchester City Council, to arrange an improper tender for the purchase of the Ducie Street School. There was a later scandal in the Press about the conversion of the property into flats. Large council grants were obtained, and the men involved ultimately made a great deal of money at the expense of the rate-payers of Manchester.

Roberts was active soon afterwards in trying to unseat me in the Conservative Association. His voice was added to the strident complaints of Miss Ann Carroll. 'I'm convinced a lot of Taylor's problems came from mischief-making by those two,' says former councillor Tom Murphy. 'There was trouble wherever Carroll went,' he says scathingly.

Her malevolence towards me is shown by the fact that she reported to the police that I had 'clocked' vehicles when trading as Vanland, that is, fraudulently adjusted the milometers to read less than the actual distance. Since she was talking about events almost twenty years previously of which she could have no possible personal knowledge, this can only be seen as spiteful calumny.

This vindictive woman also told police that there were irregularities with the finances of the Conservative Association and implied I was diverting funds for my own use. This was a rather stupid allegation, to say the least, since I poured my own money into the Association. But just how wide of the truth this was can be judged from the fact that for four years the police investigated me thoroughly from every conceivable angle to try and make criminal charges stick and yet misappropriation of Conservative Association funds was never raised. There was clearly not a shred of evidence for this hysterical claim.

In August 1984 moves were instigated by Carroll and her cronies to oust me from the chairmanship. Seemingly I had far more supporters than was supposed and the motion was roundly defeated. Carroll claims to have started receiving anonymous threatening phone calls at about this time. It's an old trick to discredit your opponent: he or she can't disprove it and the allegation doesn't even need to be true to work its venom. I dismissed it as the bitterness of a defeated rival at the time. In fact, she was more determined to do me harm than I had supposed (covertly, of course, such people rarely work in the open). She too features in the Sampson Report as a source of malicious gossip.

Tory politics came home to roost in my back yard in a rather different way than expected. By the early 1980s, the Thatcher policies had begun to bite, and there was less money in circulation. For the first time, I found myself building units that remained empty. This was ironic, since the later architect-designed buildings were much better quality than the earlier versions, which were little more than concrete boxes with a glass frontage.

The bubble had burst. Interest rates could only go up and my gearing was too high. It was the time to sell or re-finance. I decided to sell. In many ways, I think this was a bad mistake. If I had hung on, the police would have been unable to destroy me financially in the way they did.

But that is said with hindsight. The plan had always been to capitalize the profits on the Precinct, so the final sell-off marked the successful conclusion of a fifteen-year project. The development was purchased by the Viranis, a wealthy Asian family, for a consideration of £2.75 million. The sale was completed in May 1984.

4
Getting Down to Business

We now come to events that are crucial to subsequent accusations made against me by the police; the matter of the alleged fraud of the Co-op Bank involving property deals in the period 1984–86. I will keep the explanations as simple as possible, bearing in mind that the issues are fairly complex, but it is essential that the reader grasp some of the particulars, in order to understand the folly of the indictment against me. The fact that the charges which were brought were so specious and essentially trivial is the best possible proof of the fact that I had no crimes to hide. Clearly there was a desperation to get a successful conviction, in order to justify Stalker's removal, and with over a score of detectives investigating me intensively for almost five years, anything serious and crooked would certainly have come to light and been used.

After the successful sale of the Moulton Street Precinct, I decided to follow a similar formula a second time, to find sites that could be developed and sold onward at a nice profit, but this time to get a bigger spread and so make a larger profit. The difference was we were not going to do the building ourselves but to try and arrange a composite plan, working with companies which would finance sites; others that would build and still others who could help in the sales and marketing of good investment properties.

The first acquisition in this new phase was the purchase in September 1984 of 80,000 square feet of warehousing on Trafford Wharf Road in Trafford's huge industrial complex. It was a 'back-to-back' purchase, meaning that an intermediary had exercised an option he held and would buy the land from its existing owners and sell to my company on the same day, taking a profit for himself. This is common business practice and entirely above board. The introduction had been made through Vincent McCann, a quantity surveyor who was at that time scouting for projects suitable for development by us.

Until the post-war years Trafford Park had been the heartland of the manufacturing and engineering industries for the UK, but with the recession of the early 1970s, many companies had collapsed and much of the former thriving acreage of warehouses, factories and other buildings now stood empty and approaching dereliction, with bushes growing where machines had once stood and rusting railway lines wandering forlornly into an empty wilderness. The plot I bought was an old steel stock-holding warehouse, the cost a mere £160,000. It was in poor condition but usable. The plan, however, was to knock it down and redevelop the land.

In view of the decline in the area it was a considerable risk, but my gambling instinct served me well, brilliantly in fact, as events were to subsequently show. The critical factor was planning permission. In this instance, I approached the planners and asked them what they would like to see. It's better that way, because if it is commercially viable for you to fall in with their ideas, it saves a lot of hassle. They suggested retail DIY. It was the perfect time for it: major DIY operations like B & Q, Texas and Smith's Do-It-All were expanding all over the country.

Outline planning permission was finally granted in January 1985 and the value of the land, at a stroke, more than doubled. Not a bad profit. The City has a saying that it is never wrong to take a profit. A cautious man might have cashed in his chips at that point but I was never a man to stop at the first roll of the dice. I saw a much greater potential. In fact I recognized the makings of a whole 'theme' trading park, covering a vast area and reclaiming a great deal of land that was standing idle. The planners were delighted and gave it their unqualified support.

I thus set about making more acquisitions. There were several parcels of land and ultimately the enlarged site was completely to dominate the eastern entrance to Trafford Park. By this time, my new company, Rangelark Ltd, had established a working relationship with the Co-op Bank. This bank had recently gone into the commercial marketplace in a big way and were being fairly aggressive at attracting new business. Terence Bowley, the corporate business manager, had recognized the worth of my idea and agreed to back it to the full.

The arrangement struck with the bank was that of 70/30 financing. The bank would put up 70 per cent of the purchase price or valuation, whichever was lower, on suitable properties. This first purchase and the one described next totalled £260,000. To prime the pump, my share would be £78,000 but I lodged £136,000, a gesture which the bank would hardly have spurned. However, as acquisitions progressed and the stakes grew higher, the bank took over the financing com-pletely, as the inherent worth of the scheme was obvious to Bowley and the rapidly appreciating security of the land value was more than adequate to compensate for the larger share of involvement.

Not content with just one scheme, I was simultaneously looking around for other sites. In July 1984 I contracted to buy land at Pool House Farm, Poynton, just outside Manchester. The sale was com-pleted in December of the same year. It was an ex-brickworks and at that stage little more than scrub land with a giant hole in the ground. It had minimal intrinsic worth unless planning permission as a tip could be secured. An application had already been refused but an appeal was pending and the results hopeful. In due course, the appeal succeeded, permission for use as a tip was granted and the land purchased.

Tipping rights are valued according to a measurement of volume, generally in cubic metres since the UK went metric. Planning per-mission was obtained based on an estimate of a minimum air space of 150,000 cubic metres and the going rate for ordinary tipping was at that time 50 pence per tonne (1 tonne = a cubic metre, roughly). But I hit on the idea of selling tipping rights for re-inforced concrete, which was difficult to dispose of and fewer sites were available; accordingly, it fetched a higher price, in this case about £70 for a 20-tonne load. As much as half the tipping could be concrete, so even on the conservative estimate of available space, tipping would fetch £300,000. Experts thought that, ultimately, there could be as much as 500,000 cubic yards of air space, which would raise this figure to around £1 million.

There was a further potential worth in the site. It contained shale deposits, admittedly low quality, but sellable. The going rate at that time was about 50 pence a cubic yard for poor grade material; not insignificant when it was assumed that a minimum of 30,000 cubic metres and a possible 250,000 cubic metres existed. But the beauty of this asset was that, as fast as you took out the shale, the bigger the tipping space became. Increasing one would increase the other; every 10 cubic yards of shale dug out would yield £5 and net a further £20 in tipping. Remember, no test borings had been done, no one knew the real extent of the shale – it could be much greater than the minimum estimate.

These details are given at some length, at the risk of boring the reader, because they are important. If these fundamentals are clearly grasped, the enormous absurdity of the police accusation will be apparent. The final cost of the land was £100,000, the bank's share of this was £70,000 (in effect rather less, since I had put in more than my minimum 30 per cent share at that time). The police, desperate for some sort of conviction on me, dreamed up the idea that the value of the land had been fraudulently over-valued and money obtained from the bank was therefore 'theft'. This is where McCann was brought in to the 'conspiracy' to defraud; he made the introduction between myself and the vendor of the site. He is also supposed to have misled a valuer as to the extent of shale on the site (note that the bank insist they do not take the value of shale into account in making a loan).

We now consider a third site in Tottington, Bury, not far from my own home. This was 5.75 acres of land, purchased in April–May 1985, at a cost of £72,000. At the time there was no planning permission but, notwithstanding the fact that a portion of it fell within the Green Belt, permission was subsequently obtained for housing development, which was my intention from the first.

It was evident by this time that Rangelark was going to make a great deal of money in its first year. The decision was therefore made to purchase this third site through an off-shore company in the Isle of Man, Lacerta Ltd. The business term for this sort of arrangement is that it is 'tax efficient' and it must be emphasized that it is neither illegal nor tax dodging. In actual fact, nowadays the tax rates are so much improved in the UK that it would hardly be worth the trouble of carrying out this sort of investment manoeuvre, except to avoid the possibility of being crippled by exchange controls which could be brought in by some future government. But at the time it made sound economic sense.

Lacerta Ltd was funded with £85,000 from the sale of *Diogenes* in April 1985. From here on it gets complicated. The purchase of the Tottington site was imminent and so £120,000 was transferred from Lacerta's account, to reside in Rangelark's current account, in readiness. In the meantime, it would help defray some of the interest charges.

Britton, my accountant, at this time decided on a little 'tidy-up operation', as he puts it. Propwise Ltd, an earlier but still extant company of mine, owed Lacerta £39,000. Rangelark owed Propwise a similar sum. However, Propwise, since it was no longer trading, had no money of its own. To put it all straight took a few simple steps, which were done with the full co-operation of the Co-op Bank: Propwise opened a new current account, which was allowed to overdraw by £39,000. It then issued funds to Lacerta. Lacerta, now in possession of over £120,000, was able to settle its tax affairs and certain other commitments and then send £120,000 to the Rangelark current account. Rangelark, in turn, had settled with Propwise, which could now wind up its affairs properly. Some of the balance of money in Rangelark's current account was next used to purchase the Tottington site, but in the name of Lacerta, since that was the original intention and Lacerta had, de facto, provided the money. The police tried later to assert that this 'money-go-round' was cross-firing, which is ridiculous. As everyone knows, cross-firing of cheques is when there is no money extant to prime the circuit, not as in this case. It was a complicated manoeuvre, for purposes of cosmetology; but nothing more sinister than that.

It was made to appear far more dubious than it really was by two occurrences which, in an ordinary business context could be seen as nothing more than mistakes, but for a dishonest police enquiry looking for reasons to get Stalker off the Northern Ireland enquiry, were a godsend. For one thing, the cheque from Propwise to Lacerta didn't clear when it first struck the bank. It was returned 'effects not cleared'. Of course this is a very different thing from a bounced cheque but in the spotlight of subsequent events it was a very unfortunate thing to happen.

The second complication was that the bank sent an offer letter to Rangelark, several weeks later, mentioning the offer of monies for the purchase of Tottington (which by this time had already been bought). I mistakenly counter-signed this letter acknowledging the offer and so apparently involved the Co-op Bank in the Tottington site which the police were then able to argue gleefully was done without proper security. I can't remember this important letter, after so many years, but my signature exists on it and so clearly I saw it.

As Britton explains, 'I was away at the time. If I'd been present I would have realized that a mistake was being made and explained to the Bank that the Tottington site did not really concern them, that it was an off-shore purchase in the name of Lacerta.' But the blunder was made and it was to haunt us long afterwards.

Fortunately, Britton was later able to show in evidence a letter to the solicitors Adler's, stating clearly that the money for the purchase of Tottington was in repayment of part of the £120,000 loan from Lacerta to Rangelark. As a result of events to be explained in Chapter 6, the police were in possession of this letter at the time of formulating charges but chose deliberately to ignore it, since it didn't suit their purpose.

The important point for the reader, is that if I'd wanted the purchase to involve the Co-op Bank, surely I would have transferred the Lacerta money to the advances account and not just the current account. In doing so, I would have had access to a further £280,000 of bank money, because of the 70/30 arrangement.

Returning to the Trafford site, remember that at the start of this project, I was very liquid and in funds. But in deciding to go for the more ambitious scheme, I was committed to extensive borrowing from the bank. This was no problem; the bank manager liked me and approved the extended plans. The funds were there. At no stage was I overstretched, though beyond a certain point-of-no-return, the final resolution could only be by means of a successful sale, enabling the bank to be repaid. This had been the plan from the start.

Part of my ultimate problem was bank internal documentation. It appears that whenever a client visits his bank manager, as soon as he leaves, the manager writes up attendance notes which are his interpretation of what was said and what was intended. If that bank manager liked the scheme, he would tend to dress it up (as we all do); if not, he would tend to dress it down. These notes are then entered into the banking system and become ratified as 'fact'. But that is something the client has no control over at all.

For example, where I may have said Martin Edwards of Manchester United Football Club had been to see the site and was 'interested', manager Davenport's version was that Edwards was a potential buyer.

These enhancements are probably not bad in themselves. Everyone knows from experience in house buying that in property nothing is word until it is in writing. Certainly no credible financial institution would take seriously such casual remarks as evidence of value of a property – or if they did, any resultant loss would serve them right. Nevertheless, the police were later to try and make capital out of so-called misinformation supplied to the bank.

While on the subject of internal workings at the bank, it is worth apprising the reader of the existence of an 'advances department'. It exists to vet borrowings and see that documentation of security is in order. A customer never sees and probably never hears of such a section; he or she would consider himself to be dealing with a bank manager and be guided only by what he says. The existence of other sections to which he may be answerable are largely irrelevant to those outside the working structure of the bank. But herein lies another potential problem and one which was to arise in connection with the case: advances departments are by nature cautious and seem unable to understand the need for expediency or haste. To a degree they are working against the corporate business manager, though both would argue hotly that they are acting in the bank's best interests – one to get customers and the other to challenge their credibility.

'The trouble with the people in the advances department is that, left to their own devices, they would only lend money to the Pope or the Queen,' remarks Britton sarcastically. 'The bank wouldn't get many customers.'

We weren't exactly blue-chip. We were speculating for a return. You can't guarantee profits but the bank was aware of all that. They were charging us more to cover their risk. You can't expect higher interest charges unless you are prepared to accept some risk.

Bowley understood this, naturally. In fact, precisely because he understood it, Bowley was a go-getter. He had a vast in-depth knowledge of commerce and was brilliant at bringing in new business. If he believed in a scheme he would back it to the full and make it work and he tended to short-circuit the procedures required by the advances department. To him it was sheer frustration to be tied up with endless paperwork and he knew it would lose valuable clients. This cutting of corners didn't happen just with me but, as it emerged, many other good customers of the bank were treated the same way. In fact, the tension between Bowley and the advances department grew so acute that one of the bank's directors allowed Bowley to approach him directly for decisions affecting loans. Naturally, this would rankle with the 'clerks' working in the advances department and, when it came to the enquiry, several of them were willing, indeed eager, to testify what a troublesome man Bowley was and how he broke the rules.

The important point is that breaking the bank's internal regulations is not the same as breaking the law. Failure to follow procedures and mistakes or omissions associated with loans do not constitute theft. As for any harm that might have been done to the bank, Bowley's record was phenomenal. Despite cutting corners, he had no bad debts from his years as the corporate business manager; none.

So when a Notice to Complete on the Trafford site was served on 7 September 1985, which would invoke a penalty clause of £57.20 a day and expire in twenty-one days, Bowley wisely released the funds so that completion could take place before all the paperwork was satisfactory to the advances department. Most of us would recognize this expediency as plain common sense, especially bearing in mind that the funds released were £34,000 against my own input of £110,000. To the police, however, this was claimed as *prima facie* evidence of a conspiracy between myself and Bowley. But then, as we have said repeatedly, the police had their own reasons for what they were doing, and concern that the Co-op Bank had been put at risk was not one of them.

This thread is followed to its conclusion to show the absurdity of what the police were trying to prove (and I use these last few words advisedly). The situation was rendered much more complex by the fact that several transactions were going on at once and there was often an overlap between meetings with the bank manager or his deputy, applications, letters of offer and the actual movements of money. No one could possibly argue with the fact that the Rangelark account was complicated. During the course of the enquiry the police were to generate a 'paper storm' of over 7,000 documents. By selecting certain of these out of context, it was possible to put myself, Bowley and Britton in a bad light. The difficulty for us as defendants was remembering, after three or four years, what the actual sequence of events had been.

The end result, however, was that, after acquisition of several parcels of land, the Co-op Bank had loaned me £996,000 in respect of three securities which were valued as follows: £1.5 million (Trafford), £265,000 (an offer on Poynton from Cleanaway Ltd, which I rejected) and £325,000 (my home, valued by Robinson, Son and Hamer). The important item here is the valuation on the Trafford site by Bernard Thorpe and Partners, a highly respected firm of chartered surveyors. In fact there were subsequently to be several offers in the region of £1.5 million for the Trafford site, suggesting their estimate was correct and, incidentally, vindicating my early insight. These offers all fell through after interference with the potential purchasers by investigating police officers and this had much to do with the final demise of my businesses. The fact remains that, even when I had been ruined and the land sold by a receiver (which as everyone knows is not the way to get the best price for a property), it sold for £1.2 million.

Readers will be appalled therefore to know that DI Stephenson, in charge of the trawl against me, deliberately (by his own admission under oath later in court) withheld this all-important Bernard Thorpe valuation from the Director of Public Prosecutions. In doing so he sank to the depths of murk and criminality in that he was willing cynically to manipulate evidence in a way which might result in an innocent man being sent to jail.

The reason Stephenson didn't want the DPP to see that valuation was because it was central to the police's case that they somehow try to prove that I had borrowed money from the Co-op Bank beyond the value of security offered. As you will see from the above, the total security for a loan of £996,000 (later £1.1 million because of interest charges) was in excess of £2 million. Does that sound like cheating the bank?

What will now be easy to understand is why the police should have been so anxious to foul up my ability to trade. In normal business terms, I had done well and stood to make a fat profit. If the police wanted their case to stick, they had somehow to prevent me realizing that profit. Scaring off customers, which is exactly how it was done, was the level of their desperation. The added advantage was that the longer it took me to sell, the more interest would erode the profitability, since interest charges were clocking up at the rate of £2,000 a week.

To return to the narrative, from the time planning permission was granted to make Trafford a DIY cash-and-carry park, the plan was to sell it. This was instead of the original intention to find tenants and develop with a building company which, it was judged, might take too long. The company now needed to become more liquid again, before it could go on.

Very soon Guinness Peat PLC expressed their desire to buy the site. After surveys and negotiation, a price of £1.6 million was agreed and contracts were being readied. Then, inexplicably, they lost interest and withdrew. It was annoying but these things can happen to anybody.

The marketing company, Samien Properties, were not deterred and soon found another client. But that collapsed mysteriously too. This happened repeatedly and it began to look as if there was strange unknown external force at work. Naturally, at the time, I had no idea it was due to the police approaching potential buyers. Yet it later emerged, one client, who was offering £1.65 million, was visited three times by police noisily announcing they were investigating me and my companies for alleged fraud. Obviously, sensitive property companies could not risk getting involved where there was the slightest hint of taint because, at bottom, property is all about confidence and credibility at the banks. As I soon knew to my cost, it is not possible to function at all without full support from banks.

It is hard to see how the police can justify their approaches to a potential buyer in terms of an investigation of a fraud. What could a customer possibly know about a supposed conspiracy at my bank that would be of value to the enquiry? The answer is a resounding 'nothing'. It is evident that the police were engaging in nothing less than industrial sabotage, to discredit me. We now know that, at this stage, the police were tapping my phones and had rapid access to knowledge about how any potential sale was progressing. In one case, the police showed their hand rather carelessly when they visited a client within a few *hours* of the first phone call expressing interest.

In November 1985, Town and Country Properties Ltd, a subsidiary of Mayfair and City Properties Ltd, inspected Trafford. They were obviously keen to buy the site and spent over £20,000 in legal costs alone and probably twice that sum on architects' and surveyors' fees preparing their offer. By this time the site consisted of six parcels of land and titles to some were extremely complex; one of the plots, which had belonged to GEC, had been taken over by repeated mergers but not actually sold since the turn of the century. Ancient watercourses, some of which were no longer extant, had to be surveyed; rights of way were difficult to establish; other plots also had remote ownership and complicated titles. Any serious buyer therefore was committed to considerable fees in preparation.

This time matters progressed to within ten days of a sale. As Britton reports, 'There had been a meeting in London between Kevin and our lawyers and the directors and lawyers of Town and Country Properties Ltd. The final details of the contract were thrashed out. There was a lot of discussion about the wording but finally everything was agreed. All that remained was for Neville Heginbotham of A J Adlers, working for us, to go back to Manchester and re-engross the contract ready for signing. He estimated this would take no more than a few more days.'

That was a Thursday. The following Tuesday, the lawyers for the other party suddenly came back to Heginbotham with a strange condition on which they were absolutely insistent. They wanted added to the contract a proviso that if they had not let the whole site there was no need for them to complete – a condition which would have made nonsense of the whole sale. As Britton explains: 'They would only have to leave one tiny portion of the site unlet and they could have walked off with it free. They must have known it was an impossible request and clearly this was a deliberate attempt to torpedo the deal, without losing face by saying they wished to withdraw.'

Significantly, this sudden failure of the sale took place only a few days after the police searches on my offices, which would have given them access to details of the Town and Country Properties sale. There is no doubt that police did visit the company because Stuart Ely, its managing director, was later produced as a police witness. Obviously, it isn't unreasonable to draw the conclusion that this particular sale fell through because of direct intervention by the police, though Ely denied this was the case.

*

By now (May 1986, when the Stalker Affair broke), there is a considerable time overlap with subsequent chapters of this book, but it seems best to take this particular section on the property dealings through to conclusion.

Because of the difficulty securing a sale, in July 1986 the Co-op Bank appointed Cyril Neild, of Cooper's and Lybrand, as a receiver over the Trafford sale. It is important to state that this is not the same as receivership of a company; there was no suggestion, at this stage, that my companies were insolvent. However, it was clearly in recognition of the fact that something was causing difficulty on the sale of the site. Remember, the bank had been party to the knowledge that the police were investigating me for some months prior to this action (and before I myself knew). They were getting edgy about their financial exposure. Bowley was long gone, he had moved to another post in the Tyne-Tees area in late 1985.

Gradually the margins were being eroded by accumulating interest charges at the bank. There was still plenty of profit but it lessened weekly. The problem with land in receivership is that it is more difficult to get full market value. Once the story of my involvement in the Stalker Affair broke in the Press, my position became virtually untenable. As soon as a buyer heard the full story one of two things happened: either the offer was dropped to some derisory sum, hoping to cash in on my difficulties or, more usually, the buyer would withdraw, to sit on the sidelines and watch and wait, hoping to pick up a bargain when the crash finally came.

Only one group seemed persistent. Their offer was £1.6 million and they stuck to it. It was an Irish consortium, headed up by Gay McEnroe, cousin to the famous tennis player. He certainly did not give the appearance of a rich property developer; he would turn up to meetings in a battered MG 1100 car, with worn shoes and shabby clothes. He claimed to be the manager of a bank but wasn't convincing. Nevertheless, it was a hope and, to me, watching the fortunes it had taken me over fifteen years to accumulate being relentlessly destroyed, what choice was there?

Finally, that offer too lost all credibility and the receiver's patience ran out. Cyril Neild then did a remarkable thing. He put the site out to selected tenders, subject to the condition that a 25 per cent deposit was lodged and that completion was within twenty-eight days. These were harsh conditions, to say the least. Quite impractical, considering the great complexity of the site in relation to titles, etc. No sensible buyer could hope to get his surveys and paperwork straight in that time. Also, it must be said, a 10 per cent deposit was normal in the trade; so why ask for more? Finally, a most damning criticism – the majority of property people would consider it highly improper not to advertise the site publicly before selling it.

The reader could be forgiven for thinking that this, too, was part of the plot against me. There is no doubt that the police wanted to see that land sold as cheaply as possible, to bolster their weak case. Cyril Neild was interviewed at length by the police and must have absorbed some of their line of attack. I make no suggestion that Neild had been in any way 'got at' but the fact remains that his handling of the disposal of this site was, to say the least, strange. Why would he want to make the land so difficult to buy?

In the end it was sold in July 1986 to Trafford Development Corporation for £1.2 million, a loss of £400,000. I was deeply distressed and wanted to take legal action against the receiver. Since the site had not been sold subject to 'normal' restrictions and conditions, perhaps there would be a case for compensation? I was told by my legal advisers, in the light of our limited knowledge at that time, it was not so. There seemed nothing to do but grin and bear it.

Britton took a rather more cheerful line. 'There was no doubt Neild sold the land for far less than it was worth,' he comments bitterly, 'but the police wanted it dumped and yet he stuck to his guns for a remarkably long time. There is no doubt that the police were sick that it fetched as much as it did.'

But during the course of the trial, the shocking truth was finally to emerge concerning this particular transaction. All was revealed by the testimony of one man, Colin Wicks, the district valuer from Salford, a man of conscience and courage. The last credible offer on the site had been from Carter Developments at £1.65 million. The newly formed Trafford Urban Development Corporation wanted to buy the land desperately and were willing to top any other offer. The TUDC bid was £1.66 million: Wicks was instructed to value the land. Being a pedantic and cautious man, the maximum value he was willing to put on the site for government purposes was £1.2 million, despite pressure to come up with a figure of around £1.7 million (remember I had been charged with supposedly over-valuing properties, yet here was clear evidence of local government officials wanting to conspire to do the very same thing). There was a problem. It was no use expecting me to take a lower offer when Carter Developments were also anxious to buy. Perhaps the Department of the Environment would pay the difference? They said no.

Michael Shields, as chairman of Trafford Urban Development Corporation, then had another idea, which he no doubt thought was very clever but did him no credit whatsoever. Using his other hat as chief executive of Trafford Borough Council he simply revoked the planning permission already granted on the site. That crashed its value. He could then refuse all further planning permission for other buyers. To make doubly sure of getting rid of any competition, he contacted all those who were interested to say that if they went ahead with the purchase, Trafford Borough Council would issue a compulsory purchase order for the land. Mr Shields had no doubt swallowed the police line that I was as good as convicted and expected no come back.

Small wonder, then, that I was not able to realize the value of my site. Without being paranoid, it was no exaggeration to say that I was the victim of an orchestrated campaign to strip me of my assets.

Today, the scheme that was my brain child is brighter than ever. The development has a life of its own and, if anything, exceeds my original estimations. Land immediately surrounding the site is now being gobbled up at £800,000 per acre. That would make my original holding worth over £5.6 million.

The Poynton site was finally sold in 1989 for the sum of £185,000, again by the receivers. In 1989 we heard that planning permission had been granted for a forty-bed motel, with restaurant and leisure complex. That should realize a value of over £1 million.

Tottington, sold the same year, also fetched £185,000. Based on the value of plots changing hands at the time of writing, it should have yielded me around £2 million.

In total, the Co-op Bank received, for an original borrowing of £996,000, returns in the region of £1.385 million – a substantial profit. No wonder that the bank has never, at any stage, made a complaint to the police. The only loser in the whole affair has been me.

Yet, even in relation to the sale of the remaining packages of land, there was more scheming and insults which I had to endure. The Co-op Bank used part of the monies obtained from the final discharge of these securities to pay off second and third mortgages, before settling their own account, leaving a small deficit of around £40,000 on the Rangelark account. For those not familiar with the law, the Co-op Bank's first duty is to its shareholders and the first charge, meaning just what it says, is paid off before the remainder can be settled. This totally indefensible action has resulted in Rangelark ending up with a debit balance in its account when it was actually due a small credit of around £50,000. Once again, the question inevitably will arise in the reader's mind: was this part of the plot? Consider that this improper distribution of funds took place a short time before the trial and that soon afterwards extra charges were brought in against myself and Britton – 'trading while insolvent'.

We now return the narrative to the summer of 1985.

5
Put Up or Shut Up

The year 1985 began as an excellent one for me. I was on a winning streak and my property schemes were beginning to bear fruit. The Trafford land site had virtually doubled in value when planning permission for retail sales was granted in July. Our home life was happy, the girls were growing up to a promising future. It seemed the view was clear and the weather held nothing in store but bright sunshine and cloudless blue skies.

One of the many memorable events that summer was John Stalker's raunchy rendering of 'Frankie and Johnnie' at our twentieth wedding anniversary party at The Mason's Arms in Nangreaves, just outside Bury, on 7 August. My wife Beryl and I had organized a little celebration, just a quiet affair with immediate family and a few dozen friends. Those who attended were treated to a side of Manchester's Deputy Chief Constable that would hardly be guessed at from his dour, rather academic public image. His singing was received with rapturous applause.

Also present were a number of men I had known as friends for many years, yet who were later to excite so much comment. Some of them were men with petty convictions from the past and, by associating with them at a social gathering of this sort, it was said the DCC had brought the police into disrepute. The ridiculousness of this assertion is that even I didn't know about their backgrounds until it came out during the Sampson enquiry into Stalker. It wasn't exactly a Mafia convention. To get it into perspective, seven of the guests had criminal records, mostly minor; six of them had been present at my fiftieth birthday party, also cited in the Sampson Report. Three of these men were last convicted in 1966, 1962 and 1944. The crimes concerned were as petty as receiving a stolen battery, handling stolen cloth and, in one man's case, stealing potatoes at the age of ten; none had been to prison but had only received small fines. As I understand it, the slate should have been wiped clean long ago for most of these men, according to the Rehabilitation of Offenders Act, 1974. Even the man with the most serious record had not been actively involved in crime for years. He was, in the very best sense, 'reformed' and, since policing is all about getting men to mend their ways, what harm could there be in his presence? The truth, of course, is none; except when devious men are trying to twist the facts to fit their perverted schemes.

How was Stalker to know about this long-ago history? I daresay he would have come in for far more criticism if he had attempted to access criminal records to check up on friends and acquaintances.

The irony of the charges of associating with 'undesirable' people was that Stalker was a man I knew to be happy in any company, because he was totally incorruptible. No matter who he was with, he was secure in this self-knowledge and therefore had nothing to fear from being compromised. As events will show, it was men within his own profession that couldn't be trusted; not strangers at a party.

In the same year, on 1 April, I finally sold my yacht *Diogenes* to Alan Brooks, a man I had never met but who, by a twist of fate, it subsequently turned out was involved in drugs trafficking. He was eventually arrested with three other Britons on 2 February 1987, just outside Puerto Banus, and the Spanish police claimed to have cracked a major drugs ring called the Octopus, though how much of that was media hype just to make the authorities look good I'm not certain.

In fact, I already had my suspicions. In January 1985 I had granted a licence to Brooks to sail *Diogenes* in Spanish and Portuguese waters. This is normal practice when someone expresses an interest in buying a vessel. I knew something was wrong when *Diogenes* turned up in Dartmouth on 3 February. I was suspicious that the boat might have been used for drug running, and reported the incident to Jim Anderton over a drink at a Manchester City Football Club luncheon on 5 May. I remember the day well, since Jim was the guest speaker. I also reported the movements of the boat to Stalker. These were not formal statements, I hasten to add, but comments made in a social situation. Even so, I was surprised, given the serious implications of what I was reporting, that no officer was despatched to take a statement from me. At the time, I put this down to sloppy policing and gave the matter no further thought. However, when the Stalker chronology is looked at in detail, it is clear that the GMP plot against him was under way by this time. The suspicion of drugs trafficking was already being used to investigate me and my affairs as part of the campaign to get Stalker. Therefore, this action of an obviously innocent man was simply ignored, since it didn't suit the police.

Naturally, when Brooks was finally arrested in 1987, a year after the Stalker Affair had shattered their credibility, the GMP were anxious to know whether they could implicate me in the activities of the gang. Officers were despatched to Marbella, but ultimately the police had to accept that I was innocent of any involvement.

Bearing in mind the Miami holiday with Stalker and its considerable impact on the case, together with these suspicions about drugs dealing, it could be said that buying the yacht *Diogenes* was one of the worst mistakes I ever made. As an aside, I went to Puerto Banus recently and saw her still moored there, in custody, and gradually deteriorating. If it was possible for a boat to be contrite and apologetic, that's how I would say she looked. I was reminded once more of the old saying that the two happiest days in a boat owner's life are the day he buys her and the day he sells her.

Despite the successes of 1985, it was in the summer of that year that I was first alerted to certain unusual occurrences. The caretaker of 2, St John's Street, where I had my offices at the time, reported seeing men with cameras in nearby buildings photographing visitors entering and leaving the premises. It was a large building with many other occupants, so at first it wasn't evident that I was the target. As I have said, I hadn't a care in the world at the time and it never crossed my mind that anyone, never mind the police, would want to check up on me.

It emerged later that at about this time there was also sophisticated surveillance equipment deployed in the woods across the River Irwell from my home. Neighbours had noticed it but hadn't realized what was happening. Only the following May, when the Stalker Affair became public, and my name reached the newspapers and TV, did they put two and two together. It was thus reported to me some months retrospectively.

The truth finally dawned when an ex-detective friend of mine, now a private investigator who knew a great deal about surveillance, spotted cameras through a first-floor window on Longworth Street, trained directly on my office. Anyone sitting at the desk talking to me would be directly in front of the lens.

Then there were the cars, unmarked Vauxhall Cavaliers mostly. They would follow me at a respectful distance. Sometimes one would give way to another. If the tailing was supposed to be done discreetly, those concerned were hopelessly bad at it. Given the make of car, the obvious conclusion was that the police had me under observation. The immediate question was why?

True, some not quite pukka men came to the office to play a hand of cards or backgammon, though this happened only very occasionally. But Clive Lloyd, Bernard Manning and some *Coronation Street* celebrities also dropped in for a coffee and a few jokes with 'KT'. In fact, my office, at times, resembled a social club rather than an office. In the property game there are a few quick movements and then months and months of waiting while planning permission is settled, contracts are exchanged, surveys are completed or financial advances come through. My style was to work hard when there was work to be done and play hard the rest of the time.

The suspicion that it was a police enquiry finally became fact when two detectives approached my sister, Margaret Waterhouse. They were asking about my Vanland operation in the late 1960s and were, by all accounts, very disappointed that she had nothing juicy to tell. She immediately telephoned me to tell me of the visit.

Concerned, I retained Guy Robson, a solicitor of Messrs Kenneth Robson. As a result, Robson wrote to the Chief Constable, James Anderton, on 9 August, asking what was happening.

On 15 August CS Ryan replied to Robson from the Bury division, saying: 'Without more information as to the nature of the enquiry by the police, and the address of Kevin Taylor's sister, it is not possible to ascertain the purpose of those enquiries.'

Robson immediately supplied the missing details and on 6 September, Ryan replied again. 'Further enquiries have been made but I have not yet been able to establish that any officer of the Bury division has been making any enquiries regarding your client. I have therefore passed the correspondence to the Chief Superintendent (CID Command) at Force Headquarters, so that he may look into the matter further and he will no doubt communicate with you in due course.'

On 11 September Superintendent Machent wrote to Robson to say: 'Enquiries have been made but, from the information available, it is not possible to identify the officer involved.'

It was very frustrating. Clearly the police could go on playing administrative cat-and-mouse in this way until we were exhausted and gave up.

Then there were the strange noises on the telephone at both the house and office; clicking sounds and other extraneous noises that led me to believe my phone was being tapped. I attempted to enquire into it but in vain.

A year later, there was a fault on the line and the British Telecom engineer who called tested the phone and reported that there was unusual resistance on the line. Asked directly, the engineer said, yes, that phone tapping would explain the interference and unusual resistance.

In September, I told Stalker I was being investigated. Notwithstanding our friendship and presumably at this stage by no means certain that I was innocent of any crime, Stalker decided to do some checking up. Though he doesn't give names, Stalker, in his book, describes how he asked about the investigation into myself, and was told by DS John Simons that there wasn't one. There was no conceivable reason to lie to the Deputy Chief Constable at that stage, unless he was being set up deliberately for the trap which was to be sprung six months later. The specious grounds that it was to prevent me finding out would be untenable in the light of Robson's letters. The conclusion is that the target was Stalker and this conversation with Simons is further evidence of the plot. Remember that Simons was Stalker's Number Three on the RUC enquiry and would be in an ideal position to feed back to the GMP (or higher) information on the progress of the investigation.

Then, in autumn, the banks began to put me under pressure, slowly at first and then with rapidly increasing momentum. It wasn't hard to associate this sudden loss of confidence in my financial soundness with the fact that the police were investigating me. For someone with a high public profile such as myself, it was inevitable that things were being said, in secret if not yet in the open.

On 23 November that year, I organized the Tory Ball. Stalker and Anderton were both invited. Anderton said he was otherwise engaged, but after checking with the Chief Constable, Stalker decided to accept. He attended in an official capacity, and sat at the 'top table', along with David Trippier MP, who the following year was to become a junior minister in the Department of Employment. Stalker said grace at this meal, notwithstanding it was a Protestant gathering. Stalker's presence at the Ball was criticized largely on the grounds that it was showing political bias. That Anderton had given his express consent for his deputy to be there was conveniently overlooked in this derisory accusation.

Sadly, the Ball was the last time Stalker and I were to meet as friends. Stalker afterwards told Anderton that he was 'distancing' himself from me, and from then on there was no further contact. I understood the position and acquiesced to it. I was, as already pointed out, well aware of the sensitive nature of Stalker's enquiries in Northern Ireland, and would not have wished to jeopardize that investigation.

On 3 December, I received a letter from Messrs Travers, Smith and Braithwaite, representing the First Interstate Bank. They were my former bankers, but I no longer had an active account with them. At one time, I had enjoyed a £1 million facility with them and had paid the money back on the due date. The conduct of my account had always been perfectly satisfactory. The letter was to inform me that the bank had been contacted by DI Anthony Stephenson from the Commercial Fraud Squad of the Greater Manchester Police. Information had been refused without permission from me, and after discussion over the phone, it was the bank's own recommendation that I did not disclose any details to the police without proper authority. Next day, I took the letter to Robson, who then telephoned CS Ryan and asked about Stephenson. Ryan promised to make further enquiries and report back.

Instead it was an Inspector Jones who called back. He was from the Commercial Fraud Squad, and said that Stephenson was not with them, but that he would try to speak with him and get him to call Robson. It was all very mysterious and disturbing, and most of all, totally unnecessary. It can be judged only in the context that the police liked to see themselves as spies, and enjoyed creating the mystique of cloak and dagger roles. It was patently absurd in this case, since I was well aware that enquiries were taking place.

Next day, 5 December, Robson twice spoke to Jones and it was established that Stephenson was away until the following week. Robson expressed his concern, and Jones promised that someone would contact him without fail.

On 6 December, Robson was able to speak to DS Simons, head of the Commercial Fraud Squad. Four important points transpired.

(1) Simons assured Robson that the enquiries had 'gone past' me and my companies. This turned out to be a bald lie and further implicated Simons in the deceit.

(2) He refused to reveal the exact nature of the enquiries into me that he was now saying were past tense.

(3) He insisted that the enquiries actually related to one of the tenants at the Moulton Street Precinct.

(4) When Robson expressed concern at the damage that was being done to my credibility, caused by enquiries at the banks, Simons refused to comment.

Presumably he knew that any approach to my bankers at this stage was strictly improper and he was trying to avoid any admission of police guilt.

The pressure from the banks had become intense. As one bank official was later to say: 'We were concerned that Taylor's companies would come tumbling down like a pack of cards.' They wanted repayments immediately. Obviously this was not possible. Repaying bank loans could only be done by the sale of plots of land. Dark clouds were gathering on the commercial horizon and the real storm would not be long in coming.

This meant two worries for me. Firstly being investigated by the Fraud Squad (apparently), and secondly, the prospect of financial disaster, caused only and simply by those enquiries. If the reader accepts the possibility of my innocence at this stage, it can be imagined that this was a considerable strain and anxiety.

A number of friends, who dined with me frequently at this time, noted the tension beginning to show. Those in the know were sworn to silence but it was obvious to those who knew me well that the largesse and bonhomie were, by now, no more than a front. I was a very worried man, yet still had no idea why the police should be investigating me. As I later said frequently to the Press during the Stalker affair, I was a man who had never done anything wrong in my life and had never even been accused of any serious wrong-doing. All of a sudden the police had got it into their heads that I was a crook.

Christmas 1985 was a very subdued affair. On new year's eve there was a party at the house for chosen friends and family. It had none of the fizz and glitter of our usual parties.

On 6 January a meeting had been arranged between myself, Guy Robson and DS Simons of the Fraud Squad. A second officer, DI Anson, also from the Commercial Fraud Squad, was present.

Robson began by setting out what he called the 'botherations' that were troubling him with regard to the investigation. He outlined the fact that, despite police denials, it was perfectly obvious that an enquiry was taking place. At least one bank had written to confirm absolutely that it had been approached by a DI Stephenson, so there could no longer be any fudging on this issue. Robson also pointed out that the bankers were now putting pressure on me, for which there was no valid commercial reason; therefore they were doing it because of the police interest in my affairs. Furthermore, other banks were now also applying leverage.

Without calling Simons a liar to his face, Robson did draw attention to the fact that Simons' letter of assurance that there was no enquiry taking place was almost contemporaneous with the letter from the bank, making it perfectly clear that the enquiry was ongoing. He also remarked, somewhat sarcastically, that it was an odd coincidence that, as soon as a name had been uncovered connected with the enquiry (Stephenson), the police had announced that the enquiry was over or 'moved on'.

If, as appeared the case, there was definitely an investigation, the police should state what the suspicions were, and what were the grounds for that suspicion. In other words 'put up or shut up'. But to go on with the cloak and dagger nonsense was futile and the damage being caused to my business standing, considering that I had been charged with nothing, was intolerable.

At that point Simons asked that I leave the room and Robson, rather surprisingly, agreed to this strange request. I absented myself, but what neither Simons nor Robson knew was that I had left a tape-recorder running in the briefcase which I had left behind in the room. Later I was able to replay the conversation.

Simons started out by saying in supercilious tones: 'I have no wish to speak to Mr Taylor, one way or the other . . . I have only really come to see you, because you were in difficulty and to find out what was going on. . . . All I can say is this, that if the police are making enquiries, they have obviously not reached the stage where it would be necessary to speak to Mr Taylor. If they ever do . . . they will certainly make it known to Taylor, as they would with any other person, and put any accusation forward, probably with a solicitor present.'

Robson brought Simons back to the matter of the banks, and the harm being done. 'We, of course, can't control Mr Taylor's financial situation and his relationship with his bankers. . . . But if we, the police, feel it is necessary we will do so, and as you well know, we are entitled to do so.' His manner was cold and haughty.

Robson pointed out that his client could hardly approach each bank in turn and ask what the enquiry was about. If there had been no police approach, my very question would alarm the bank, and be prejudicial to my good standing with them. In any case, the banks were hardly likely to be a source of information about a criminal investigation, so that if they (the police) wouldn't say what was going on, then, in effect, there was no way to clear up the situation.

Again, Simons repeated that the police were entitled to make their enquiries, and 'make them we will'.

Robson switched to the fact that the same day, 6 December, my sister had had a visit from someone wanting to interview her, no name given (later found to be D Sgt Ware). Simons suggested that she should have challenged the officer and got his identity.

When Robson countered that this was hardly likely to be revealing, since Mr Stephenson was 'somewhat elusive', Anson broke in abruptly, the first and only time he spoke.

'Where did you get that name?' he demanded of Robson. Presumably Anson was a bit slow on the uptake and hadn't grasped that Stephenson had given his name to the First Interstate Bank. Robson pointed this fact out politely.

These same topics went backwards and forwards, concluding with Simons repeating once more his stand of early December: that he couldn't say what his enquiries were. Robson offered me for interview on the basis that there was nothing to hide. Simons' words are worth repeating verbatim from the transcript: 'I don't wish to speak to Mr Taylor at this moment in time. Obviously you have given me the opportunity to do so, and you will make a note of that.'

Taken along with subsequent correspondence, this offer of co-operation on my part was to assume enormous significance in the years to come in establishing that the police had acted improperly and in bad faith.

The meeting concluded as unsatisfactorily as it had begun. The mystery was as deep as ever. Even more perplexing was why Simons should have wanted me out of the room. He was obviously uncomfortable in my presence. Yet there seemed no reason why an officer engaged in a bona fide enquiry should want to hide any of the remarks made to Robson. The big question was – was it a bona fide investigation?

Against what he called a 'wall of silence', Robson decided to follow up his conversation with Simons by writing to the Chief Constable, James Anderton, on 13 January 1986. He wrote at length to Anderton:

J. Anderton, Esq.,   *13 January 1986*
          STRICTLY PRIVATE PERSONAL AND CONFIDENTIAL

Dear Mr Anderton,
     I refer to my telephone conversation of the 9th instant with Chief Inspector Harris regarding my client, Kevin Taylor, of Wood Mill, Summerseat, Bury.
     Earlier last year my client became aware that certain enquiries were being made about him, the matter coming to a head in August when his sister, Margaret Waterhouse, was interviewed by a police officer as to our client and one of his Companies.

As a result of his concern, I wrote to you on the 9th August and eventually received contact from the Bury Police to whom I was able to supply a little more information, but who quite understandably, without actual details of a particular officer, were not able to assist further. I can only assume that the letter was passed to Bury because that was the area in which my client lives. Bury however, sent the papers to the Chief Superintendent (C.I.D. Command) at Force Headquarters and eventually on the 11th of September I learned from Branch Headquarters, that it was not possible to identify the officer involved.

It appeared that enquiries were still being made but nothing could be done until the 4th December when my client received a letter from solicitors in London acting for a bank with whom my client deals, stating that on the 29th November, that bank had received a phone call from Detective Inspector Stephenson of the Commercial Fraud Squad.

As a result of that, I immediately made further enquiries and was eventually able to speak on the 6th December to Superintendent Simons of the Commercial Fraud Squad who indicated at that stage that:

(a) Enquiries had gone past my client and the relevant Company, Propwise Ltd.

(b) He could not, quite properly, indicate the nature of his enquiries.

(c) He was unable to comment on my concern about further enquiries being made of banks in respect of my client and/or his Companies.

A meeting was subsequently arranged at this office between my client, Superintendent Simon, a colleague of his, Mr Anson and myself. This took place on the 6th January.

In the presence of my client I outlined his particular concern, which was that his bank seemed for no good reason, to have hardened their attitude towards him and this was quite frankly affecting his business. The only reason as far as we could see was that the banks had been contacted in respect of our client. We were anxious to know the position in relation to our client and I offered him up for interview. Mr Simon declined to interview my client and indicated that he could not disclose the nature of his enquiries, nor for that matter could he say one way or the other, whether my client is still subject to enquiries. If however, a need should arise for my client to be interviewed, I would be contacted. I expressed again my concern and drew attention to the fact that as a result of enquiries, if such were continuing, my client could suffer real losses. Superintendent Simon found himself unable to comment further.

You will understand my concern about this situation and its effect on my client and I am now firmly of the view that I would like to speak to you to discuss the situation at large, as soon as is possible.

I look forward to hearing from you.

Yours sincerely,

Guy Robson.

It later transpired that Stalker had seen this letter on the day it had arrived (15 January). Anderton was absent, and although the letter was marked 'Strictly Private, Personal and Confidential', Stalker had seen fit to open it. Next day Stalker told Anderton that he had opened the letter, and pointed out that he was not mentioned in the letter, but because of it and previous conversations, he was distancing himself from me. Anderton must have been laughing up his sleeve at this remark, since he was well aware that the push against Stalker was under way and he himself was fully committed to the scheme to undermine the DCC.

On 31 January, Robson approached Mr Clement Goldstone of counsel. His advice pointed out the impracticability of proving a negative. So on 3 February, Robson wrote to Anderton again by recorded delivery, calling attention to the fact that the letter of 13 January had not been answered. He repeated my considerable concern about the matter, particularly as I had received no response about my predicament, and he concluded by warning that, if he did not receive a satisfactory response within fourteen days, there would be no alternative but to submit a report to the Home Secretary.

Was it a coincidence that four days later a reply was received from Anderton (date/timed at Robson's office)? This letter was also, curiously, dated 3 February. On 4 February, Anderton wrote again, apparently in response to the recorded delivery. Neither letter is very helpful. The letter of 3 February is reproduced here:

> *Dear Sir,*
>
> *I have your letter of the 13th January, 1986.*
>
> *It has long been the practice of police not to either confirm or deny that enquiries are being undertaken and I hope you will understand the reasons for this policy.*
>
> *In the event of it becoming necessary to interview your client you will, of course, be informed.*
>
> *I hope you will appreciate that in the circumstances it would not be appropriate for me to discuss the matter with you.*
>
> *Yours faithfully*
> *J. Anderton*
> *Chief Constable*

The reader's attention is called to the undertaking by Anderton that, should an interview be necessary, Robson would be informed. In the event, Anderton was flagrantly to violate this undertaking.

The Robson correspondence, as it became known, has been given in some detail, since it has enormous bearing on later proving the existence of a police conspiracy to pervert the course of justice.

To tie this narrative into Stalker's chronology, it should be pointed out that the 15 February was the date Sir John Hermon sent John Stalker's interim report in to the DPP.

A few days later, on 28 February, a verbal exchange took place between Anderton and myself. The occasion was a Variety Club of Ireland dinner dance at the Piccadilly Hotel. Anderton, who is a fairly physical man, grabbed me by the arm as I was walking past, and said: 'What's the matter Kevin?' (We'd known each other for years and were on first name terms.)

I replied, 'Jim, you know what's the matter. I'm not a crook: your force is investigating me, and it's damaging my businesses.'

Anderton's version, given in the Sampson Report, is that I made an open approach to him to complain about the effects the police enquiries were having on my businesses. In deciding who is telling the truth, the reader should bear in mind that, up to this point I had carried on my approaches quite properly, despite all the frustrations, via my solicitor. I knew that you couldn't expect to get anywhere approaching the Chief Constable in that fashion.

One morning in early March, my accountant Derek Britton entered the office and found signs of a disturbance. On close scrutiny, he realized that the filing cabinet had been entered and the files tampered with. Nothing was missing; it wasn't a burglary in the classic sense. Whoever had forced their way into the office had taken what they wanted – information. At the time, the significance of this event was not clear, but it was to emerge that this crime had almost unquestionably been carried out by the police, without search warrants. Vital information which was later to be used by the prosecution could only have been obtained in this way. We made this startling accusation several times in our later court actions and it was never denied. If all this seems too far-fetched for the reader, it has since been established by independent researchers, not working for me, that GMP do indeed use civilians for breaking and entering. The technique is to saturate the area with plain-clothes men, in case a uniformed bobby chances by, and then send in the burglar. By this means information can be obtained illegally, without the bother and restrictions of search warrants, which can be used later to collect useful material in the orthodox legal manner. Such an abuse of the law would have seemed unbelievable to me years ago, but now, after many dealings with the police and coming to terms with their methods, I have no reason to doubt our intelligence on this particular point. Of course, I can speak only for the Manchester police, but there seems no reason to suppose it is confined to this region.

On 12 March, unknown to me, Orders of Access were issued under the provisions of the Police and Criminal Evidence Act 1984 (PACE), in respect of my bank accounts and those of my businesses. At that time, I was trading as Rangelark Ltd, but Mistform Ltd, MBE Properties Ltd and Propwise Ltd, all concerned with the Moulton Street Precinct, were still extant. American Express was also served with an Access Order and here the police covered their trail badly. Two statements taken from an Amex official were concerned entirely with the holiday in Miami with John Stalker, which was clearly not the purpose for which the orders were granted. This abuse of process was a great help in proving that the police had acted improperly, giving fraudulent reasons for their enquiry. It quite clearly ties in the charade of investigating me with the plot to depose John Stalker.

The most important point, however, is that in order to secure the Access Orders a police officer (in this case it was the mysterious DI Anthony Stephenson) had to place relevant information before the Recorder of Manchester, Judge Presst QC. This deposition was made under oath, as with swearing out a search warrant. In the fullness of time, it emerged that in issuing the Access Orders, Judge Presst directed that the information deposed by Stephenson was to be placed in a sealed envelope, and that this envelope was never to be opened, unless on his instruction. Eventually the contents of this sealed envelope were to assume enormous importance for me and my attempt to fight back against the police conspiracy.

Why did Judge Presst ask for the depositions to be kept secret? The reason for this was something we were to discover later.

Greatly concerned about how these Access Orders had been obtained, on 24 March Robson wrote yet another letter to the Chief Constable, as follows:

> For the Personal Attention of the Chief Constable
> *Dear Mr Anderton*
> Kevin Taylor
> *I refer to your letter of the 3rd February, the contents of which I was grateful to note.*
>
> *However, our client received a letter from Barclay's Bank PLC dated the 14th of March advising that the Bank had been served with an Order under Section 9 of the Police and Criminal Evidence Act 1984 granting access to ledger accounts, accounting documents, correspondence, minutes and business records to your force in respect of our client's own account and those of three limited companies with which he is connected.*
>
> *Clearly this was highly distressing to our client and on making further enquiries he is aware that certainly one other bank has been served with a similar Order.*

Whilst I appreciate that it is not the practice of the Police to confirm or deny that enquiries are being undertaken, it must now be the case that enquiries are being undertaken.

That being the case I must refer to my letter of the 13th of January.

As you know, on the 6th January, I tendered my client for interview to your officer. I subsequently repeated that tender in my letter of the 13th January and I am, therefore somewhat surprised that the need should have been found for an application to have been made to a Circuit Judge, presumably ex parte [ex parte means secretly in camera without the other party present].

As I said above, I do feel that an interview is now appropriate on, of course, the basis that such an interview be conducted in the presence of his Solicitor, as stated in the letter of the 3rd February.

I look forward to hearing from you as soon as it is conveniently possible.

Yours sincerely,

Guy Robson

On 2 April Anderton replied, finally admitting there was an enquiry. He repeated that if it should be necessary to interview me, he (Robson) would be notified as soon as possible.

Robson wrote back on 25 April, pointing out the help and co-operation offered on several occasions. He stated he was concerned about the nature of the evidence that may have been put before the judge in obtaining the Access Orders under the PACE Act. Clearly those wedded to the knowledge that I was innocent of any crime would have the view that any such evidence must have been shady to say the least.

Anderton replied on 28 April. It is a haughty and dismissive letter given here in full:

Dear Sir

Re: Mr Kevin Taylor

With reference to your letter of 25th of April I have to inform you that it is not my policy in the particular circumstances of cases of this sort, to disclose at this stage any information you seek respecting points at issue. If and when it is necessary for your client to be interviewed by investigating officers of the Greater Manchester Police Force you and your client will, of course, be advised and relevant information communicated to you.

This latest letter of yours which has been sent to me personally at my office now prompts me to raise an important matter. Whilst I fully appreciate that it is the rightful prerogative of any legal representative to write to me personally as Chief Constable in the interests of or in connection with a client, your persistence in doing so in the case of Mr Kevin Taylor is, to say the least, unusual and, in my experience as Chief Constable of Greater Manchester during the past ten years, also quite unprecedented.

I am sure you will appreciate that officers in the various investigation branches in my Force conduct many enquiries of different kinds involving numerous people, and subject to my being satisfied as to the propriety and necessity of these investigations, and that there is orderly and correct supervision of them, I must allow them to continue towards a proper conclusion.
    Yours faithfully
    J. Anderton
    Chief Constable

There seemed little else that could be done except wait anxiously for events to develop.

The reader will recall from the previous chapter on Trafford, that at this stage the police were visiting potential clients, in some cases intimidating them and waging a campaign of harassment against my companies. Sales were collapsing mysteriously as a result.

Was this what Anderton considered a proper enquiry with 'orderly and correct supervision'? Or was there an orchestrated campaign of intimidation operating under his command?

If there was any doubt, it was dispelled by a startling incident which took place about this time, which considerably increased my alarm. A petty crook, someone I had never met before in my life, dashed into the Rangelark office at St John Street, very agitated indeed. He claimed to have just been released by the police after being picked up and held in a secret location for four days. He'd been interrogated extensively about Kevin Taylor, he said. A lot of pressure was brought to bear on him to say something incriminating but he had refused, never having met me and knowing nothing about me. Ultimately the police had released the man, realizing they were getting nowhere. He had located me and come immediately to tell me what had happened. Whatever the truth of these sensational claims, he was clearly a very frightened and demoralized individual and did not intend to stay another day in Manchester. Unfortunately, we made a serious error in considering the man's claims not sufficiently credible and so not taking a signed statement from him. But at that time the enormous scale of the police operation and the depths of its dirty tactics simply hadn't been appreciated. We still had no idea where it was all leading.

Meanwhile, for Stalker, time was running out fast. On 30 April 1986, Sir John Hermon failed to keep an appointment that had been made weeks earlier. Very dissatisfied, Stalker returned to Manchester but not before obtaining a number of Special Branch documents that he had been seeking. The all-important tape of the hayshed shooting had still not been forthcoming. Back in his office in Manchester, Stalker telephoned Belfast and made another appointment with Hermon for 19 May. In fact, he was never to see Hermon.

Forces were now on the move that were to make history in Britain that summer.

6
Searches

On 9 May 1986, the bombshell exploded. At around 8.00 am, six police officers, including a policewoman, arrived at Wood Mill, our family home, with search warrants. Beryl was in her dressing gown when Trevor Goodwin, who looks after the house and lives in the adjoining cottage, called from the telephone at the bottom of the stairs to report anxiously what was happening.

I had just got out of the jacuzzi and was back in the bedroom. I dressed and went downstairs. Beryl followed a few moments later. By this time the police had entered beyond the front porch. The principal officers were shown into the smaller of the two lounges. Alarmed, Beryl asked me what was going on. I told her that the police had a warrant to search the house. Beryl asked the principal officer, DI Murray, to show her the document which gave him the right to enter her home. He did not answer but, with yet another demonstration of the extraordinary arrogance and insolence which was to characterize the whole investigation, he interrupted her question, demanding to know if there was anybody in bed. Beryl told him that our younger daughter, Emma, was ill in bed at the time. The strain of all the police enquiries, which had come at the time of the final build-up to her 'O'-Level exams, had taken its toll on her health.

'If you don't want your daughter embarrassed, get her out of bed at once,' Murray snapped.

Beryl stood her ground and repeated her request to see the search warrant, which she was quite entitled to do. Murray, apparently incensed that anyone should stand up to him, even more truculently barked his instructions to 'get your daughter out of bed immediately'.

At this point I intervened. 'Perhaps you'd better get Emma out of bed, love,' I said to her gently.

Bowing to the pressure Beryl went upstairs and got Emma out of bed and so did not have the opportunity to read on the document:

'Sworn in front of D. Fairclough Esq, the Stipendiary Magistrate at the Manchester Magistrates' Court'. She might have been puzzled at the letters DIU (Drug Intelligence Unit).

This was to become very significant in later establishing the existence of a police conspiracy, and that the warrant, and others like it, had been obtained by laying false evidence before the magistrate. In the event, the idea of drugs charges would have made the subsequent 'search' more puzzling, rather than less so.

Meanwhile, the police had already begun to search downstairs. They started in the dining room where there was a sideboard. One officer concentrated on this room, which is not large and adjoins the lounge in which the initial confrontation had taken place. Two or three officers searched the lounge itself. They seemed to spend a long time at a small bureau, in which a large number of photographs were kept, mainly of holiday times and family events when the children were just babies.

Two officers and the policewoman looked at every photograph one by one. It took a long time: there were literally hundreds in the bureau. Some photographs were chosen and taken away. We were given a receipt on the back of the warrant, describing the articles so taken, generically, as 'photographs'.

While this was going on, another officer was searching the kitchen which adjoins the dining room in an 'L' shape; other officers went upstairs. Beryl was asked to accompany the policewoman while she searched the girls' bedrooms.

Beryl complained on Emma's behalf, that the invasion of privacy and general atmosphere of threat and confrontation was very distressing for an adolescent girl. The policewoman seemed to understand, and commented that in Emma's place she would probably feel the same.

'I noticed that the search of the girls' bedrooms, or in fact, of the two spare bedrooms, was not very thorough,' Beryl was later able to report. 'I got the impression from the policewoman and from her colleagues upstairs that the search was perfunctory and unenthusiastic. When they got to our bedroom, the search of the wardrobes, which were very cramped, was less than professionally thorough.'

On the dressing table were a few papers and a photograph. One of the officers pondered over these. Beryl walked over and picked up the photograph.

'Memories of happier days?' asked the officer in not unfriendly tones.

'Yes, it was our last holiday,' Beryl informed him.

Two of the officers discussed the photograph together, and decided to leave it. By this time, Beryl had come to the opinion that they were interested in photographs more than anything else. This is important in relation to what happened to John Stalker a few weeks later.

Downstairs, watching the remainder of the search, I was forming the same impression. Even more disturbing was the fact that the police seemed to know what they were looking for and where to find it. Almost immediately one of the officers entered a small cupboard under the stairs, where we kept most of our family photograph albums. Yet the door to this storage room was particularly well disguised in the wooden panelling. In all other respects, the search was a token one, and soon over. The whole business took little more than an hour. There were no sniffer dogs; not one floorboard was raised. This was strange, to say the least, for what purported to be a drugs investigation.

At one point I lost my temper and snapped at Murray: 'This has been going on for two years and I am going to find out who keeps pushing this. When I find out, I'll have someone out of Chester House.' Given the duress of the situation it seems a natural thing to say, but great play was made on this remark in the Sampson Report, as if it meant something sinister. It need hardly be said that, since the collapse of the malicious prosecution, I may yet see this prediction fulfilled.

The only documentation the police took away for their efforts was a big black bag full of old bank statements and returned cheques, also from under the stairs. These all dated from the early 1970s and by no stretch of the imagination could they be relevant to the ultimate charge of defrauding the Co-operative Bank, or any of my companies or affairs. They were not used in evidence. The conclusion was that they were removed merely as a smokescreen, to make the search seem more credible.

Instead, most of the search time was spent on family albums and photographs, of at least ten or twelve volumes, of which the police took away three, leaving the rest behind. The three that were taken away contained photographs of John Stalker and his wife in various social and holiday engagements with Beryl and myself.

In fact, the whole pretence of a warrant and a search was such a patent sham, and the actions of the police so impossible to rationalize, that I realized from that moment there was unquestionably a police conspiracy with some ulterior purpose in view. What that purpose might be, I could not guess, and I had to wait a few more weeks before matters were to become clear.

There are two important points to call to the reader's attention. In a statement on oath on 7 May 1986, Detective Inspector Anthony

Stephenson, under the order of seniors – who we shall name – stated that he had 'reasonable cause to believe that a serious arrestable offence had been committed, namely to obtain dishonestly from the Co-operative Bank PLC, the sum of £240,000 by deception, and that there is material: ledger accounts, accounting documents, correspondence minutes and business records at premises, Kevin Taylor's home, Wood Mill, Summerseat, Bury, which material is likely to be of substantial value to the investigation of the said offence and is likely to be relevant evidence.' I say that photographs of Stalker and my family could not possibly fall within this purview.

Secondly, if the warrant was obtained falsely, the search constituted a violation of privacy and trespass, and anything removed from the premises had been stolen by the police. It is a condition of any search warrant that entry can be gained no other way and therefore I say that Stephenson was false in this also, bearing in mind the correspondence already existing between the Chief Constable and Guy Robson and my obvious willingness to co-operate.

Furthermore, the Co-op Bank had not made any complaint of a fraud and there was no reasonable cause to believe one had been committed. What Stephenson's investigation amounted to was, in fact, a massive trawl through my affairs to try to find a crime, not establish one, which is illegal and unconstitutional. The real purpose of the search was simply to get dirt on Stalker.

For a long time, it remained a mystery to me how the police knew exactly where to look for the items they wanted, if they had never visited the house previously. I did not associate it with the break-in at our office reported in the previous chapter. It was only after the start of the trial that I met a man who had spent years investigating GMP and claimed to have conclusive evidence of the police hiring burglars to work on their behalf. As I have said, a professional would be sent in and the area saturated with plain-clothes men, to make sure a uniformed patrol didn't stumble across the crime, in order to obtain valuable material about a supposed suspect. Could this be what was used against me, to gather information that could not be obtained legally? Some facts on this case are hard to explain any other way.

Meanwhile, on the same day as the fiasco at the house, other search warrants were also executed as follows: the offices of Rangelark Ltd, my principal company; the offices of Britton and Co, my accountant; Britton's home; at the offices of A J Adler, my solicitor; at the home of Edward Neville Heginbotham, a legal executive working at Adler's; at the home of Colin Peter Brown, my chauffeur and former 'companion'; and at the offices of Charnock, Stocks and Simon, the registered office of Compallex Ltd, a company of which Heginbotham was a director.

In a gangster-like swoop the police had not only moved in on my lawyers but the lawyers' accountants. It was a day that sent shock-waves round the legal profession of Manchester. If the police could assume such far-reaching powers, no one was safe. Confidential files on clients, essential to judicial fairness and democracy, were no longer immune and privileged.

Present when Adler's offices were searched was the managing clerk, Neville Heginbotham, who stated: 'I have known Kevin since 1968, and regard him as a personal friend, as well as a business client. Since 1978, my firm has done a lot of work for Kevin Taylor and his companies, principally to do with Moulton Street and Rugby Street developments at Strangeways, and the Edward's Street Precinct.

'I had the conduct of the acquisition, leasing and licensing of land plots and wholesale warehouses. I know of no case of controversy or dispute of any material importance in regard to that development programme, which took fifteen years to complete. The benefit that Taylor's activities brought to the Salford community are self-evident: what were once derelict or semi-derelict and unused areas are now thriving and prosperous.

'Taylor is a forthright man, whose manner I admire, and whose honesty and integrity is, in my opinion, beyond doubt.'

Heginbotham had no foreknowledge of the events of 9 May 1986. DI Stephenson and two other officers arrived during the lunch break, when only he, a secretary and the firm's cashier were present.

Stephenson advised Heginbotham that he had a warrant to search the offices and to take away papers and documents relating to my affairs and companies. Attached was a schedule of these companies, of which two – Guinness Peat PLC and Compallex Ltd – Heginbotham knew that I had no involvement with.

Heginbotham read the warrant and asked what the letters ('DIU') next to Stephenson's name meant. Stephenson replied 'Drugs Intelligence Unit'. Heginbotham asked what this had to do with me, whom he was quite sure was in no way involved with drugs. Stephenson gave no satisfactory reply.

Heginbotham went on to challenge condition (c) on the warrant, namely that there was reason to believe that entry to the premises would not be granted without a warrant. Heginbotham complained that entry to A J Adler's would not have been denied for the purpose of any legitimate inspection of the documents, files or papers relating to myself and my companies, had the firm been approached with such a request beforehand.

Stephenson replied: 'We were not to know this.'

Heginbotham, again on the attack, challenged the falsehood of this assertion. He knew very well that Guy Robson, representing me, had been writing to the Chief Constable of GMP, offering to co-operate fully with any enquiry. The series of correspondence from a few months earlier now began to assume great importance. It meant there was no logical reason for the police to force entry to my home and my offices, unless there was some ulterior motive for doing so.

Stephenson grew manifestly uncomfortable. He commented to the effect that if a person received prior warning he might endeavour to remove or destroy documents. Heginbotham rejoined sarcastically that this was hardly a tenable justification, since I had known of the enquiry since July of the previous year, and would have had ample time to get rid of any incriminating evidence.

Again there was no satisfactory answer from Stephenson. Heginbotham wouldn't let up. He registered his protest at the obtaining of the warrants in the presence of the other two officers, who were by now beginning to squirm in their seats.

Nevertheless, he was obliged to spend time recovering files and documents in respect to the scheduled list of companies. Stephenson also wanted to take away the firm's ledger but Heginbotham was not willing to accept this, saying that it would have a frustrating effect on the firm's ability to trade within the provisions of the Solicitors' Accounts Rules. Stephenson seemed unwilling to see reason at first, but after much resistance, he agreed to a compromise, whereby Adler's agreed to allow photocopying of the relevant entries in the ledgers. For some obscure reason, unless it was just that of retaliation, Stephenson insisted that the photocopying had to be done at police headquarters in Oldham. A member of Adler's staff was dispatched for this purpose.

Stephenson called on a second occasion, but this time he came alone. On entering Heginbotham's office, he noticed a copy of the Police and Criminal Evidence Act 1984 (PACE) lying on the desk. A discussion ensued about the sections covering legally privileged material and Heginbotham stated that, in his view, the articles taken from his office fell within the privileged category. Stephenson, predictably, argued they did not, and claimed legal advice had been taken on this point beforehand. That being so, he and his legal advisers were wide of the truth. In December 1988 Lord Justice Parker, sitting in the Divisional Court in R v Guildhall Justices, ruled that in no circumstances could search warrants be applied for to a magistrate in relation to solicitors' offices or in circumstances where special procedural material was to be sought and that such applications should be made to a circuit judge under Section 9 of the PACE Act 1984. Special procedural material would also have included the search of Derek Britton's offices, shared with me at 2, St John Street, Manchester.

Stephenson explained he had come to collect the charge certificate affecting second mortgage by Rangelark Ltd, in favour of Compallex Ltd, over land at Trafford Park and Poynton. Strictly speaking, he should have held a new search warrant for this, but Stephenson seemed ignorant of this important point of law, as of other professional details. Probably he was used to the fact that heavy-handed police tactics got the results he wanted and that, most of the time, people are too ignorant of the law, or else too intimidated, to argue.

Heginbotham decided to concede on this occasion without being disputatious. 'Of course, we had nothing to hide,' he argues. 'Our point of view all along was that we would never have refused to co-operate with the police; they just didn't ask. Presumably, the bully-boy tactics suited some ulterior purpose they had.'

This point about re-use of search warrants is worth noting. It cropped up again in relation to a visit to the home of Geoffrey Stocks, an auditor at Compallex Ltd. Once again, Stocks repudiates the police assertion made under oath – that there was reasonable cause to suppose that he and his client's company were unwilling to co-operate. Stocks also goes on to point out his understanding of the operative words of the warrant: 'You are hereby authorized to enter and search those premises, and search for and seize the material on one occasion only, within one month of the date thereof.' He had reason to believe that the warrant served on him had expired because it had already been used on one occasion prior to this visit to his office, and subsequently his home. It would be so easy for the police to hoodwink the public in this way, because in the heat of the moment, the opportunity to check such details is often missed.

Before leaving the search of Adler's, it is enlightening to give details of further police *faux-pas*. Without authority and possibly in error, the police removed six files relating to the Co-op Bank PLC, also clients of A J Adler (quite unrelated to my dealings with them). Since the Co-operative Bank was not listed on the schedule attached to the warrant, the warrant did not, therefore, cover documents relating to the Co-op Bank.

Eleven days later, Heginbotham wrote to Stephenson, care of the Chief Constable, James Anderton, and requested immediate return of the files, pointing out the error. A reply came dated 27 May, and signed by DS Simons, stating that sanction for removal lay in the working of the PACE Act. The Act allows that, where a constable is searching premises under statutory powers or with the consent of the occupier, he may seize any article (other than items which the constable has reasonable grounds for suspecting to be subject to legal privilege), if he reasonably believes that it has been obtained 'in the consequence of the commission of an offence' or that it is evidence in relation to an offence which he is investigating, or any other offence, and that it is 'necessary' to seize it in order to prevent it being 'lost, damaged or destroyed' (Section 19 (II) iii). This very wide power is not limited even to serious arrestable offences. The police may now seize evidence implicating anyone in any crime when lawfully on premises (*The Police and Criminal Evidence Act 1984*, Professor Michael Zander). Notwithstanding, Simons, under whose authorization Stephenson appeared to be acting, promised that if any additional document should be required, arrangements would be made to supply copies.

Heginbotham wrote back trenchantly, arguing that the police were not legally on the premises, and that the warrant was invalid. The magistrate was in error in issuing the warrant, and had no discretion to allow the search of solicitors' offices, since all material in them is subject to legal privilege. Once again, he requested return of the files. Having received no reply, Heginbotham wrote again on 6 October 1986, calling attention to Simons' promise that copies would be made available. This time the reply came – curiously also dated 13 October 1986 – from CS Peter Topping – again stonewalling this simple and reasonable request. He ended the letter by stating: 'If the production of any original document is required for legal purposes please telephone this office so that any necessary arrangements can be made.' He chose to ignore the fact that, without sight of the files or knowledge of what they contained, it would be difficult for anyone to know whether what was in them may or may not be needed for legal purposes.

In fact, apart from a few papers released as a token, merely to be able to say, 'We returned certain documents,' the police refused to give back any of the many files and documents seized at my offices and from other premises that day. Twenty-seven boxes of papers were removed in all, including even our telephone books and diaries, which effectively prevented us from continuing to trade. Viewed against the obvious intent of the conspiracy to destroy my means of financial survival, this seems just another deliberate ploy. It certainly hastened the inevitable demise of my companies.

Still, I had no idea why all this frightening persecution was happening to me.

7
Ten Days in May

My immediate response to the searches was to instruct and retain a new solicitor, Ian Burton. He was a specialist in criminal litigation. It was evident that the matter had assumed a dramatic and far greater significance than had been supposed and I needed all the help I could get. I contacted Burton on his car phone at 9.00 am on the day of the searches, while the police were still at Wood Mill. It was agreed that he would meet me later, with Britton, at the offices of Rangelark Ltd.

Burton's first action, on arrival, was to speak with DI Waterworth, the man in charge, and demand to see the authority to conduct the search at my business premises. Waterworth showed Burton the warrant and explained that he was almost finished. Burton asked for the names of other officers involved and was told that DCI Norman Born was in overall charge of the case.

Burton's reaction was surprise: that a supposed conspiracy to defraud the Co-op Bank of £240,000 was ostensibly being investigated by the DIU, a specialist squad set up to look into the resources of major drug traffickers. An experienced criminal lawyer, he could sense there was something wrong.

Burton took me to one side and asked me point blank if I had any involvement in drugs. I told him the idea was preposterous. He wanted a frank and open appraisal of the situation; whatever there was to tell, now was the time to tell it. I protested my complete innocence and told him I was utterly mystified at the events of recent months and why matters should now suddenly have come to the boil so dramatically. Evidently a massive police operation was in full swing against me but how or why it had even begun, never mind gathered such momentum, was totally baffling.

Several possibilities suggested themselves as logical explanations of the mystery. I must inevitably have made a few enemies over the years, especially in the political arena, but it was difficult to imagine that sour grapes or a private vendetta could have escalated to such proportions. So far the enquiry had gone on for several months, involved a number of detectives, a massive phone tapping and surveillance operation and a major trawl through my banking institutions, probably at a cost of several hundreds of thousands of pounds. Committed to this degree of involvement, the police must surely have been concerned that they would be able to justify an enquiry of such proportions. I began to worry that, if they found nothing to charge me with, they might plant false evidence in order to avoid the embarrassment of failure and this fear weighed heavily on my mind in the ensuing months.

The obvious thing to do was to try to learn more. Burton telephoned police headquarters and arranged to meet DCI Born, the operational head of the DIU, the following Thursday, 13 May. The meeting took place at Manchester City Magistrates' Court.

Unfortunately, Born was unhelpful. He told Burton the enquiry was of a highly sensitive nature. There was no explanation of what 'highly sensitive' might mean, but in the light of Stalker's removal from the Ulster enquiry two weeks later, the reader is left to draw his or her own conclusions.

In addition to refusing to disclose the nature of the enquiry, Born would give no guidance as to when it would be concluded. He did, however, assure Burton that there would be no direct approach to either myself or Derek Britton without notifying him first. Since no further details were forthcoming, Burton had to be content with these meagre crumbs of information. I was far from happy. On the face of it, the police were able to visit a citizen with terrifying summary executive powers and yet were not required to offer any explanation of what they were doing or why.

As an active Conservative politician and an honest businessman, I had always assumed that stories of police harassment and persecution of individuals were nothing more than left-wing propaganda, to discredit the Establishment. Now it began to look as if there might be something in these claims.

Burton had already been told of events leading up to 9 May. He knew that Guy Robson had written to the Chief Constable on no less than three occasions and each time received an assurance that no action would be taken by the police without first approaching Robson on my behalf and that these undertakings had now been shockingly violated. As Burton later deposed in an affidavit: 'My confidence in the assurances of the Chief Constable, Mr Anderton, was somewhat lessened by the apparent disregard of these assurances in the subsequent approach to Mr Taylor and Mr Britton on 9 May 1986.' In plain English: the police in general and Jim Anderton in particular were hardly to be trusted in any assurances or undertakings they might give.

As a result of instructions from myself and Britton, Burton wrote to the GMP Drugs Intelligence Unit, marking his letter for the attention of DCI Norman Born. In this letter he stated:

> At this stage, we must say that we are a little concerned that Mr Taylor's legal advisers were not notified that the Police were to call at Mr Taylor's home and business address on the 9th of May, particularly in view of a copy of a letter we have in our file from the Chief Constable, dated the 4th of February 1986, a copy of which we enclose for your attention.
>
> The correspondence that we have referred to, clearly sets out the fact that Mr Taylor is only too willing to co-operate in providing any documents that might be required of him in relation to whatever enquiries are presently being conducted by the Greater Manchester Police and it is therefore somewhat surprising that the offer of assistance was not taken up and that it was thought necessary to go to the lengths of obtaining warrants to search premises.
>
> It will be apparent from the correspondence that you have received from Messrs Kenneth Robson and from the conversations with ourselves, that our client is more than a little concerned that your enquiries have now been proceeding for some many months and he has not yet been given the opportunity of putting his side of things. Mr Taylor is actively concerned in the business world and because of the recent Police activity and in particular, enquiries made of his various bankers, his business activities are being prejudiced whilst some question mark hangs over his integrity as a direct result of Police enquiries.

And he concludes by saying:

> We would ask for a specific undertaking that any future contact with our client, Mr Taylor, or his accountant, Mr Britton, be through this office and that should it prove necessary to see either Mr Taylor or Mr Britton for the purposes of interview, or obtaining any further documentation, that an appropriate appointment to see them can be made through this office.

To that letter, there was no oral or written acknowledgement of any kind from the police.

On 14 May, John Stalker was told by Sir Philip Myers to cancel his next planned meeting with Sir John Hermon in Belfast. No explanation given. The meeting was rearranged, instead, for 26 May.

On 15 May, Burton, who regularly played squash with CS Arthur Roberts, got into veiled conversation with him about me and my predicament. Burton said that he had heard wild rumours concerning myself and the Deputy Chief Constable. He told Roberts he was representing me in case his opponent felt compromised. Roberts said not and the game went ahead. Roberts won.

Back at HQ, Roberts and DCS Peter Topping, head of CID, were discussing matters in hand and Roberts is supposed to have told Topping of rumours he'd heard – that the DCC had been on holiday with 'a villain' and there was some talk of drugs. At first he didn't realize that Topping was deeply involved and told Topping also about the squash game with Burton. What followed is important, because it is believed to be one of the main events that gave Anderton the ammunition he needed against Stalker.

Topping minuted the conversation with Roberts and sent a copy to Anderton. It was later a source of bitter contention as to what was actually said. Topping's minute contained three points:

(1) that Taylor was saying Stalker came to his parties and had paid for Stalker's holiday in Miami

(2) that Taylor was threatening that if nothing was done to squash the investigation, he would 'blow out Stalker and his associates' and

(3) that he talked constantly of his friendship with Stalker.

I have never met Roberts and know nothing about him but it is worth pointing out that these supposed remarks sounded very like those *claimed* to have been made by me to a CI Hughes at the opening of the Herriot's Danish Food Centre and raises the possibility that these two officers may have got together to concoct a story. The restaurant opening was a festive occasion and I certainly can't remember any conversation taking place with Hughes. However, I would hardly be likely to threaten to harm my friend John Stalker and subsequent events showed that I went to a great deal of trouble to protect him.

As to the last point, it is clearly ridiculous. It was well known within GMP that Stalker and I were friends and had been for nearly sixteen years. On his invitation I'd been to mess dinners at Chester House in the presence of many of the most senior officers, including Jim Anderton. Why would I be boasting about it now? The only person to whom the fact that Stalker and I were friends seemed 'news' was Topping, as documents unearthed later were to show.

Roberts, when he found out about this minute, contested furiously that he had ever raised points (1) and (2) and that, like me, he thought (3) just too silly to comment on. He complained that Topping ought, as a common courtesy, to have checked the minute with him, before giving it circulation. Roberts was friendly with Stalker and it could easily be interpreted as making trouble for Stalker. Roberts felt that Topping had been guilty of deliberate and covert misinformation. By the end of this book, readers will hopefully have drawn their own conclusions about Mr Topping and his *modus operandi*.

For the forces arraigned against Stalker, Topping's memorandum was a powerful tool. Of course the fact that he wrote it himself doesn't mean he wasn't implicated in the plot to get rid of Stalker. The reader will learn in due course that Topping was in fact deeply committed to the covert investigation of his senior colleague. Arguably, therefore, this memorandum was just a ruse. It did, however, pass the ball into Anderton's court. The Chief Constable cannot escape the blame for what was to follow.

On 19 May a meeting was held at the Royal Hotel in Scarborough between HM Chief Inspector of Constabulary Sir Lawrence Byford, Sir Philip Myers, Anderton and others, to discuss the Stalker case. Significantly, Sir John Hermon denies any involvement with Stalker's removal at this stage. However, I will give evidence later in the book that he was almost certainly present at this meeting in Scarborough.

In fact, weeks later, on 20 June the Secretary of State for Northern Ireland Tom King revealed that it had been Sir John Hermon who statutorily removed Stalker from the enquiry into his force. Given this degree of double-talk, I can't help wondering if Stalker's seniors grasped the irony of the fact that they were doing far more harm to police integrity than the man they sought to impugn for having casual social intercourse with former petty crooks.

As a result of the Scarborough meeting, James Anderton agreed to lodge a formal complaint against Stalker. Part of the information used in evidence was photographs taken from the search on my home, on 9 May, one of which showed Stalker present at a party in the presence of (though not talking to) an ex-police officer who had been convicted of obtaining money with menaces. This weird use of 'evidence' supposed to be from an independent fraud enquiry was the culmination of what must have been ten days of frantic activity, following the raids on my home and offices. It pointed inescapably to the conclusion that the heavy-handed and prejudicial police investigation into me was nothing more than a smoke-screen to unseat Stalker.

Considering Anderton's obvious foreknowledge of Stalker's impend-

ing suspension, a strange event took place a few days later. Stalker
had been told by Myers to cancel his appointment in Belfast yet again.
It was rescheduled for 2 June and this time Stalker had made up his
mind he was going, come what may. Meanwhile, on 27 May, Stalker
and Anderton had dinner with Peter Taylor and Colin Cameron of
the BBC. It was an incidental engagement that had been arranged
weeks before the RUC drama had developed and concerned the
programme *Brass Tacks*. Anderton wasn't very happy about the way
the producers had dealt with policing issues. Throughout the meal
Anderton maintained a flow of polite and friendly conversation, which
included Stalker, and no one guessed what Anderton knew. Peter
Taylor, in his book on Stalker (*The Search for the Truth*), describes it as
brilliant acting.

On leaving the restaurant, Anderton handed Stalker a file to take
to a meeting he'd asked him to attend at the Home Office the following
Friday. He must have known that Stalker would never attend the
meeting. That meal eventually passed into GMP parlance as
'The Last Supper' and the file was christened 'The Poison Chalice'.
The whole event causes a strange disquiet about the mentality of
Manchester's Chief Constable.

On 29 May, exactly nine days after the searches on my home and
offices and three days before he was due to interview Sir John Hermon
under caution regarding a probable conspiracy to murder within
his constabulary, John Stalker was told by Colin Sampson, Chief
Constable of West Yorkshire Police, that he was being removed from
the Northern Ireland enquiry 'for ever'. Allegations had been made,
he said, which could constitute a disciplinary offence. The events
which followed are well documented in Stalker's book and elsewhere
and represent another sad chapter in the tortured history of the Irish
people and the perversity of British so-called justice, with which they
have become all too familiar.

From my point of view, the furore of publicity was as disastrous as
it was misleading. The newspapers and television channels carried
headline stories about supposed disciplinary actions against Stalker,
based on associating with 'undesirable persons'. Always in this context
my name kept coming up, as did those of members of the so-called
'Quality Street Gang'. Piccadilly Radio even went as far as to call me
a criminal, a mistake for which they can expect to pay heavily in the
fullness of time.

CS Topping in his book wickedly accuses me of originating these
press stories. How does he explain that it was leaked to the Press, on

19 June, that a preliminary report had gone to the Director of Public Prosecutions? The only people who could have known about the existence of that report were the DPP's office, an unlikely source of the leak, or the GMP officers involved. Ian Burton, my solicitor, tried to get fair play and complained in the local Press: 'It's a poor do when we have to learn about this development from newspapers and the police don't even have the courtesy to tell us.'

In fact this leak was one of many through the ensuing summer weeks, which amounted to a virtual 'trial by media' for me. The *The Daily Mail* were particularly bad in this respect and seemed to have the inside track for information. Margaret Henfield's by-line appears next to a number of these scurrilous articles. Stalker himself was to complain of this woman's manner and journalistic methods in his own book. When the 'Octopus' arrests took place in February 1987, she tried to tie me in to the drug-ring, for which there was not one shred of evidence. Indeed, as it becomes increasingly obvious the police were desperate to nail me for anything they possibly could, the reader may be absolutely certain I was not connected in any way with trafficking in drugs. Yet this woman printed her story anyway. It seems self-evident that she had a hidden motive for circulating rumours on behalf of the police.

If I had any shred of commercial credibility left, it now evaporated once and for all. It was impossible for me to trade. Even if I'd had prime land for sale at a knock-down price, nobody would touch it. I was finished as a property developer.

Nor were all the press stories confined to the Stalker connection. My family was particularly pained by a *News of the World* article claiming the famous fiftieth birthday party had been a sex orgy, with men and women romping in the swimming pool naked. My wife Beryl, described as an attractive brunette, swam 'near naked', the lurid article said (doesn't everybody?). The truth was that children were present and also elderly in-laws; the whole party was perfectly above board. We always observed the strictest decorum at the house; this was only sensible, since I had such a high political profile. At the time, of course, the public at large were not to know where the truth of what was being reported lay.

Nobody was fooled by the accusations of disciplinary offences on Stalker's part. Somebody wanted Stalker off the case before certain evidence came to light that might incriminate senior officers of the RUC, perhaps even very senior officers of the RUC, and, by the most impudent and breathtaking effrontery to all that is proper, that somebody had succeeded, at least for the time being. As subsequent events unravelled, that evidence never came to see the light of day and it was finally buried for ever by Colin Sampson's findings. The Bible has a saying: 'What shall it profit a man, if he shall gain the whole world and lose his own soul?' I fervently hope that Mr Sampson didn't sell his to the Establishment for that magical tap on the shoulder. Only time will tell.

What disciplinary offences was Stalker supposed to be guilty of? the public were rightly asking. Associating with Kevin Taylor? But I wasn't a criminal, despite the heavy innuendos. Besides, Stalker had had some suspicions that investigations were underway, but as he reveals in his book, he had been told categorically in December 1985 that no such investigation was taking place into my affairs. Later, it emerged that this assurance was a lie, possibly to trap Stalker into a compromising position. But Stalker had immediately distanced himself from me and told his boss, so how could he be considered irresponsible?

Taking free holidays with me? That was hotly denied by both of us. And where was the proof? It had been explained clearly that John had contributed to his share of the cost of the trip. There was no question that I 'bought' Stalker, or that he in any way returned hospitality with any special favours. Our friendship was an unremarkable but genuine one, begun fifteen years earlier, long before Stalker was in any position to influence matters within the GMP.

In the meantime, Colin Sampson headed up an enquiry into Stalker and his background, using the resources of the West Yorkshire Police. It should have been done before Stalker was removed but at least here was now the possibility that the truth would be established and the whole ghastly mess could be cleared up quickly.

Until the findings of the Sampson enquiry were made public, the Press were having a field day. For weeks, rumour and speculation were rife. The Masonic plot was one of the favourites. In a leading article on Friday, 25 June 1986, James Cusick of the *Manchester Evening News*, reported that Norman Briggs JP, chairman of the Manchester police authority and the man who had actually removed Stalker from the Northern Ireland enquiry, had a prominent listing in the Masonic year book. He also named Sir John Hermon, Roger Rees, clerk to the Police Authority, DS James Grant, head of the GMP Operational Support Group, Sir Philip Myers, HM Inspector of Constabulary, to whom Stalker directly reported, CC Colin Sampson himself and last, but not least, CS Peter Topping and DS John Simons, whose names the reader will already have met several times. Topping was to sue the *Manchester Evening News* over the implications of this article but, interestingly, he did not sue Martin Short, author of *Inside the Brother-*

hood, though on page 257 of this book he virtually accuses Topping of boasting about his Masonic favouritism.

James Anderton is on record in 1984 as saying: 'I am not a Freemason; I have never been and never will be.' He is also reported as saying: 'Membership of this organization, having regard to its structure and practices, is generally incompatible with membership of the police service.' Notably, these words were spoken before he converted to Catholicism.

As the intensity of the 'Masonic plot' theory increased, Colin Gregory, chairman of the East Lancs Province of Freemasons, held a remarkable press conference, the first in the Manchester Temple's fifty-seven year history. It was intended to squash the speculation. Unfortunately, pronouncements of this sort rarely have validity. How could Gregory have known whether or not a cabal of his fellow Masons were in cahoots? It's the old problem of the impossibility of trying to prove a negative. In fact this theory has a lot to commend it and certainly, to date, there is no proof it wasn't a Masonic plot. None of the evidence of a conspiracy brought forward in this book excludes the possibility of Masonic influence but it is worth pointing out that I myself am a Freemason, though I have not actively participated in ceremonies for many years.

Counsellor Norman Briggs, said to have been upset by allegations that he might have been part of a conspiracy, decided to get out of the limelight. He went on holiday. Suddenly, however, on 1 August and before the Sampson Report was completed, Briggs died of a heart attack. It is widely supposed that he was a victim of the pressure of events.

Another tenable theory was the involvement of MI5. Again press rumours abounded. In one lurid piece under the headline: 'Stalker: Why MI5 tried to silence him', sources 'close to the Royal Ulster Constabulary' were quoted as saying that Stalker had to be silenced because he had stumbled across things he shouldn't have:

(1) The fact that MI5 was running a private cross-border shooting war against the IRA, deep inside southern Ireland and actually in Dublin itself. This was separate from the alleged 'shoot-to-kill policy' within the RUC.

(2) That MI5 specialists were regularly sent from Ulster to Dublin, to carry out covert operations including burglaries of Libyan terrorist suspects living there.

(3) That rather than betray good sources, MI5 allowed a number of IRA murder plots to go ahead when they could have been prevented.

The article went on to speculate that 'the men from MI5 panicked and went too far in their efforts to stop John Stalker' and that the plan to ban him from completing his Ulster enquiry had backfired on them. 'Now Whitehall security chiefs have been forced to launch a rearguard "cover-up" of MI5's hamfisted campaign,' it was reported.

The most remarkable claim in that same article was that someone had tipped off the newspaper that the hayshed bug had even picked up chit-chat among MI5's own men, staking out the barn, revealing details of at least three covert cross-border operations, one as far afield as Killarney. If true, this would explain a great deal. It was a secret of sufficient national security interest for them to want to stop transcripts of the tape-recordings from becoming public.

Easier to swallow is the supposition that MI5 didn't want any of its current Ulster operations or sources compromised. Whatever the truth of MI5's involvement, it seems certain that Stalker's plight must have been known in detail at Cabinet level and, with the enormous media outburst of those weeks, the prime minister could not possibly claim to be unaware of events at that time. Further, it is my certain belief that the name of Kevin Taylor was known to our first citizen and my role in the downfall of Stalker could not have escaped her, especially considering my former prominent role in the Conservative Association of Manchester.

I feel strongly that it would be untenable for her to argue she did not participate in these events simply because she made no positive steps to direct matters. There is such a thing as passive involvement and in that sense at least my fate was partly her responsibility and the fault of the ruthlessly pro-authoritarian style of government which she has evolved since coming to office.

The bitter irony is that I would agree with her in part. I have often said that if a businessman in Manchester is destroyed, it is of less importance than the fact that people might die in Northern Ireland because of damaging revelations about the security forces. Only because of the emergence of an apparently deeper plot, charged with the basest of human motives, was I goaded into retaliating by embarking on what Peter Taylor of the BBC described as a 'guerrilla war' in the courts, to try to stop my police oppressors. We shall come to these matters in Chapter 9.

The first hint of this 'other' conspiracy came from a remarkable encounter between myself and a plain-clothes officer, who must of course remain nameless. Rather than trust to the phone, which he had good reason to know would be tapped, he arranged to meet me in a well-known and trendy champagne bar. The officer expressed his condolences for the plight I was in and seemed apologetic and embarrassed by events that were taking place. The conversation was brief and furtive. Finally, the man told me there were certain officers at Chester House (headquarters of the GMP) who were out to destroy me. 'These are the men involved,' he said and produced a short typed list of names, some of whom I knew, but most of whom I did not. The encounter ended as abruptly as it had begun and the man melted into the crowds and out onto the street.

I have been advised that it is not safe to reproduce this list in case the man can be identified from it, but suffice it to say that one by one the names on the list have been authenticated and their involvement proved beyond any reasonable doubt.

The question of phone tapping calls up another curious occurrence which took place in the few weeks after the Stalker suspension. By this time, my financial state was dire. Although I still had – on paper at least – tangible assets, accumulating bank interest had largely eroded their worth and Trafford had been sold at an absurdly low price. Banks had closed ranks on me: I couldn't trade. Nothing had gone either in or out of my company account for almost a year and consequently no salary had been drawn. I was, by this time, being supported by gifts and donations from friends. It was humiliating and demeaning for a man of my former means to have to accept such aid but that was the only way I could keep going. Immediate relatives also did what they could.

However, a wealthy businessman, not family but an acquaintance of mine, telephoned and offered assistance. We arranged to meet twenty minutes later in the Piccadilly Hotel. The man, who of course will remain unnamed, affirmed his belief that I was innocent of the charges being implied by the press and explained that he knew of my difficult financial plight. He wanted to help.

I was bombshelled when the figure proposed was an unencumbered interest-free loan of £70,000, with the words 'If you can pay me back, good; if not, it doesn't matter.' It was a great act of charity and I was very moved. Apart from the extraordinary generosity of this gift, it also helped to know that there were people around who felt I was innocent and caught up in something far bigger, something that affected us all, one way or another. A cheque was arranged for the next day.

That night the benefactor in question received a mysterious phone tip-off from an anonymous caller: 'Did you meet a man connected with the Stalker affair this afternoon?' the voice asked.

'Yes, as a matter of fact, I did.'

'Your entire conversation was recorded,' announced the informant and rang off.

Once again, some thoughtful copper had decided to leak helpful information, via a third party. Further proof that there was a conspiracy going on at Chester House and ordinary decent policemen didn't like it. The implications of what this 'mole' had said were staggering; within twenty minutes of the original phone call, the detectives had manoeuvred themselves into the Piccadilly Hotel and were able to make a successful recording of our meeting. The impact of this degree of sophistication in electronic surveillance I find alarming, to say the least. Big Brother is here, now!

This event was virtual proof that my phones were being tapped, despite denials, under oath in a court, by the detective inspector in charge of the investigation. He testified that my phones were not tapped, no application was made for a legal permit for such tapping and that no application could have been made without him knowing. In other words, if my phones were being tapped, the police were doing so in flagrant violation of the law.

I had been aware for many years that chief constables had delegated powers to authorize phone tapping, under the Prevention of Terrorism laws. It was my understanding, from information given to me by Stalker, that about ten years ago GMP were using over 10,000 phone taps a year. I wonder what this figure is today?

Because of the unwelcome police scrutiny, it was decided that the £70,000 loan should be made in the form of a money draft. To give some idea of my difficulties at this time, it should be said that I found it almost impossible to cash the draft. No bank seemed to want to deal with me. Finally, when I found a willing bank, it emerged not long afterwards that they had at once called the police and reported their belief that I was up to something to defraud the creditors of my companies. Possibly a convenient leak of this transaction gave rise to the newspaper rumour on 24 August that I had 'milked' my companies, which was untrue and never part of the police accusations against me. It was just scurrilous newspaper mud-slinging.

My generous business friend, too, had a less than happy ending to his act of kindness. Though he had no connection whatever with any of my business affairs, the police visited him several times for questioning. He describes these interviews more as deliberate and threatening harassment than attempts to get worthwhile information.

*

Meanwhile, amid a blaze of publicity, Colin Sampson's investigation into the allegations against Stalker got into full swing. Hundreds of people were interviewed, including all the guests at my fiftieth birthday party, four years earlier, and the anniversary dinner at the Mason's Arms in Nangreave. Astonishingly, detectives turned up in restaurants and clubs, wanting to know if Stalker had had complimentary food. 'Did he pay for his own sausage rolls?' was the enquiry at one football club. It became a joke and tee-shirts were seen on the streets of Manchester stating 'I've never met John Stalker' and 'Kevin who?'

There were more rumours of police offers to release or go easy on criminals if they would put something incriminating about Stalker and myself on paper. One man was to depose some years later that he had been offered freedom if he would testify to something which incriminated me. He was in jail after being convicted of fraud to the tune of £300,000. Apart from accentuating the general corruption of the police involved, the mathematical immorality of this is that my own fraud charge involved only £240,000.

So dirty were the tactics at this time that Foo Foo Lamar (Frank Pearson), a well-known local drag artist, was asked if he knew of any homosexual suspicions in relation to Stalker or me and whether we had been seen in gay bars or dancing with other men. It is frightening to think that it would only have taken a mischief-maker to play along with this nonsense and some sickening dirt may have stuck.

Perhaps it was a measure of the respect with which I was generally held in Manchester that no one (it later emerged) had taken the opportunity to shop me. Carl Nigitus, features editor of *The People*, was able to confirm this aspect of the case: 'Certainly if Kevin Taylor had been guilty of any criminal involvement, we would have expected to hear of it from a number of individuals, looking for money to spill the beans to the newspaper. In fact we received no such calls. Not even one.' Perhaps, in all the millions of words written and spoken in connection with the five-year investigation into my affairs, these are more eloquent than any in establishing my real innocence.

I myself was interviewed for the Sampson enquiry by CS Robinson and another detective whose name I cannot recall, on 7 July. The interview took place in the offices of Ian Burton, my solicitor, and I made a comprehensive sixteen-page statement about my relationship with Stalker. I was interviewed again on 14 July concerning flights to and from Miami and a third time on 17 July about the Ball at the Piccadilly Hotel and the alleged misuse of police cars. I told the officers concerned that, to my knowledge, over the years Stalker very rarely

95

availed himself of the right to have a police car but preferred to use his own vehicle, whereas Jim Anderton always, whatever function or wherever he went, used a police car.

I was interviewed for the fourth and final time on 29 July, again about police cars. It is important to state that at no stage in these interrogations was I asked any questions in relation to the alleged crime of fraud against the Co-op Bank. Indeed, the police still maintained an elaborate cloak-and-dagger charade and refused to speak to me directly on the issue or say what the line of enquiry was. During the whole of the Sampson enquiry into Stalker, I remained in complete mystery about my own fate.

Amusingly, about this time reporters got hold of the fact that Anderton and I had spent many occasions drinking together. I was quoted as saying that he had always been very polite and chatty to me when we met, that I had known him for some years and considered him to be a friend, though Anderton, in the same article, was frantically denying any such association. I had no idea at this stage of Anderton's involvement in the plot to ruin me. In fact, even with all the evidence before me, it took a long time to come to terms with this shocking realization. As friends will know, I had always held Anderton in the highest regard and considered he was a very good officer.

As it happened, Anderton's credibility was suffering badly in the media. So, on 11 July, concerned about morale in his force, he called together his top officers for a pep talk. Anderton told them that the start of the enquiry was 'The blackest day of my life' and that 'Duty, that stern mistress of the soul, demanded that I send Stalker home'. During his ninety-minute speech he claimed that 'No one would be happier if John Stalker walked through that door with his reputation untarnished.'

Margaret Henfield (yes, her again), in almost sycophantic tones, reported in the *Daily Mail* next day that 'The Chief Constable was heartened to receive confirmation of his view that morale in the force remains at a high level.' In fact those who were present at the talk made it clear to us that Jim's message was received with silent hostility and incredulity. Amazing what a sympathetic reporter can do for your sagging public image.

In fact, despite all the sickly cant from Anderton, at the very moment he was speaking those words, officers under his personal direction were hard at work trying to piece together enough of a case to destroy his deputy, using any means, fair or foul.

Anderton himself, it was to emerge, had put false information in front of Norman Briggs, the chairman of the Police Authority, in order to force the pace regarding Stalker's removal. As Peter Taylor reports in his book, Anderton had told Norman Briggs, probably on the day after 'The Last Supper', that Stalker had been on holiday on my boat while it was under surveillance by the US Federal enforcement agencies for suspected drug-running. In fact this has never been the case; the allegation was a complete invention. It was no more than black propaganda, to discredit Stalker in a highly prejudicial manner. Anderton covertly accused his deputy, without giving him a chance to defend himself, probably in the belief that he would never be found out. In fact, Anderton was to be called to account for this remark within a matter of weeks (Chapter 8).

Two days after the 'morale-boosting' speech, the two Special Branch men responsible for the false cover stories concerning the RUC shootings, whom Stalker had asked to be relieved of duties fifteen months earlier, were finally suspended. This was apparently at the instigation of Colin Sampson, who by now had taken over the RUC enquiry. No one could accuse Chief Constable Sir John Hermon of acting with alacrity in respect of disciplinary matters within his force. He protected his men in a way which could have been seen both as admirable or dangerously partisan, according to the view you took. Stalker points out the irony of the difficulty of getting these men suspended over such a serious breach of regulations, compared to his own case, where he was removed solely on the basis of rumour and speculation, without even an enquiry.

It was now up to Colin Sampson to produce the evidence that would justify what had been done to Stalker, albeit retrospectively, if in fact there was any. These were anxious weeks for Stalker, but I, too, waited apprehensively for the next move. Apparently, I had been caught up in events far bigger than I had imagined and I felt like the proverbial pawn in a sinister game of chess being played out somewhere across the Irish Sea.

8
Lies from Beyond the Grave

The Sampson Report was finally ready in August 1986 and the Police Committee met to discuss the findings on 22 August. It voted overwhelmingly, thirty-six to six, to allow Stalker to return to work. Clearly, the majority of members found the case against Stalker was unproven.

On the 23rd Stalker returned to work, but only to meet the cold hostility of Anderton, once his friend and mentor and now his implacable enemy. Stalker's account of Anderton's conduct in the ensuing few months makes disturbing reading, considering the Chief Constable's frequent moral posturing in the press at this time. It was during Stalker's re-instatement that he gave his famous 'prophet of God' speech and launched his far-from-Christian attack on AIDs sufferers, accusing them of living in a 'cess pit'. Ultimately, by psychological attrition, Anderton was to get rid of Stalker. Despite the vote of public confidence in him, Manchester's Chief Constable was not about to be swayed from his purpose. On 18 December, Stalker resigned from the police. He finally left the force on Friday 13 March 1987.

Stalker's return to work did nothing to solve my problems. Business virtually at a standstill, unable to sell any of my land assets and with interest accumulating rapidly on the bank loans, by the end of the summer of 1986, my affairs were desperate. I was being accused in the newspapers of being a criminal, yet no charges had been brought and, consequently, there was no opportunity to defend myself. Some of the suspicion was beginning to stick. There must be something there, otherwise the police wouldn't keep at it, was the general view. Perhaps this was another reason why the enquiry ultimately dragged on for three more years: to allow speculation and rumour, unquestionably fired by judicious leaks from Chester House, to work their mischief.

Now he was re-instated, Stalker could, theoretically, demand a full account of the investigation into me from his subordinate officers. Stalker was quoted as saying: 'I shall be making general enquiries of a number of senior officers about organized crime in Manchester.' (*The Guardian*, 25 August.) In fact, as Stalker says in his book, Anderton had forbidden him to look at the Taylor dossier. Stalker denied he was even interested in the file. It might have been better if, in the name of truth, Stalker had replied: 'Why not, Jim? Is there something you are trying to hide?'

In fact Anderton was deeply implicated in what was happening on my case at this stage. We now know that on 24 July 1986 he had actually attended in person a conference concerning me at the Director of Public Prosecution's office. This was without precedent: that such a senior officer should be involved in the day-to-day details of what was supposed to be, in police terms, a very minor fraud case. The reason is easy to appreciate, however, with a fuller knowledge of events. By this time Anderton must have realized that the Sampson Report was scraping the barrel with regard to Stalker. He therefore switched his line of attack to me and his anxiety to advance the fraud case must have risen to a frenzy.

In fact, to the credit of Sir Thomas Hetherington, the prosecution against me was not allowed to proceed as Anderton would have wished. The police, characteristically arrogant and cavalier, evidently had no concern for the niceties of whether or not the DPP agreed that sufficient incriminating facts existed to allow a prosecution. They intended to charge me, come what may. This was brought home shockingly when my solicitor Ian Burton learned from David Leigh, a senior reporter with *The Observer*, that a Superintendent Harrington, spokesman for the police at Chester House, had declared boldly: 'We intend to charge Taylor; we don't know with what at this stage but we will be charging him.' The inference was that the police were going to go on and on until they had made something stick. Leigh was so disturbed by what he heard that he had no hesitation in passing on the comment to my lawyers. To hear that the police intended to charge me, regardless of the fact that I had not yet even been interviewed, displayed what was, to Burton, an unparalleled and unacceptable degree of prejudice against me.

Significantly, Harrington lost his post the day after this incident was made public. It was 'civilianized', to use the official jargon.

On advice from my lawyers, I refused to be interviewed after this point. In view of the police stated aim there seemed little point in submitting to an interrogation which might possibly help them bolster a weak case but which could do me no possible good. Remember, they had all the documentation of my years in business, whereas I had nothing to go on and would have had to rely on memory of events two or three years earlier. A skilled interviewer, selecting just those documents that told the story from the prosecution's side, and not allowing the interviewee to see what was coming in later questions, might successfully trap his victim into an inconsistency. This could hardly be said to serve the cause of justice. As one lawyer was to state: 'This is kindergarten detection; it comes from reading too many pulp novels. Why should anyone believe that inconsistencies prove guilt? Often, with the whole picture to hand, such inconsistencies evaporate under the light of fuller information. This is especially true when the accusations may be very complicated, as in this case. The whole exercise becomes little more than a memory test.'

True to form, the police nevertheless devised a way of getting round my right to silence. With evidence which came out in the trial, it became clear that the police had visited the Inland Revenue, persuaded them to issue winding-up orders on my companies and then got the information they wanted from my examination by the official receiver. The man bravely reporting this outrage said in evidence that specific instructions were sent down from his seniors in London that I was to be asked certain questions and the replies made available to the police. Once again, it seemed irrefutable that a massive high-level conspiracy existed against me, able to subvert the officers of any government department they chose, including, in this case, the Department of Industry. One of my lawyers pointed out to me that the last Western government to use the Inland Revenue service as a means to disable or attack its enemies was the Third Reich.

On 24 August, the leaker was at work again. Barry Penrose, an investigative journalist for the *Sunday Times*, said he had been told I was likely to face charges 'in the autumn'. Once again, the police were trying to force the DPP's hand and pre-empt his right to choose whether or not to prosecute. The leak was a complete fabrication, to bolster their sagging case. The DPP was to hold out against pressure from the police for a further fifteen months. It wasn't until the very day of his retirement from office that Hetherington allowed the case to go forward to the point of charging me. The reader can draw conclusions as to the meaning of this obvious reluctance.

The Penrose article also reported that the file was with senior prosecuting counsel, who would be formulating the charges. This may have been correct. The DPP does not rely on his own judgement in respect of complex charges of this nature, but depends heavily on the advice of a top prosecuting lawyer. In my case, this man was Michael Corkery QC, listed in *Who's Who* as the Crown's principal prosecutor. His involvement from this stage forward was not casual. Far from it; police notebooks were to reveal details of many meetings with the police in which Corkery actually instructed detectives to look in certain areas, re-interview some of the leading witnesses, 'strengthen' statements, etc. In the light of what we now know, his recommendations were, at best, ill-advised. Incidentally, Corkery himself was to prosecute the case in the Manchester Crown Court. It seems unlikely and bizarre that such a top barrister would be sent to the provinces on what was really a very minor fraud case. This speaks volumes for the concern about the outcome and argues a very strong interest, outside the GMP, in the case.

Burton was angrier than ever about the dissembling and delays. There seemed little point in speaking to Chester House, the source of all the disinformation and black propaganda. Accordingly, he spoke directly by telephone with Mr D G Williams, controller of the Fraud Investigation Group of the Crown Prosecution Service, and asked for guidance as to what was happening. Williams replied: 'I hope in a matter of weeks, as opposed to a matter of months, to be able to indicate whether or not the enquiry is long term as opposed to short term.'

Since the enquiry had already been going for more than a year, this response was as unhelpful as it was non-committal. Burton followed up this phone call with a letter on 3 September, addressed to Williams in the following terms:

> Kevin Taylor has now, to our knowledge, been under active investigations by the Greater Manchester Police since the early Summer of last year. Indeed, if one is to have regard to the press reports, Mr Taylor has been under investigation since 1984. We note with some considerable surprise, from our telephone conversation, that the best that can be done to advise us of the present position concerning the enquiries is that you are able to say that in a matter of weeks, rather than months you feel you should be able to let us know whether the enquiry is to be short term or long term.
>
> The enquiry must, of course, in the past tense, be long term, since it has been going on for between one and two years. The police, during the course of the enquiry, have obtained various Orders enabling them to obtain information from our client's various bankers. The effect of the enquiries have been that Mr Taylor is now unable to obtain proper banking facilities, his businesses are suffering, and indeed in relation to the major asset of Mr Taylor's main companies, the bank have appointed a receiver. The damage that has occurred to our client as a direct result of the police investigation and the attendant publicity in relation to the recent 'Stalker Affair'

is almost incalculable. It is questionable whether Mr Taylor will be able to recover financially from the effects of this enquiry.

We are, you will appreciate, concerned to know just how much longer the enquiry is to go on and also, if there is any good reason that Mr Taylor cannot now, after all this length of time, be told the nature of the enquiry.

We are sure that you will appreciate that there is little that we can actually do on Mr Taylor's part to force the position. We cannot insist that he is arrested; that is not our function. But surely, it cannot be right that this matter is allowed to drag out interminably? We must ask that a more positive indication is given as to when matters will be concluded and what the investigation is about.'

No satisfactory answer was ever received.

Then, as the storm clouds gathered, towards the end of August, a clandestine copy of the Sampson Report came in to our hands. At the same time Stalker was also shown a copy of the report and he was clearly shocked. In his book he describes what he read as 'repetitive and superficial . . . imprecise and one-sided and . . . probably the most subjective file of papers I have ever seen submitted by a senior police officer'. He continues in his condemnation: 'I was appalled; my first thought was how on earth had this disjointed, inaccurate and poorly detailed report ever been endorsed by the Police Complaints Authority as having been completed to their satisfaction? It certainly fell a long way below the standard I would accept from even a very junior officer.'

He goes on to complain bitterly that it contained many damaging and selective arguments about his conduct that he had never been given an opportunity to answer. If that was true about Stalker, it was even more so about me and this must not be overlooked. According to Stalker, 'The bulk of it concentrated on building up a picture of Kevin Taylor and the people he knew, several of whom had been in trouble with the police in the past, but most of them many years before.' Stalker sums it up by stating, 'Sampson's Report emphasized that Kevin Taylor has no convictions, but went on to try and establish him in the eyes of the reader as a man who is criminal in everything but name.'

In short, it was a malicious and mischievous document. It had done a great deal to destroy the reputation of us both, as undoubtedly it had been intended to do. However, notwithstanding its disinformation, the Sampson Report was actually a godsend to me and my advisers. For, buried among all its inaccuracies and slanders, were certain clues that began to shed light on what had been happening to me. There were clear pointers to the origins of a conspiracy to get at Stalker via me, and, astonishingly, it had its genus in a tiny piece of tittle-tattle in the summer of 1984, only two weeks after Stalker had started work in Northern Ireland. To learn more, it is necessary to turn back the clock to 1983, and enter the shady world of police informers, confidence tricksters, IRA bombers and insurance fraud.

The story begins with a man I had never met, one David Bertlestein, alias David Burke, alias David Burton. He was a professional confidence trickster and fraudsman, a police informer and notably a consummate liar. He had once claimed to have been the chauffeur to the Kray twins, but this was nothing more than whimsey, though that didn't stop Sampson swallowing it hook, line and sinker. He quotes it in his report.

Bertlestein apparently made a secondary living from the police by acting as paid informant. When business was slack, he would sell stolen goods to someone and inform on them to collect the reward. He was also said to be adept at picking up tips from one policeman and selling them to another. DS Bernard McGourlay, deputy co-ordinator of the Regional Crime Squad until his retirement in March 1985, says of Bertlestein: 'I would regard him as a dangerous informant. For example, he might make allegations of drug dealings, and one had to be careful to consider whether he had told the same story to the Drugs Squad, and also to be concerned as to whether he was actually involved in the job or had set it up. One had to be very careful with him, to ensure that the officer conducting the enquiries was running the informant, Bertlestein, and that it was not the case of the informant who was running the officer.'

Nevertheless, Bertlestein did occasionally provide some valuable tips and so this odious individual was tolerated. It appears that he was an RUC informer, with some access to knowledge of the activities of the IRA (or knew someone who had such), and more than one of his tip-offs had come good.

His most important information concerned the long-firm fraud involving a fancy goods company called Cut-Price (Wholesale Fancy Goods) Limited of Progress House, Mount Street, Salford, trading as Pricerite. At that time so many companies engaged in long-firm fraud operated from these premises that the building was christened 'LF House'. Long-firm fraud is a crime in which goods are taken on credit, with no intention of paying, and then sold on, often at less than the invoiced cost price. This is kept up as long as possible; until the creditors put a stop to it, in fact.

In this case, Mark Klapish, the operator of the fraud, got a bright idea for covering his tracks, in which it was arranged that the IRA would bomb a warehouse in Belfast, and the owners could claim insurance compensation and argue that the missing stock (what was invoiced minus what had apparently been sold) had been destroyed by the bomb. As a result of Bertlestein's information, Mark Klapish was found guilty of conspiracy to defraud the Northern Ireland Office of £8,500, and jailed for four years. Bertlestein, who had been employed by Klapish as the 'blower man' (the buyer who orders credit goods from the victims via the telephone), pleaded guilty and the court was cleared while DS McGourlay told the judge that Bertlestein was a paid informant. He thus received a mitigated sentence of two and a half years.

He later died in Preston Prison, in March 1985, of what were said to be natural causes. But who knows; maybe his life as a police 'grass' had caught up with him, and retribution had come at last. The importance of this 'lying pest', as one officer described him, is that in 1983, as reported by Sampson, he began to put it about that the Quality Street Gang allegedly had a certain senior police officer 'on a pension', and that I was mixed up with the Quality Street Gang. This remark was not taken up at the time, quite rightly, because it was meaningless padding. However it was resurrected later by DCS Topping, when looking for something with which to dish the dirt on Stalker.

It was true that at the time Bertlestein gave his evidence the police were having trouble with surveillance of certain people. They seemed to be one jump ahead of the law. In fact, when the officer in charge of the Pricerite case went to arrest Mark Klapish, he reputedly said, 'I've been expecting you, Mr Burgess.' The facts all pointed to the existence of a police informer who was tipping off potential suspects. How convenient for the GMP, if it could have been Stalker.

DS McGourlay, Bertlestein's principal handler, in a statement made in November 1986, dismisses the suggestion that Bertlestein said any such thing as 'absolute rubbish'. In fact it can be disclosed that the subverted officer did exist and was almost certainly a detective who had left the force some time before the Stalker Affair finally broke. His name is on file but for obvious legal reasons cannot be given here. Also, incidentally, McGourlay stated categorically in the same affidavit that he had never heard of me at the time of Bertlestein making these claims (1983), which is important, because McGourlay was his main 'handler' and probably the only individual with the skill and experience to find his way through the minefield of lies.

By a curious coincidence, McGourlay was to learn of my name a year later and from a very different source. It was actually on Saturday, 9 June 1984. Again, the Sampson Report is unreliable and fouls up the details, but here is what actually happened.

McGourlay had been playing golf with two men, Gerry Wareing and Des Lawlor, and at the nineteenth, the three of them were chatting over a 'pint'. In the conversation, Wareing, who McGourlay had never met before, was boasting he knew a Kevin Taylor who hosted lavish parties and that he had met one of McGourlay's bosses there. Also that he knew plenty of crooks, and that these men, too, sometimes turned up at the same parties. McGourlay later reported, 'I was concerned by the inference that one of my superior officers was associating with criminals, and I felt I needed to know the name of the senior officer concerned. After leaving the pub and walking over to our cars in the car park, I asked Wareing the name of my boss who had attended the parties. He replied: "John Stalker."'

McGourlay was worried that Stalker might have unwittingly associated with criminals. He had, and still has, the highest regard for John Stalker and felt that the Deputy Chief Constable should be warned that the innocent link might be compromising.

If it had been a junior officer, McGourlay says, he would probably have approached the man in person, to enquire if there was any truth in Wareing's assertion. As it was, he did not consider that his rank entitled him to speak to the Deputy Chief Constable directly on such a potentially sensitive personal matter. So, he reported the gossip to DCS Peter Topping, head of 'Y' Department (Complaints and Discipline) at that time. Topping reputedly wrote to Anderton, who appeared to do nothing. Topping began to do a little snooping on his own account which was to have such profound repercussions in May 1986, two years later. This was the true start of the Stalker Affair.

Stalker was not warned, which would have been the proper thing to do. Topping, who would certainly have known the correct procedure, since he was in the complaints department, should have told ACC Ralph Lees what he knew, and Lees should, in turn, have either asked for clarification himself, or passed the matter on to the chief constable. The Chief Constable, when matters were reported to him, should have asked for proof of the allegations, and then called Stalker and asked him for an explanation. If he was not happy with Stalker's explanations, he should have then called in an external police force to investigate. A retired chief superintendent has assured me that it is 'extremely unusual' for there to be an internal police enquiry under cover into a senior police officer of the same force, especially by men who were his junior, in rank and experience. Yet this is exactly what happened to Stalker and with such disastrous consequences.

Perhaps he meant to say, 'there is no proper precedent for such an activity', the reason being that what we are considering here is not, in truth, an 'internal enquiry', but a plot to assassinate the professional standing of a senior officer. Remember, Stalker had only just started his RUC investigation in Ulster; there seems little likelihood at this stage of him being an embarrassment to the RUC, MI5, the army or the government. This was a GMP affair and a matter of professional rivalry and intrigue.

By a strange coincidence, Topping claims Bertlestein had started to assert that Stalker was 'bent'. Over subsequent months (until Bertlestein's death in March 1985) Topping's men went to interview him in prison. There were two separate visits in February and March 1985, and by another curious coincidence (if you believe in far-fetched accidents) this was about the time Stalker heard of the 'hayshed tape' and had started trying to get it.

Could Topping have known about the hayshed tape? Yes. We name DS John Simons, Stalker's Number Three, as a likely 'mole' in the camp. He was thick with Topping, the men are reputedly related, though this has been denied to the media. In 1969, these two friends planned to leave the police force together, and set up a road haulage company. They were only persuaded to stay on with some difficulty by DCI Tom Butcher, who, by another of the curious twists of this story, ended up with another senior GMP officer, John Hall, in the Security department of the Co-op Bank and would have been one of its officers at the time of this investigation.

It is noteworthy that DCS John Thorburn, Stalker's Number Two, and one of Britain's top detectives, did not favour Stalker's choice of Simons for the investigation. 'It's your choice, John,' were his exact words. In fact, Thorburn may have been right with his doubts and suspicions, as this story tells. Sadly, Thorburn was ultimately to leave the GMP, an enormous loss to the Manchester community. He resigned in disgust, tired of the lies and deceit at Chester House.

Although there were endless denials that Simons was involved against me, he was the man who consented to be interviewed by Guy Robson in January 1986. As head of the Fraud Squad he was unquestionably involved in the DIU action into me. We even have a letter bearing his signature with the letters DIU at the top. Yet, he kept Stalker deliberately in the dark when it would have been the most natural thing in the world to warn him that there was trouble brewing at home. The fact is that neither he, Topping, Lees or Anderton wanted Stalker warned.

In the meantime, Topping had told McGourlay to 'have a look at Taylor'. The first step was to go through records and see if there was any criminal intelligence on me or my known associates. Nothing was recorded under the name Taylor, but on checking against the name of persons who were believed to be associates of mine, there was a name McGourlay recognized as a petty criminal.

A sergeant and constable were detailed to watch me and find out more about my habits. A week later, they reported back to McGourlay that to continue surveillance would be risky, that there would be danger of being spotted if they pursued their observations.

McGourlay told them he would accompany them to assess the situation, and on a Saturday afternoon towards the end of June 1984, he met up with the two officers at Summerseat in Bury, some distance away from my home at Wood Mill. The three of them walked along the disused railway track beside the River Irwell, and being unable to see the house clearly, went through the trees to get a better view.

While observing the house, they saw 'a heavily built man come out of the house and walk along the drive and through the garden'. It wasn't me but Trevor Goodwin, a somewhat obese retainer whom I had taken in when he had been evicted from his council flat for keeping a dog. He was a useful odd-job man and acted as caretaker, living in the cottage adjacent to Wood Mill. Goodwin is mentioned in the Sampson Report as a petty criminal – he had been fined many years before for receiving stolen note-paper. A villain indeed!

There were also two large Rottweiler dogs.

McGourlay agreed that continued surveillance of the house would be difficult without being noticed, and reported this to Topping. And that was really the end of that, as far as he and the Regional Crime Squad were concerned.

McGourlay retired in 1985, believing that enquiries into me had been concluded. He was devastated to learn that his report had been instrumental in the chain of events that led to Stalker's downfall. Asked to make a guess who might have re-instigated the enquiries into me, he named the chief constable, Jim Anderton.

Now the pot was beginning to simmer; it was dramatically to boil over nearly two years later. I was the key to the scheme against Stalker. There was not a shred of evidence I was involved in any criminal activity, except for the word of a dead man – a notorious liar and a con-man – of whom one police officer commented: 'Bertlestein would tell you what Bertlestein thought you wanted to know.' What was it, then, that Topping wanted to know? What was on the tapes recorded in Preston jail? The Sampson Report refuses to say, and insists their content is 'extremely sensitive, and confidentiality is absolutely essential'. Could the line of questioning on those tapes be the proof that is needed that a conspiracy against Stalker existed before there were adequate suspicions about me that might conceivably have justified removing Stalker from the controversial enquiry into Ulster? If Sampson was joined to the Stalker plot in May 1986, then – to use Mandy Rice-Davis's memorable phrase that was so devastating to Lord Astor's denials of impropriety – he would say that, wouldn't he?

The other possibility which will occur to the reader is that maybe the material was sensitive in the context of the Ulster enquiry. Remember, despite RUC contradictions, Bertlestein was emphatically an RUC informer, and was able to pass on tips about IRA activities from time to time. He could also have been a source for MI5. This would be an electrifying possibility, and could represent the first point at which Hermon's 'Get Stalker off my back' desires crossed with a 'Stitch up Stalker' conspiracy within the GMP.

Here is a good point to call the reader's attention to the remarkable coincidence that DI Murray, said to be the MI5 liaison officer for the GMP, and the man who headed the search into Wood Mill, was one of the officers who interviewed Bertlestein in Preston jail.

Unfortunately, internal evidence within the Sampson Report suggests this second possibility is not really the case. In one of his worst blunders in the report, Sampson dismisses the possibility that Bertlestein had any RUC connections. The most elementary detection would show otherwise. Several people have found the evidence easy to come by.

Unless one accepts the possibility that Sampson was being very clever in diverting attention from the Northern Ireland connection, the conclusion must be that the reason he would not disclose the Preston tapes is that they would have revealed the existence of an anti-Stalker conspiracy.

The rest of the report was full of insignificant nonsense, innuendos, rumour and what Stalker accurately describes as 'dross'. Nevertheless, this remains one of the most dramatic and important documents of the entire case. The first few pages of the Sampson Report leave little doubt about the timing and what the true purpose of the search warrants and Access Orders granted against me really were: to collect the dirt on Stalker.

One startling revelation (paragraph 28) is that Anderton was said to have been keeping Philip Myers (later Sir Philip), the regional Inspector of Constabulary in charge of RUC enquiry, informed on the progress of the allegations against Stalker as early as March 1985. Given the general standards of accuracy of the report, it may be tempting to dismiss this as nonsense. As Stalker points out in his own book, in May of that year Anderton and Myers were encouraging Stalker to apply for the chief constable posts in Strathclyde and Bedfordshire. This seems unlikely if they were concerned about his background and connections. However, if this statement should prove to be true, the implications are sensational. It could not possibly be construed as trying to get Stalker off the RUC case, but Anderton trying to stab his imagined rival in the back.

What is also significant about paragraph 28 is that it states clearly, 'The developments following the execution of the search warrants called for a reappraisal of the situation.' Anderton is thus in the thick of the plot here and it was he who informed Myers of the 'developments' that led to the meeting in Scarborough on 19 May 1986, when it was decided to take steps to remove Stalker.

Anderton, naturally, was incensed by the leak of the Sampson Report, since it showed him in a bad conspiratorial light. He asked for the matter to be investigated by the West Mercia police. A report was submitted to the DPP but no action was taken and his obvious frustration and anger remained unappeased.

Just how obsessed Anderton was with getting rid of Stalker is shown by the fact that, professing Christian or not, he was prepared to spread disinformation about Stalker to the Police Authority chairman, Norman Briggs. He told Briggs in May that, 'The yanks were watching the boat,' meaning that the US enforcement agencies had the *Diogenes* under surveillance for suspicion of drug-running. True to form, Anderton denied having said it. He expected his dissembling to be unchallenged, since Briggs had died before the day of reckoning. Fortunately, however, there were others able to substantiate that he had indeed uttered this accusation. One of these was Edward Gallacher, a member of the Police Authority representing Stockport. On two occasions during the height of the Stalker Affair, Gallacher had appeared on TV, pressing to establish what the allegations against Stalker were and putting pressure on Briggs to come clean with the Police Authority.

Like many other members of the Police Authority, he was deeply unhappy that Stalker's removal was a *fait accompli* at the time they were first told of it. The authority moved formally to suspend Stalker mainly to give him much needed protection that was lacking while he was merely on 'leave of absence'. Gallacher says that he remembers being present at a full meeting of the authority on Friday, 22 August 1986, when the Sampson Report was discussed at length. David Moffat had taken over from the late Norman Briggs at this point and was acting chairman. Anderton was excluded at first by a Labour Group resolution, since Gallacher and his colleagues wanted to question Sampson without Anderton having foreknowledge of what Sampson was saying.

Then Anderton was brought into the meeting. Gallacher went straight for the throat and asked Anderton where the reference to the yacht had come from. Anderton was evasive and, when Gallacher explained his line of questioning, Gallacher reports that 'Mr Anderton did not reply but affected a confused look.' But his inquisitor was not to be put off. Gallacher pointed out that Norman Briggs had said that Stalker had been on a boat that was being watched by the Americans in connection with drugs trafficking and that he had been told this by the Chief Constable, whereupon Anderton affected a facial mannerism of surprise and said, 'I don't recall giving that information.'

Unfortunately for Anderton, Roger Rees, a solicitor and clerk to the Police Authority, was also present at this meeting. After several more denials from Anderton, Rees intervened: 'Perhaps I can interrupt, Mr Chairman. At a meeting with Mr Briggs, Mr Anderton and myself, the Chief Constable did, in fact, pass on that information.' Anderton was caught out. The matter was allowed to drop because, in Gallacher's words: 'It was clear that Mr Anderton was preparing himself to proclaim persecution and his proverbial defence, "Am I on trial?"'

This part of the story is given in some detail, to show what kind of man Anderton is and what he may be capable of when he sets his mind to mischief. It is a vital point because, as Gallacher states, 'I can say without hesitation that had the Labour Group known that such information concerning the Americans was unreliable, we would have pressed for John Stalker to be put back to work the following day.'

Nor was that all.

Gallacher again: 'During Mr Anderton's appearance before the committee, he was vociferous against Stalker, putting the knife in throughout the meeting. I recall in particular the issue of Mr Stalker's use of police vehicles. He [Stalker] had justified this by reference to potential IRA threats. Anderton dismissed this explanation by proclaiming that Stalker had had no trouble with the IRA and hadn't complained to him of such. Mrs Audrey Walsh, a Conservative member of the authority and chairman of the magistrates' delegation, countered Mr Anderton's suggestion, by stating that she had in fact discussed such potential danger and its connection with Mr Stalker's use of police vehicles with Mr Stalker and she disagreed with Mr Anderton's observations.

In short, during the entire two hours he was being questioned by the Police Authority, 'Anderton made it quite clear that he wanted Stalker out and conducted himself during the meeting as a prosecutor.' It seemed obvious to others then, that, despite the cant, Anderton's attack on Stalker was a personal one, no matter what additional interests were served by it. It was in a very real sense *his* campaign and, as chief executive officer of the GMP, he must be held largely to blame for what was done, as it unfolds in this story.

9
Guerrilla War

At this point I'd like to introduce Charles Buckley. Among the many colourful and eccentric characters who have peopled this story, and have helped to make it more cheerful, he is surely one of the stars. With his habit of interjecting: 'Do you take my meaning, dear boy?', invariably shortened to 'Do you . . .?' for his friends, and a disarming charm and suavity, his portly, pipe-smoking form ambles through the rest of this narrative.

Born in 1942, with the best of 'breeding' (his word), he started in the north in 1960, articled with a man he considers to be the finest post-war solicitor in Manchester, Arnold Gordon. Buckley became a senior partner in 1979, and was co-founder of Elliot and Co. in 1968.

Over the space of ten to fifteen years, he handled some of the best-known cases in the north of England. He was involved in successfully defending Barnes v Williams' and Glyn, the biggest banking action since the War, and in 1980 he received a commendation from the attorney general for his handling of the case involving Lord Kagan's family.

Then disaster struck. He lost a lot of money in a business venture involving a crooked accountant. The man later went to jail for other offences. Buckley's affairs were put into disarray, and the Law Society intervened. Buckley maintains they acted improperly and had it in for him, because he had on one occasion defended a number of prominent solicitors against the Law Society. In any event, their action ended up with Buckley being bankrupted, and he was unable to practise until discharged. The officer of the Law Society involved, significantly, was later dismissed for this and other gross errors.

In May 1986, with three years still to run until his practising license was re-instated, and just back from New York where he had been studying for entrance exams to the New York bar, Buckley saw me being interviewed on television about the Stalker Affair.

'It was obvious Taylor was in trouble,' says Buckley. 'Accusations were flying everywhere, no charges had been brought, and I could see the man was floundering. He needed help.'

He promptly phoned me and I arranged to meet him and his wife in the house of an intermediary. 'I sent for him,' says Buckley imperiously.

I explained to him how the probe into my affairs had wrecked my financial standing. It meant, to put it bluntly, I had no money left with which to pay him. There would be no fees beyond reasonable expenses, Buckley reassured me.

'Helping Taylor for next to nothing was my way of paying back the £300,000 of help I'd received from the Legal Aid fund,' Buckley later explained. More importantly, perhaps, he was gripped by the story I had to tell. There were certain parallels with his own misfortunes. Whatever was happening to me, it was intriguing and definitely some sort of conspiracy. To him, there was an intellectual challenge and therefore the case had merit in its own right.

'Besides,' as he was often to say subsequently, 'the Taylor thing helped the three years until I could restart my own practice to pass remarkable quickly.'

Buckley told me I must fight or hang. Probably, he had his own case in mind. In the course of his bankruptcy litigation against the Law Society, Buckley had probably caused that august body more harm than any other solicitor has ever done, such was the ferocity of his counter-attack. He was the proverbial bulldog – when he sank his teeth into something, he would not let go, but became a persistent, painful wound in the hindquarters.

Buckley set to work right away, initiating letters and enquiries, and soon began to imprint his mark of authority on the case. One of his first interests was the circumstances of the issuance of the fraudulent search warrants, which were processed by Mr Paul Firth, deputy clerk to the justices. 'There is no doubt,' according to Buckley, 'that great consternation exists in the magistrate's court as to the circumstances and propriety of these applications.' Mr Eric Ball, a long-standing and trustworthy clerk to the justices said: 'Charles, I want nothing to do with those warrants. I totally dissociate myself from them.'

One of Buckley's letters was to Philip Dodd, chief clerk to the justices. It was couched in the most unflattering terms imaginable and probably did nothing to endear my cause to this man. In this long and technical letter, which I won't quote in full, Buckley pointed out that the magistrate appeared to have exceeded his authority and towards the end stated flatly: 'You may have conducted yourself in such a manner as gives rise to more than marginal, but less than complete, suspicion of a cover up and *ipso facto* that you have something to hide in your public office.' Mettlesome words and an augury of what was to ensue in the coming months.

The important thing about the warrants, however, was not the circumstances in which they were issued but the letters 'D.I.U.' which had appeared on each of them. On the face of it, this was evidence that drug-dealing had been the weapon used to coerce the magistrate. Since I knew I was innocent of any such activity, there existed the high probability that an officer of the law had sworn false information in order to obtain the warrants.

'If we could show that he had lied to the magistrate,' explained Buckley, 'we would be a long way to proving that a conspiracy existed within the police and that a group of officers were abusing the law.'

To understand our immediate battle strategy, the reader needs to know several important points of law. There is no better way to have these details explained than to let Buckley himself do the talking:

In England, we have no formal process of discovery in criminal cases, unlike the Americans who have the Freedom of Information Bill. We have no judicial weapon, apart from the subpoena, to produce witnesses or get hold of documents in a case, and this right can only be exercised during a trial. Consequently, the defence has to fall back on the informal process of delving and digging, interviews and, sometimes, just plain chance or good luck.

The reason for this anomaly is largely historical. It is simply that, in the past, it has always been assumed that the police would do any investigating. It was not until 1982 that the Attorney General reissued Guidelines on matters affecting the discovery process, which allowed a different, much fairer position. His role is, in effect, the public conscience and he acts as a sort of contraceptive between the law (that is the government, the judiciary and the police) and the public interest. He stated that a duty was imposed on the prosecution to disclose information material to the defence.

Notwithstanding, until recently, the Attorney General's Guidelines have always been very narrowly interpreted, which gave very wide scope for the prosecution to withhold the names of witnesses, their statements and other unused material from the defence.

It wasn't until the case of Ex parte Hawthorne, Regina – v – Leyland Justices in 1978, that things changed dramatically. In this action, a Manchester firm of solicitors took an appeal to the divisional court based on the fact that the prosecution had failed to disclose an important witness and won because of this 'failure to be frank'.

The point about Ex parte Hawthorne and the fact that the magistrates decision was quashed, was that the judge stated unequivocally that there was a quasi-judicial role invested in the prosecutor. This very significant case therefore established the important principle that the DPP had to act fair-mindedly. That is, one step backwards in the role of an umpire, and not in the position of 'winning at all costs'. This effectively put a halter around the neck of the police.

Along parallel lines there was also an evolution leading to the introduction of judicial review, which in effect allowed decisions in any tribunal to be reviewed and challenged in the High Court (Supreme Court Act 1981). As a result, a new climate was created, making judicial and quasi-judicial bodies gradually more accountable to the principles of fair-mindedness and justice.

In a way, this was legal *Perestroika*. However, the judges must use their new powers with great caution; if they over-play their hand, the government will begin to legislate against it and they will lose this important quasi-constitutional instrument.

So we now have three important remedies for the defence:

(1) Ex-parte Hawthorne, saying material evidence must be revealed to the defence.

(2) Judicial review.

(3) The Crown Prosecution Services and Director of Public Prosecutions having to act judicially.

Thus we have gradually moved towards the position where the need for a defendant to present his case in the best possible light outweighs the high public interest for secrecy on the part of the prosecution. Discovery has become, if you like, an inevitable part of the process of criminal law. And if ever there was a case in which discovery was vital, it is that in which the defendant's principal defence consists of an indictment against his persecutor, as in Kevin Taylor's case.

Taking stock, there was *prima facie* evidence of a police conspiracy of some sort, at this stage by person or persons unknown, but strongly implicated were Anderton, Topping and Stephenson, the latter in charge of the investigation.

Piecing together the evidence sifted from the Sampson Report and events that were known up to this point, the following facts built up to a tenable hypothesis:

(1) The police had searched my house, offices and other premises, applying a search warrant that could only have been obtained fraudulently, by claiming that I was suspected of drugs trafficking.

(2) The search at my house had been concerned primarily with obtaining photographs of John Stalker, later used in the Sampson Report. Obviously, there were grounds for suspecting that the search, at least in respect of the house, had a different reason from the one given to the magistrate. This would render the warrant invalid.

(3) The police had been using a media campaign to try to force the DPP's hand, implying they had little substantive evidence of any kind. Of course, in my camp, where my innocence was accepted, this went without saying.

(4) The enquiry had now been known to be going on for over two years and no charges had been brought. In the light of the Stalker Affair, it was not unreasonable to assume that the entire investigation was not bona fide, but a smokescreen to justify actions taken against Stalker.

(5) The police were taking actions under the guise of 'making their enquiries', that were difficult to interpret in any light other than being intended to destroy my financial standing.

(6) That, despite every offer of co-operation on my part (Robson's correspondence), the police had refused to follow it up. Instead, in disregard to the Chief Constable's assurances that no action would be taken without contacting my solicitors first, they had chosen in cavalier and high-handed fashion to go straight to search warrants. This implies further corruptness on the part of the police, since in order to obtain the search warrant, the officer who swears it out has to declare 'that entry to the premises would not be granted unless a warrant was produced'. In the light of my attempts at co-operation, this could only have been a perjured oath.

Certainly there were enough points here to cause disquiet in even the most impartial observer. Unfortunately, police internal matters are impossible to investigate from outside, especially if you happen to be a suspect who may eventually be charged. Buckley had an almost impossible task to face.

'What I had to do in September 1986 was conjure up a means of getting at the truth,' Buckley explains. 'From the extraordinary arrogance and contempt meted out to Taylor's previous lawyers in their dealings with the police, I knew we were dealing with guilty men, and because they were guilty, they would inevitably make mistakes. It was simply a case of me throwing out the rope and they would hang themselves.'

On 23 September 1986 an application for discovery of certain documents by means of an originating summons was made in the Chancery Division of the High Court. I appeared as plaintiff and it named James Anderton and the Greater Manchester Police Authority as defendants. The latter were included on the assumption they were rightfully responsible in law for the misdemeanours of officers serving under their imprimatur (sanction). The case was heard on 15 October, before Mr Justice Scott.

Battle was joined by means of statements in affidavit. The principle evidence for my argument came from depositions by my lawyers, supported by copies of the all-important Robson correspondence and a lengthy fifteen-page statement also from myself, explaining events to that date and why I supposed that the searches had not been bona fide. The affidavit referred to the Sampson Report and information discovered from it and the Stalker connection. I described the general drift of enquiries in relation to the Co-op Bank and the supposed fraud of £240,000 but pointed out it was mystifying, since:

(1) I had never had that amount advanced by the bank,

(2) the then present incumbent corporate business manager John Cowburn had stated there were no problems with my accounts when he took over, and that

(3) the bank had proposed later to lend a further £200,000 to purchase an additional package of land, *after* the supposed fraud.

The defendants' case was in the form of an affidavit from Roger Rees, clerk to the Greater Manchester Police Authority, protesting the Authority was not vicariously liable for what the police did and in any case had no powers to order them to disclose the documents being sought. In fact, early on in the proceedings, it was agreed by Robin De Wilde, acting for me, that the Manchester Police Authority could not reasonably be joined to the action, since it was accepted that none of the documents sought were in the possession of the Authority and they were removed.

A short five-page statement came from Stephenson. There was nothing from Anderton.

The thrust of my assertion was to be that DI Stephenson, heading the investigation, must have said something improper to the stipendiary magistrate in order to obtain the search warrants for my home and offices; that it was difficult to see in what terms the request to the magistrate were couched that could possibly have covered the removal of photographs of Stalker from Wood Mill; and that the obtaining of search warrants was fundamentally improper since it was in violation of one of the conditions specified, namely that entry to the premises will not be granted without a warrant. Details of the correspondence between Robson and the chief constable of Manchester were produced, to show that there were no good grounds on which to make this last assertion.

The trouble was that it wasn't possible to prove our case without seeing the documents. Yet the judge was only likely to accede to this very unusual request if there was *prima facie* evidence of malice. It was a catch-22 situation.

The matter which most interested Mr Justice Scott was that of public interest immunity, that is where the police were entitled to keep their documentation secret on the grounds that not to do so would allow a potential criminal to use such information to his advantage and wriggle off the hook, though this is very different, of course, from escaping prosecution because it was found that the police had acted improperly.

In his judgement, delivered on 16 October, His Lordship quoted from Lord Reid as to why the police were entitled to some degree of security: 'The police are carrying on an unending war with criminals, many of whom are, today, highly intelligent, so it is essential that there should be no disclosure of anything which might give any useful information to those who organize criminal activities, and it would generally be wrong to require disclosure in a civil case of anything which might be material in a pending prosecution. But after a verdict has been given, there is not the same need for secrecy.'

De Wilde's counter-argument was that on the facts of the present case, the public interest immunity which may have attached originally to the information deposed before the magistrate must be taken to have been lost by the fact that there had been unreasonable delay. If the police were not able to bring a prosecution, or if the investigation should prove to be no more than a smoke-screen in connection with the removal of John Stalker, then immunity must lapse sooner or later.

The judge countered that, since only six months had elapsed since the execution of the search warrants and two years in total since the initial investigation, he didn't regard this as an unreasonable delay for a case of complex commercial fraud.

But the most important point in the proceedings, and one on which the application for discovery eventually failed, was that DI Stephenson, in his affidavit, stated that papers were before the Director of Public Prosecutions and that a decision to bring charges was expected any day: 'I anticipate that within fourteen days from 30 September 1986, I shall have all the statements of evidence necessary to sustain, in my opinion, a successful prosecution of Kevin Taylor.' Remember this statement was made under oath. Just what a flagrant falsehood it turned out to be will be discerned if the reader turns back to the first chapter of this book.

Mr Justice Scott, of course, well understood and allowed into the judgement the fact that, if the search warrants had been wrongly sought, then an offence would have been committed by the police, namely trespass to property and to goods, wrongful detention of goods and abuse of power. Therefore it would have been a momentous decision for him to find in my favour and against the police.

In typically ornate legal language, he summed up his decision with the words: 'My conclusion on public interest immunity is fatal to the plaintiff's application for discovery now of the information or informations in question.'

I had lost the first round but there was no bitterness whatever on my part. Of all the judges we dealt with in these preliminary proceedings, Mr Justice Scott remains in my mind as the most courteous, understanding and sympathetic to our cause.

Buckley was undaunted, in fact surprisingly buoyant. He explained to me that, in his affidavit, Stephenson had effectively 'fingered' Anderton. Paragraphs 4 and 5 inextricably link the chief constable to any subsequently proved wrong-doing on the part of the police, especially in relation to the Access Orders at the banks. These are worth quoting in full:

> 4. I carried out a considerable amount of research and conducted enquiries into Kevin Taylor's activities which culminated in my preparing a report to the Chief Constable in February 1986, which report concluded that I had reason to suspect that offences had been committed by Kevin Taylor and others, in particular in relation to the bank account of Rangelark Limited, maintained at the Co-operative Bank. I requested authority in the report from the Chief Constable to apply for an order under Section 9 of the Police and Criminal Evidence Act 1984 for access to a number of bank accounts held in various names or organizations which were controlled by Kevin Taylor.

5. I received authority from the Chief Constable to make the aforesaid applications and I served notice in accordance with the Police and Criminal Evidence Act 1984 on the parties concerned and, on 12 March 1986, I appeared before Judge Presst who granted the orders applied for upon information given by me under oath and I served the orders on the banks to which the orders related and examined the accounts, the subject of the orders.

Attention now shifted to what was said to Judge Arthur Presst QC, the Recorder of Manchester, and the motive for saying it became of crucial importance to the viability of the defence.

Meanwhile, early in September 1986, James Anderton had been complaining in the papers that he was being harassed. Journalists, he said, had been hounding him: 'I am not aware of any other comparable case of any inquiry involving a police officer of any rank where any figure central to that inquiry, particularly a chief constable like myself, should thereafter be harassed and hounded day to day by the media to answer questions said to arise from widespread public concern,' he bleated and insisted once again that everything had been above board in Stalker's removal.

Events of the recent past, he said, could not be dealt with 'by seeking one of the main participants and opening him up to public inquiry and investigation through media interrogations because I think it is outrageous and no individual, let alone a chief constable, should be subjected to that kind of treatment . . .'

This, remember, is from the man who laid the complaint against Stalker that was ultimately to hound him out of the force, despite being acquitted of the malicious accusations. From my point of view, finding myself nothing more than a pawn in Anderton's campaign against Stalker, I could be said to have been very much 'hounded and harassed', by Anderton and his boys. It seemed that Manchester's Chief Constable was happy to dish it out but didn't like being on the receiving end. Well, if Buckley got his way, Anderton was going to have to defend himself and his actions – or go to jail.

In the opinion of Mr Philip Cox QC, Leading Counsel, there was now in our hands sufficient evidence on which a summons could properly be brought against the Chief Constable James Anderton, head of CID Peter Topping and the man leading the investigation, Detective Inspector Anthony Stephenson. The charge: conspiracy to pervert the course of justice. So, on 14 October, almost coincidental with the hearing of the discovery action in front of Mr Justice Scott, the summons was issued, naming my wife Beryl as the principal prosecutor.

'It had to be Beryl who took the action on behalf of Rangelark as one of its directors,' explains Buckley. 'The company was really the complainant. It had a grievance; it had been destroyed by this charade of an inquiry. Taylor couldn't bring the action, otherwise it would just be seen as an attempt by him to frustrate a police inquiry of which he was the subject.'

It was a bold, imaginative action and so startling that several courts were too frightened to handle it and refused. Co-operation was secured finally in Bury Magistrates Court, ironically my home ground. Here the team had a stroke of luck. The Clerk, Ian Webb, whose later behaviour made it clear he would certainly have refused, was away at the time. Instead William Knowles, his deputy, took the court. Not without some anxiety, he allowed the summonses to be taken out. The opening battle had been lost but the guerrilla war was on.

The first step was in collecting affidavits. Here again, Buckley was gradually drawing the enemy forward, getting them to make repeated statements in which they might drop their guard. Anderton swore only a very limited affidavit, protesting that the action was outrageous; that it has caused great distress to him; and the action should be stopped because it would subject him and his men to 'unnecessary and unwarranted humiliation'. A media prima donna, protecting his cherished image probably caused him as much anxiety as the gravity of the charges against him.

Topping's affidavit was whining in tone and he was anxious for the judge to know that he was 'deeply aggrieved and angered' by the issue of the summons. He was also careful to put the blame for anything which might be irregular on Stephenson's shoulders by saying, 'I have given Mr Stephenson no directions about how he should carry out the enquiry or what steps he should take.' He even contradicts this affidavit himself in his own book published two years later, where he assumes responsibility for the enquiry. Also, the reader should be reminded that DCS Topping was present in the Co-op Bank in December 1985, along with Stephenson, before legal access orders were granted.

DI Stephenson provided two affidavits (18 November 1986 and 27 January 1987) and, as predicted by Buckley, these contained slips that would later prove very useful, as far as establishing a conspiracy was concerned. He confirms acting entirely on the orders of Topping and Anderton and his sworn statement meant that both senior men must be implicated in our later revelation that Stephenson deposed inaccurate and false information in front of Judge Presst. He also stated on oath, 'I honestly and truly believe' that the material seized in the search at Wood Mill was not subject to legal privilege and was needed 'for the purposes of my investigations into Mr Taylor's commercial activities'. The reader will no doubt recall that the majority of what was removed from the house was photographs of John Stalker and Co. What these have to do with a commercial fraud no one can know. His claim is as farcical as it is disingenuous.

Stephenson then committed an even bigger error in reference to the photographs by saying they provided criminal intelligence. He seemed unaware that the law forbids seizure of goods for criminal intelligence but only in support of known or suspected crime. Unless going to a party is against the law, the good detective had neatly shot himself in the foot.

Stephenson repeatedly claimed, as in the 18 November affidavit, not to have been involved in the investigation into Stalker. Yet facts show otherwise: his dirty fingers turn up time and time again in the Stalker pie. No sooner had the infamous Access Orders been granted by His Honour Judge Presst than Stephenson assigned himself to Miss Angela Simpson, a fraud investigator for American Express (Amex), and hot-footed it down to see her. The result? Two lengthy statements concerning only the use of my Amex accounts for the trip to Miami with Stalker and nothing about my commercial affairs. Incidentally, we were eventually to get sight of the relevant page of her diary, in which is written: 'Stephenson Manchester 10.30 re drugs Kevin Taylor'. There was no doubt here, then, that the police were using the suggestion of drug-running to blacken my name. We will return to this theme many times before the story is told in full.

Roger Rees, solicitor for the Greater Manchester Police Authority, supplied the fifth defence affidavit on the case. It was factual and precise, arguing that summons was frivolous and vexatious. Notwithstanding that it was brought by Beryl on behalf of Rangelark Ltd, it was really an action instigated by me in order to frustrate the police investigation, it was argued.

On these grounds, Anderton and co. successfully applied in December 1986 for leave for a judicial review of the Bury magistrates summonses in the divisional court, seeking to have them quashed.

Before the hearing, a very frightening incident took place. I was in a Manchester snooker club one evening, playing a game of cards, when a man burst into the room. He pointed a gun at my head and, in a thick Belfast accent, said, 'I'm going to kill you, you stone-faced bastard!'

After the first few seconds of shock it was obvious he didn't intend to kill me, otherwise he would already have pulled the trigger. I tried to stay calm and reason with him, on the grounds that keeping him talking meant he would be less likely to lose control and shoot. After some of the most frightening minutes of my life, I eventually managed to escape, down a fire-escape at the rear of the building.

I know there were a number of off-duty policemen in that room, who did nothing. Yet the incident was not reported or, if it was, no one was sent to take a statement from me. This raises the question: was it arranged by certain police officers, simply to frighten me? The gunman had come straight for me, in a room full of people, so there was no question I was his target. What possible reason could there be for this act if he had not been instructed to carry it out and were the policemen in the room simply observers? I have no answers.

'JR One' (as we christened Judicial Review Number 1) was heard in February 1987 in front of Lord Justice May and Mr Justice Nolan. Philip Cox QC appeared for Beryl and Rangelark Ltd, Andrew Collins QC for the defendants. It was a tough and tense battle, three senior police officers literally fighting for their freedom. Yes, the cards were stacked very much against us. No one had ever tackled the Establishment in quite this way before. But then, the Establishment had set a precedent by the shameful abuse of police powers. It was an important move, therefore, on moral grounds, as well as a brilliant tactical manoeuvre by Buckley.

The first day found the judges acutely hostile, with an ill-concealed scorn for Buckley and his methods. At one point the judge severely castigated him in open court in regard to vituperative letters he had written on behalf of the defence. It must be said that Charles gives a lot of offence with his letters, but it is, of course, a deliberate affectation, designed to get results.

Collins, to give him credit, argued his case forcibly and convincingly for the defendants. Heavy emphasis was put on the fact that an attempt to obtain sight of the evidence put before the stipendiary magistrate in Manchester for the purpose of obtaining search warrants had already been blocked by Mr Justice Scott. This was just another dodge to get round public immunity privilege, it was claimed.

It was a lost day as far as I was concerned. However, the next day, when Cox began to elaborate on our evidence of a possible police conspiracy, the judges noticeably altered in demeanour. Remarkably so. The letters exchanged between James Anderton and Guy Robson early in 1986 (quoted in detail in Chapter 5) were read out to the court, to the obvious discomfiture of Andrew Collins.

Young Kevin Taylor, aged 18.

My wife, Beryl, and I outside our former home, Wood Mill, near Bury.

Beryl and I in happier times, with our two daughters, Kay Maria and Emma.

John Stalker in the Bahamas, 1982.

The family boat, *Diogenes*, moored in the Bahamas.

With Sugar Ray Leonard, before he regained the World
Championship from Tommy 'Hitman' Hearns in Las Vegas.

Our first Rolls-Royce, outside our
semi-detached house in Failsworth,
Manchester.

For fun, I flew this Cessna 172 in the
Grand Canyon.

Relaxing on the Bahama Banks in 1981.

Beryl and friends with 'Ol' Blue Eyes' in Las Vegas.

We loved the elegance of our drawing room, the scene of many memorable parties.

The original stone woollen mill, before we converted it into our home.

Wood Mill, after the conversion, the source of much pride.

One of the lads at Loxford Boys Club where I was President. It was in the notorious Moss Side district of Manchester.

With the Lord Mayor of Manchester, at an old people's charity club where I was also Chairman.

Sir Walter Clegg (left), former Speaker of the Commons, Fred Sylvester (right) Conservative M.P. for Worthington, with their wives and Lynne Perrie (Ivy Brennan in *Coronation Street*) supporting me in fund-raising for the Manchester Conservative Association.

My friends, John Stalker and Angelo Dundee, Mohammed Ali's manager with P.C. Burke, who trains the young boxers in the Manchester boys' clubs.

Beryl and I with John and Stella Stalker on New Year's Eve, 1984, at the Piccadilly Hotel, Manchester.

One of the many formal occasions when John Stalker and I would have a glass in our hands.

MENU

Artichaut Sauce Ravigotte
Gonzalez Byass Elegante Fino

Bisque d' homard
Muscadet
Julien Damoy 1978

Canneloni
Chianti Ruffino

Pintade au Vin
Courgettes Sauté
Pommes de Terre gratinée Anna
St. Emilion

Sorbet de Pommes au Calvados
Veuve de Vernay Demi Sec

Blue Stilton
Celery
Port

Café
Cognac

Best Wishes.
Jim Anderton
Chief Constable.

Senior Officers' Mess, GMP, Gourmet Evening 28th November 1980 menu, signed for me by James Anderton.

During my Chairmanship of the Manchester Conservative Party, Lynda Chalker, the former Minister of Transport, was our guest at a fund-raising dinner.

David Hood, my leading barrister at the trial.

Bottom right: James Anderton, Chief Constable of the Greater Manchester Police. A controversial man, who played a critical role in my destruction. (By courtesy of Manchester Evening News)

Charles Buckley, my able solicitor, whose detective work so assisted me in my trial.

Down on my luck outside the 'labour exchange'.

Below: Detective Chief Superintendent Peter Topping, former head of CID in Manchester. We carefully examine his activities against me in this book. (By courtesy of Manchester Evening News)

But it was the information laid by Stephenson before Judge Presst in March 1986 to secure Access Orders to my bank accounts that assumed critical importance during this action. The prosecution, in this case Beryl, asserted that what had been said to Judge Presst must *ipso facto* have been suspect, since it implied a suspicion that I was involved in drugs and those concerned knew that I was not and never had been involved in such activities. Therefore false evidence must have been sworn under oath and this argued strongly there was a conspiracy to pervert the course of justice.

In order to lead away from this very dangerous point, Andrew Collins, presumably on instruction, so he cannot be blamed for it, had in his opening made a statement which was to go on record and which was to be catastrophic for the credibility of the enquiry: it was that *Kevin Taylor was not under suspicion of trafficking in drugs*. This expedient and seemingly kindly remark does enormous damage to the police bona fides since, as I have already hinted in referring to Miss Angela Simpson, it was to prove later that the suspicion of drug-dealing was used repeatedly to gain co-operation at banks and with others, to open doors which legally ought to have remained closed. It was a clever trick, designed to show me in a 'false light', as American lawyers say. Everyone hates drug-dealers and nobody minds bending the rules and working with the police to bring them to justice. Of all the tricks used by the police conspirators in their campaign against me, this was probably the most contemptible and foul.

It should be noted that we included this remark in an affidavit of mine, used on a subsequent occasion, to give the prosecution the opportunity to withdraw, amend, vary or qualify what was said. They never did.

Matters got worse. When the court heard about the DIU's so-called search warrants and the abuse to which they had been put, Lord Justice May actually made an utterance to the effect that the police had 'a lot of ground to make up'. In fact it became so bad for the defence that Andrew Collins QC stood up and, to the astonishment of all, asked the judges if it would be possible for Stephenson and Topping to be put forward for trial but Anderton kept out of it (presumably to avoid too much police humiliation, since Anderton at this time was president of the Association of Chief Police Officers). Collins was later overheard saying to my barrister in the robing rooms that he had been so concerned about the set-backs that he had called Chester House for guidance and had been told to offer the two underlings, to protect Anderton. What it is to be a chief constable!

(Incidentally, Andrew Collins was also heard to remark: I hope the Taylors never get sight of what is in that envelope!)

At the end of the hearing therefore, we had scored so many points it was considered that ours was the victory. This is important: as everyone knows, legal decisions are a matter of excruciating technicalities, verbal pyrotechnics and more than a dash of whimsey or even prejudice but, at the end of the day, lawyers know when they have won fair and square. The prosecution know it and the defence knows it. The rest should be mere formality, a ratification of the outcome of the judicial process. Imagine the consternation therefore when judgement from Lord Justice May was handed down several weeks later, finding totally in favour of the police.

The delay was certainly suspicious. It seemed to be too many weeks in coming, but even so it was a staggering and unforseeable decision. When I read the judgement, it seemed that I was reading about a different case from the one I'd sat and listened to. Barristers shook their heads. Many senior men at law, even very Establishment figures, were heard to remark that I had had a very raw deal.

The Stalker connection, it was stated by Lord Justice May, was 'irrelevant'. This accorded with his remark in court that 'Stalker was history'; no doubt a very sincere wish of the government at that time, but hardly correct. The principal points on which Lord Justice May sustained the quashing of the summonses was that the information had been improperly laid before the Bury magistrates, preferring to believe the vague testimony of Knowles (and Webb who wasn't even present when the summonses were issued) against the word of Ian McCulloch, a barrister, who had actually made the application on behalf of Rangelark.

The unsuccessful action in front of Mr Justice Scott to try to discover the documents used in issuance of the search warrants was held to be highly significant to the present action. Lord Justice May insisted this earlier action should have been disclosed to the Bury magistrate and withholding it was clearly 'conscious and deliberate'. Yet that had been a civil matter and the present case was a criminal one, which some might say put them poles apart.

Most damagingly, perhaps, it was stated that the prosecution's only aim was to seek discovery of the vital Presst document. The issuance of the summonses was therefore held to be an abuse of process and the fact that the police had violated the pre-requisites laid down by Parliament as necessary for the giving of Access Orders was simply ignored as unimportant.

*

That summer, there was another bizarre development to the narrative. According to the bank, a man allegedly describing himself as a CID officer from Scotland Yard, a Mr Tom Wareing, had actioned Isreal Reyes, Head of the Organized Crime Bureau in Miami, to secure information concerning my bank account in Florida. I had run a small dollar account at the Barnett Bank for the purpose of serving my yacht, paying berthing charges, repairs, etc. It was inactive at this time, since I had moved the boat from Miami years before.

The first we knew of this was when I received a letter from the Barnett Bank. Although it was a registered air-mail letter it had taken weeks to arrive and bore two mechanical date stamps, one for 23 June 1987 and one for the 28th. It seemed obvious that somebody had deliberately interfered with the mail and delayed my receipt of this letter, which was to tell me that documentary disclosure had been sought but pointed out I had the right, under US law, to object.

By the time this letter was received we were out of time and lawyers acting for the Barnett Bank told us it was now too late and they had already given disclosure on 30 June. Not that anything damaging was revealed in inspecting this account; its use had been perfectly legitimate. But to realize that the hydra-like conspiracy against me was big enough to corrupt public officials across the Atlantic was unnerving, to say the least.

We instructed lawyers to make enquiries and found out that the subpoena had been granted on 1 December 1986. By repeatedly telling the bank that he would be producing a temporary restraining order (the equivalent of our injunction) preventing disclosure, Reyes had managed to delay the bank telling me about the subpoena almost six months, until it was too late. In fact he never did produce a restraining order; he had no valid grounds on which to obtain one. He had simply deceived the bank until his aim had been achieved.

When we asked who had originated the request for a subpoena for disclosure we were told: a Mr T. Wareing from Scotland Yard. We immediately rang Scotland Yard but they could find no trace of an officer called Wareing – his identity was a complete mystery.

That might have been the end of it but, not long afterwards, papers from the DPP's office suddenly surfaced bearing the name T. Wareing of the Crown Prosecution Service. Charles Buckley got on the phone immediately, seeking clarification from Wareing at the DPP's office. But as soon as Buckley mentioned the Kevin Taylor case, Wareing went wild and screamed, 'I will not discuss this matter with you,' and banged the phone down (I could hear his frightened voice myself, on the intercom set). Just the sort of reaction one would expect from a guilty man.

I have to say that one of the hardest stresses to come to terms with in this whole sorry business has been the obvious involvement of certain individuals at the DPP's office and the CPS in the campaign against me. It was particularly disturbing, because the Crown Prosecution Service was set up precisely for the purpose of preventing the wrongful prosecution of individuals by over-zealous or corrupt police, yet here was one of its own officers, ostensibly mixed up in the abuses.

What could I do? Very little, it seemed. In Britain today, there are very few rights for an individual and no real accountability of the police. One of the reasons that other European countries are sometimes reluctant to extradite terrorists and other criminals to the UK is because we, alone of civilized countries, have neither a bill of rights nor a written constitution to protect our citizens from wrongful arrest, harassment and oppressive interrogation, which by its nature and duress is calculated to force a suspect to say whatever the police want, regardless of the truth. To send individuals into such a backward and oppressive country as ours would, in other words, be contravening their own human rights laws.

Furthermore, what the public doesn't realize is that in this country we now have a potentially dangerous organization in the form of the Association of Chief Police Officers, which is pushing for a unified national police force. It would have incredible powers and would be answerable to no one for adherence to the law, even in simple civil matters, such as damages or other indemnity claims. We are coming perilously close, in my opinion, to a state police force, such as the Gestapo, KGB or Boos (South Africa).

Leave to appeal against the quashing of the Bury magistrates' summonses was naturally sought but was refused by Lord Justice May and Mr Justice Nolan, though Nolan did say it would be in order to re-issue the summonses after the conclusion of my own trial. In July 1987, on the same day leave to appeal was refused, following Buckley's advice, I took yet another action ('JR Two'), this time seeking a judicial review of Judge Presst's own decision in regard to the Access Orders (remember that judicial review allows the decision of any lower court or tribunal to be challenged and possibly overthrown). Undeterred by the setbacks, Buckley's ingenuity had come up with yet another scheme to get at what he wanted.

In fact, we were technically out of time for such an action. A request for a judicial review must be brought within three months of the decision sought to be impugned and it was now over a year later. Nevertheless, Buckley felt that, since we had not been told of the decision sooner, it wasn't unreasonable to apply as soon as was practicable after it had come to light. Note that the hearing before Judge Presst in March 1986 had been held *ex parte*, that is without my knowledge. Elementary justice would then surely allow that I could retrospectively challenge such a decision, if it was felt to be a mistake.

Mr Justice Mann refused the application, saying it was 'academic', but his decision was over-ruled in November by Lord Justice Parker and Mr Justice (Paul) Kennedy, who gave leave to go forward with alacrity. Here it is worth quoting Buckley, when he says, 'It is remarkable what a beacon of light Lord Justice Parker has become in matters affecting civil rights, quite out of character with his supposed difficult and eccentric nature.' Since I had been arrested only the week before, Lord Justice Parker remarked that the matter, in the meantime, had become 'no longer academic'.

The proceedings were held in February 1988, in front of Lord Justice Glidewell and Mr Justice French. There was a slight element of farce in court. Halfway through, Glidewell attempted to draw the whole thing to a close and give his judgement then and there. Anthony Scrivener QC, acting for me, was forced to remind His Lordship that there was a right of appeal to the House of Lords and that if he (Glidewell) didn't mind he (Scrivener) wanted His Lordship to hear the whole of the case that had been prepared. His Lordship allowed himself to be persuaded by such importunings, and graciously agreed to listen to the complaints, even if perhaps merely going through the ritual motions for the sake of form. In the course of events, he described what I was doing as opportunistic and, to coin a phrase, said it was a 'breathalyzer attack' on the technicalities of the Police and Criminal Evidence Act, 1984.

It was during these proceedings that Andrew Collins, acting for the respondent DI Stephenson, remarked that consideration would be given to disclosure of the contents of the sealed envelope. In reply Mr Justice French uttered a memorable and magnanimous remark to the effect that: 'Mr Collins, it is not a question of deciding if you will release the contents, the question is surely whether you have a duty to disclose them under the Guidelines.' Words such as these were of enormous comfort to me and my team, battling to get the few meagre scraps of justice that fell from the tables of the high and mighty.

Astonishingly to me, Glidewell refused even to look at the contents of the sealed envelope, which had been brought to the court. Needless to say, the result of the judicial review was a foregone conclusion: I lost again.

With confidence in British justice predictably declining, Buckley judged it time to consider suing for fair treatment outside the UK and its legal system. In January 1988 it was decided to put matters before the European Commission of Human Rights, at the Council of Europe in Strasbourg, to let them decide objectively the rights and wrongs of the struggle with the police. A dossier was prepared, the necessary paperwork put in motion and the case of Kevin and Beryl Taylor *v* the United Kingdom passed into the machinery. The main complaints cited in the application were violations of Articles 6, 8 and 13, covering the right to a fair and public trial within a reasonable time, respect for privacy and property and defence against the national authority where its officers are in violation of its own legal processes.

The first stage was simply to be granted leave to proceed. It was to be almost two years later, during the course of the trial itself, that a decision was returned. The Commission, which included a British judge, declared the application inadmissible. It was not dismissive or high-handed but pointed out that according to Article 27 paragraph 3 all domestic remedies must be exhausted and it was judged that this was not yet the case. As to being denied the right to pursue criminal proceedings against the police for abuse of process, the Commission said it was unable, under its Articles, to guarantee citizens that right. It was a fair and sensitively worded judgement and by no means closed the door to future help from the Commission, if all other remedies and appeals failed. It would be fascinating to know if the British government were consulted before or during its preparation.

There was still plenty to do. Buckley assigned himself the task of following up some of the witnesses mentioned in Sampson's report and re-interviewing them. In many cases what they said in reality bore little or no relation to what Sampson claimed they had said. There was a major legal problem in respect of the Sampson Report: whether it would be permissible to use the report itself in evidence. As Buckley states: 'I have always thought the first fourteen pages of the Sampson Report one of the most dramatic documents on the Taylor case. The rhythm and momentum of those twenty-three paragraphs show beyond any peradventure or shadow of a doubt that the real purpose of the Access Orders and search warrants on Taylor was to get material to dish the dirt on Stalker.' Clearly it was very important evidence for us.

Unfortunately, the report was then thought to be a privileged document, and as such would therefore not normally be allowed as evidence in court. Indeed, the fact that we, the defence, were even in possession of it was somewhat dubious (legally speaking), never mind arguing from between its pages. Adlers pursued the matter at some length with Mrs J. Douglas, the Treasury Solicitor. Her immediate response was that the Police Complaints Authority could not waive public interest immunity and neither could any member of the Authority agree to give oral evidence. If subpoenas were issued, these would be contested and it would be up to the court, in the end, to decide where the public interest lay. Her letter concluded by stating, 'I do not know from whom you obtained a copy of this report but you are not authorized to receive it [and] not entitled to retain it. I have therefore to ask you to return that Report either to me or to the Police Complaints Authority or to the Greater Manchester Police whom I am advising of this request. I assume that you have not any further copies of the Report nor extracts from it other than the copy to which you refer. If you have then I should be obliged for their return as well. I should also be obliged if, when returning this document, you would explain the circumstances in which it came into your possession.' (31 October 1986).

It was a potentially dangerous situation.

After several delaying letters and lengthy consultations with leading and junior counsel, Adlers finally wrote back on 21 November with a skilful, carefully worded letter. It pointed out that advice had been taken and that counsel had stated that it would not be necessary, at least for the time being, to procure production of the report in court; but, rather cutely put, they were 'unable to advise me that I should return the copies of the Reports in my possession' since I had come by it lawfully; that it was now 'in the public domain', quoting its use in newspaper and television journalism. The letter also pointed out that in general law there is no privilege or confidentiality attaching to calumny. It went on to argue that all concerned were, in effect, officers of the court and included an undertaking not to publish the report.

It did the trick.

We had a little ammunition and some understanding of the enemy's position and weaknesses. We were ready for the next stage of the fighting campaign: the committal hearing.

10
The Committal

On Monday, 19 September 1988, almost a year after the arrest, the case came to a committal hearing in front of Mr David Loy, a stipendiary magistrate. This is essentially a parade of police proof in front of a magistrate, who has to decide whether there is sufficient evidence that an offence or offences have been committed to justify submitting the defendants to a trial in the Crown court.

It is interesting to note that, on the first day of the proceedings, I asked an usher for directions to the courtroom. When I gave my name, the usher nodded and said knowingly, 'Ah yes, the Stalker case.' So it was well known in judicial circles, right down to the ancillary staff, that the proceedings against me were a kangaroo court procedure related to the dismissal of John Stalker. Everyone knew it; yet there was a juggernaut in motion which it was impossible to stop.

At the suggestion of Charles Buckley, the defence had elected for an old-style committal. This meant that, instead of just a review of documents, the police would have to call a number of witnesses and we would get a chance to cross-examine them and assess the strength of the prosecution case. In doing so, a slight risk was incurred in that the defence might have to show some of its hand. Also, if a police argument was roundly defeated, it would allow time before the actual trial for them to try and prop it up again. On the whole, however, the down-side was minimal, compared to the possible advantages obtained from knowing what evidence was to be used. Additionally, there was always the possibility of further revelations of police misfeasances.

I was represented by a junior barrister called David Hood, Britton by Martin Steiger, Bowley by Peter Lakin and McCann by Guy Robson. Britton, Bowley and I were on Legal Aid. McCann was to get Legal Aid but had to put down a £14,000 deposit, a substantial punitive fine, in effect.

Surprise, surprise! The opposition were represented by the highest-paid prosecuting counsel in the land, Mr Michael Corkery QC, and his 'junior' was Michael Shorrock QC from the Manchester circuit. I understand from my lawyers it is without precedent that two QCs should be appointed to a simple committal hearing of this sort. It could only be expected in a case of treason or national security and was only one step removed from the case being conducted by the Attorney General or the Solicitor General himself.

The first day and a half was taken up by the opening address for the Crown prosecution, delivered by Michael Corkery. During his remarks Mr Corkery made a serious error, which could only have been deliberate, because he was well versed in the particulars concerned. He claimed that at the time he was speaking there was still over £1 million outstanding to the bank. In fact, this was totally false. The debit balance at that time was around £185,000, and the bank still had adequate security to cover the borrowings.

'It was awful,' says Derek Britton. 'You wanted to stand up and say "That's wrong" but you weren't allowed to. So the magistrate, the Press and TV got it into their heads that we still owed all that money. Everybody else in the courtroom knew it was rubbish.'

The remainder of the speech was similar, basically innuendos, rather than facts, that were designed to put the defendants in a bad light. Some may argue that it is the prosecution's job to try to paint the defence as villains, but most readers will be shocked to know that it is permissible for a QC to say whatever he wants, presumably on the justification that we had yet to prove it was lies.

By an unfortunate quirk of circumstance, Corkery's speech was not properly recorded by the court. All the evidence and verbal statements brought before the magistrate during the proceedings were being transcribed by a rather primitive system using a telephone line to clerks in the basement. It was an extremely archaic method and fraught with possible disruptions. In the event, Britton's barrister, Martin Steiger, had taken copious notes and these were accepted by the rest of the court as a fair representation of what was said.

On the second day the examination of witnesses began. Conspicuously absent was Hylie Shepherd, chief inspector of the Co-op Bank. His exclusion was a virtual confession of guilt by the police; they were afraid their own offences in obtaining information illegally at the bank would emerge under his cross-examination. In fact, for a long time, we felt that Mr Shepherd must have conspired with the police. Later, during the trial, we were to hear testimony that made this possibility seem remote.

Instead they opened the batting with David Davenport who was assistant to Bowley at the time of the matters in question. Interestingly, Davenport's written statement began with the words: 'I am married and I have two children . . .' It seems a strange remark with which to begin a statement and raises the possibility that he was feeling threatened or under pressure in making his statement.

Davenport was supposed to say all sorts of incriminating things about the way Bowley conducted matters, but it became very evident during cross-examination that what Bowley had done with me, he had done with many others. His divergence from bank procedures was simply a matter of expediency to get the job done without being strangled by the advances department and not part of a plot. Davenport was to remain on the stand for the rest of the first week and the beginning of the following week. As a police witness, he was somewhat disastrous, and before the end of his testimony, had become virtually a witness for the defence.

The disturbing way in which Davenport departed from his written statement to the police was repeated again by several subsequent witnesses. It seemed fairly evident that the police had dictated a statement for witnesses to sign and they had signed it, perhaps under duress, or feeling they had little choice. These changes of testimony were to become a feature of the case and evidently caused much consternation and frustration on the part of Corkery, who repeatedly watched his evidence crumble into dust under cross-examination.

Some witnesses had been asked to make a second statement by the prosecution in order to 'strengthen' them. Several of these second statements bore a remarkable similarity to each other, containing identical emotive phrases, such as 'If I had known these things in advance I would have acted differently . . .' and 'What was said was intended to deceive me . . .', which all added to the belief that they were dictated to the witnesses rather than spontaneously given. It would be very easy for the police to influence witnesses in this manner. Most people never see a policeman in their lives and, if they were to be suddenly confronted with a senior CID officer at their place of work, they would naturally try to be co-operative and do the right things. Probably they would be afraid for their own job security when accusations started flying. It works as a kind of oppressive blackmail. The fact that they were put under some sort of pressure is demonstrated by the way the testimonies changed under oath. However, just how much duress was not to emerge until the trial itself, a year later.

On day eight, Steven Wood, a securities clerk, took the stand. It emerged at this time that Bowley had been doing over £65 million worth of business with a back-up staff of only four. The pressures on

Bowley's team, which included Davenport and Wood, must, therefore, have been considerable, and it seems hardly surprising that mistakes were made and procedures violated. Probably the Co-op Bank should accept most of the responsibility for the irregularities, because of being so parsimonious with staffing levels. Wood wasn't particularly hostile to the defence but his important testimony concerned a meeting which had taken place on 3 May 1985. Britton and I had attended; Bowley and Wood had represented the bank. During the meeting I asked Wood to leave the room. The police obviously wished to infer that this was the moment at which I recruited Bowley for the dishonest schemes. But asked why he thought he'd been sent out of the room, Wood seemed in little doubt that it was because, far from trying to recruit Bowley, I intended giving him a thorough dressing-down for being slow making funds available. In fact, I was threatening to go to the British Linen Bank instead. It was obvious, said Wood, that I was having trouble restraining myself from strong words while he was present in the room.

A succession of witnesses from the advance department followed, most of whom had never met me. They were only too willing to testify that Bowley had violated rules and hadn't followed procedures. This must have rallied police morale somewhat.

Cowburn, Bowley's successor, took the stand (days fifteen and sixteen) to say that in his opinion cross-firing of cheques had occurred but then damaged his credibility as an expert witness by showing he didn't know the difference between corporation tax and land development tax.

However, possibly the most damaging witness of all for the police (all witnesses were supposedly for the police) was Roger Gorvin, a director of the Co-op Bank (days sixteeen to eighteen). He was well aware of the tension between the Corporate Business Department and the advances department and it emerged that there was a special direct line from Bowley to him, for use in the event of any damaging delays which might jeopardize customer relations. He admitted that Bowley had violated procedures but with the full consent of the bank, and that he had done it often, not just in relation to me. Gorvin made his admiration for Bowley quite clear under questioning by Corkery, which went along the following lines:

'Mr Bowley was the finest corporate business manager the Co-operative Bank ever had.'

'How long had he been corporate business manager?'

'Twelve years.'

'And what were his duties?'

'His job was to go out and get new business.'

'Was he successful?'

'Yes.'

'How much so?'

'He brought in £65 million a year of new business.'

'Was that good?'

'Exceptional. The average high street bank only produces £2–3 million a year.'

'And what was his level of bad debt?'

'Phenomenal by banking standards. He had no bad debts whatever.'

'But what about Taylor and his companies?' pounced Corkery.

'We didn't lose any money with Mr Taylor. We made money. Mr Taylor was a valued and successful customer.'

At the end of the bank witnesses, the case against Bowley looked so shaky that the police, in desperation, took Bowley to Bootle Street Police Station and charged him with false accounting in respect of two specific offences. It was an act which Mr Corkery described in candour to the magistrate as a 'belt and braces' exercise. The prosecution offered to drop all other substantive charges, if Bowley would only plead guilty to the false accounting. The point of this is that, provided at least one charge was successful against him, his worth as a defence witness would be diminished. On the other hand, if Bowley was to get off altogether, there could be no case against me.

Then came a succession of expert witnesses in relation to the valuations on various properties. Much was made of the question of shale on the Poynton site, the absurdity of which is that the Co-op Bank said repeatedly it did not rely on the existence of supposed shale deposits in accepting a valuation. Thomas Holt of Peter O'Hare Associates valued the site at £210,000 (more than adequate) but Holt was to claim this was based on Vincent McCann stating that there were 300,000 cubic metres of shale; in fact there were said to be an estimated 30,000 cubic metres at this stage. It seems a simple case of Holt getting the decimal point wrong when he wrote it down in his notes but the police wanted it to be seen differently. McCann had deliberately misled Holt, they said. It was asserted that McCann had withheld a report by David Appleton concerning the shale, as if he were somehow required to disclose it. In actuality, Appleton was a landscape architect, not a chartered surveyor, and McCann was quite right not to interject his report as an authoritative one. This, actually, was the total extent of the case against McCann. Laughable.

The Poynton transaction also illustrates the carping and delays caused by the advance department. The O'Hare valuation, they said, was not done for the bank and therefore could not be said to be truly independent. Another survey was needed. Meanwhile, naturally, the land would have been sold and the opportunity to buy it lost for good.

There were numerous other minor witnesses, brought in to comment on different matters. We left most of these expert testimonies unchallenged. No jury was present but our view was that most of the evidence was so ridiculous and self-defeating it could be seen for what it was, and was best ignored.

Nevertheless, despite the police evidence being cut to shreds, it was obvious after a few days that Loy was not going to throw the case out. In fact, instead of being irritated with the obvious prosecution antics, he seemed to go out of his way to be smiling and polite to Corkery; 'Yes, Mr Corkery . . . no, Mr Corkery,' while being very taciturn and abrupt with the opposition lawyers. He even told Peter Lakin to take his hands out of his pockets. This is not to suggest that Mr Loy was being unfair, merely that his sympathies and antipathies were clearly on view.

Another very disturbing aspect of police conduct was that DI Stephenson would take witnesses into a room just before they took the stand and give them coaching as to what to say. This was obviously to try and prevent any further disasters for the prosecution. The police argument was that they were simply 'refreshing the witness's memory'. Commonsense says differently.

On the afternoon of day twenty-five Simon Houlston took the stand. He was an estate agent who had acted on my behalf and then ended up acting as estate agent for the other side, as these people do on occasion. He was a poor witness for the police and seemed more anxious to make a good impression than answer questions, constantly fiddling with his Rolex watch and adjusting his cuffs to make sure that his gold bracelet was on view.

Robert Arnold, the person I had bought Poynton from, dented the police case badly when he testified he had tried to buy the site back for £40,000 more than he had sold it to me for (day twenty-six). It was typical of the many examples of the way the police tried to take part of the evidence out of context and so blur the overall picture, which didn't add up to what they were trying to prove.

On day twenty-seven, a Dr Varey of Cleanaway was called. His testimony centred around the fact that I was supposed to have refused him permission to survey the Poynton site. Varey had offered £265,000 for the tip and I had refused the offer, believing it to be worth far more. In fact Varey was probably the person best qualified to value the Poynton site, since he was an expert concerning tips and tipping rights. Significantly, his offer was higher than any previous figure and made the estimation of police experts' valuations of (variously) £20,000 to £60,000 seem foolish and amateurish, were it not for the knowledge which emerged in court, that the police deliberately withheld information about tipping rights and shale from these 'experts'.

On day twenty-eight, the first witness was Crooke, a planning official in Bury. The Bury Council had tried to buy the Tottington site with the intention of using urban development grants to enhance the land and then sell it back to me at profit. Naturally, I dismissed this impudent scheme, but Crooke was called to testify that in the proposed cost of purchase was included £20,000 'commission'. It was heavily inferred that this was destined as a reward for Bowley. In fact the sum was for Derek Rothwell, who had introduced me to the site, a perfectly normal and widespread practice, called a 'finder's fee'. But the inclusion of this accusation, which inevitably had to be withdrawn, was an example of the desperation of the prosecution, cobbling together any story, no matter how hysterical or wild, and wasting the court's time and money by putting it forward.

On day twenty-nine came Slade, the police accountant. Based on the information given to him, he said Rangelark had been trading while insolvent. The defence counsel, in cross-examining him, asked about the land banks. 'What land banks?' was his reply. He hadn't even been told they existed. Slade had supposedly produced a balance sheet but it was based on the assumption that Rangelark were land-lords and drawing rent (which wasn't true at any stage). The land development sites had been entered merely as 'fixed assets'. In actual fact, they were the stock in trade of the company, which transformed the accounting picture completely. Slade virtually admitted he'd been misled by the police, that he'd been given 'incorrect or insufficient information'. Once again, important material that didn't suit them had been suppressed by the police. Yet Bowley was facing trial for exactly that thing.

The situation with Slade was an example of the dangers of the old-style committal, with cross-examination. The defence might inadvertently reveal how shaky the prosecution case is on some key point. As Britton says, 'Slade's brief was so narrow and wrong, we could have done with him not being there at the committal. It would have been better to let him go to Crown; a few key questions then would have destroyed him as a witness. As it was, we alerted them to the weakness of his crucial evidence and gave them the chance to shore up the damage before the actual trial.'

But there was no doubt whatever that the witness of most concern to the defence was DI Anthony Stephenson, the man in charge of the case. Because his testimony was so crucial, Buckley took the precaution of hiring a top shorthand reporter, who took down the entire cross-examination, verbatim. It runs to dozens of closely typed pages and is a fascinating document, giving much insight into the mentality and methods of the man leading the enquiry against me.

It has drama in its own right but since the revelations of his cross-examination during the trial proper are even more sensational, there is little point in quoting large extracts from his testimony here. The most important details, from the point of view of advancing the narrative, are given briefly. For example, he admitted deliberately withholding the Bernard Thorpe valuation of the Trafford site at £1.5 million from the file sent to the DPP's office. Indeed, it was most necessary, although he didn't say so, because the DPP would hardly be likely to permit a prosecution if he had been aware of its existence. In other words, Stephenson was guilty of cynically manipulating evidence with the aim of getting an innocent man sent to jail.

He revealed that the Drugs Intelligence Unit, in three years of intensive activity, had arrested or charged no one with drugs offences. Its sole target, as revealed by the Sampson Report, was me.

On a number of occasions, Stephenson was so put out that he refused to answer. The defence wanted to know, for example, where he had got his detailed facts in the Informations for the Recorder of Manchester. Stephenson claimed it was from an 'informant' and refused to say who.

But one of the most important events from the whole committal proceedings was that Hood successfully obtained sight of Stephenson's notebook. He asked that they be lent to Fred Fox, a retired Manchester police inspector and now a clerk with Adlers, the instructing solicitors, to take down some details concerning the questions being answered, and he put the request so politely and ingenuously, it could not be refused.

In fact Fox had them for the best part of thirty minutes and scribbled furiously everything he saw concerning the case, while the cross-examination continued. What was revealed in the notebook was nothing less than sensational: *that Stephenson had been present in the Co-op Bank gathering information on 16 December 1985, four months before the Access Orders were granted.* Securing Access Orders from Judge Presst was thus little more than a cosmetic job, to regularize this breech of the law. Even more incredible, the notebook showed that next day DCS Topping, the man in operational charge of CID, had also been present with Stephenson on a clandestine visit to the bank. The head of CID was inciting the bank to break the law and reveal confidential information about my accounts illegally. What more proof could be needed that a serious and sinister plot was under way and some very senior officers had dirty paws.

Corkery came into the fray when his witness was clearly having a bad time, and called attention to the fact that the notebook was still with the solicitor's clerk, who was making notes and that this might violate the confidentiality of other matters. However, the magistrate accepted that Fox was making notes of matters confined solely to the case in hand and allowed him to continue.

This simple gesture of human trust was of inestimable value to the defence. Police notebooks were to become a major feature of the trial and, along with the Robson correspondence, the Sampson Report and the Presst information, probably no other documents were so crucial in ultimately winning the case.

If the reader has not guessed it, the real reason that Topping was at the bank, of course, was to pull rank and bring some pressure to bear on Hylie Shepherd to get the Co-op Bank to make a formal complaint. The police were trying to bully him into doing their dirty work. The bank refused and never altered from this stance. If they had, the consequences could indeed have been disastrous for me.

But the greatest milestone of the case was also to come at the committal. This was the disclosure of the contents of the sealed envelope. Before the hearing, Buckley had been at work on a bifurcated correspondence between him, Judge Presst and the Director of Public Prosecutions' office. By dint of skilled writing, Buckley managed to convince the DPP's office that Judge Presst might well rescind his order not to open the sealed envelope. Indeed His Lordship wrote most kindly to Adlers to say that in asking for the envelope to be sealed, 'It was not my intention to conceal the contents of the envelope in any subsequent legal proceedings.' He also wrote to Roger Rees, the Police Authority solicitor in Manchester, in peremptory, almost staccato tones, ordering that his direction that DI Stephenson's information be placed in a sealed envelope be 'revoked forthwith'. Conscious that if the decision was foisted on them it would look bad for having refused, to pre-empt any embarrassment the Crown Prosecution Service finally agreed to allow disclosure.

When we finally read the information Stephenson had sworn on oath, it became obvious why the police had been so desperate to prevent it becoming public. It contained so many lies, some blatant and some subtle, that there has been no hesitation on the part of every lawyer who has read it in condemning it. It is probably the most crucial document in the whole case and the one which reveals most clearly the determined effort of the police to get what they wanted, without any regard to truth or justice.

The document runs to nine pages and there is little point in reproducing it here in full. However, the first few paragraphs are worth mentioning in detail. It begins with Stephenson saying, 'I am currently concerned with enquiries into the financing of unlawful drug trafficking' and that 'The main enquiry centres upon the commercial activities of one Kevin Taylor.' What possible grouping of words could give the judge a more sinister impression of me or accuse me more openly of being involved in drugs? He says this without one shred of tangible evidence that such a story is true, indeed he was later to admit he knew it was not true. If there was any doubt at all that the police had used this trick to open judicial doors where the police had no proper authority, the publication of this document finally dispelled them, for ever.

In paragraph two he also describes me as purporting to be a respectable businessman. That one word 'purporting' is a subtle contrivance to further undermine the judge's opinion of me and in using it Stephenson makes a lie out of his 12 January 1988 affidavit, in which he said he had described me to the Recorder of Manchester as 'a respectable businessman'.

He stated that the Access Orders were required because 'other methods had been tried without success.' This was untrue both in fact and as a matter of record. Firstly, no policeman ever approached me and asked me for permission to review my accounts. It would certainly have been given. Secondly, the Robson correspondence told quite the opposite story and was, not surprisingly, withheld from Judge Presst, despite the fact that the Act states clearly that it is incumbent upon the police seeking an order 'to disclose to the Court all relevant matters relating to this condition'.

The application was also made technically invalid by the fact that, in issuing notices to the banks that an application for the Access Orders was to be made, Stephenson omitted to tell the recipients that they had the right to appear before the Court to raise objections. Instead they were told by letter, 'If you have any objections to the applications being made, please notify my office by telephone within seven days of the date of this letter, so that arrangements can be made for the Court to be made aware of any objection.' This is quite outside the provisions of the Act and, of course, designed to obfuscate the necessary procedure and intimidate anyone wanting to object.

It was easy to understand now why the police had wanted the application for the Access Orders to be made *ex parte*: if I had known of the application and been allowed to hear what was being said, I could have exposed all the lies being told to the court. Stephenson did his dirty work in the comfortable belief that what he was swearing would never see the light of day and could thus never be challenged.

Ironically, Stephenson deposes such detailed minutiae of my affairs in the document that it is quite obvious that he already had the information he needed from the bank. So why bother with the application? Just to make it all nice and legal . . . after the fact? Does it help the reader to work out what was going on, to be reminded that the time these orders were applied for were only a few weeks before Stalker's removal and that these Access Orders were to be used to gather evidence against Stalker? Stephenson even mentions in his deposition that my boat had been used by criminals and 'a senior police officer', whom he does not name. But could anyone seriously believe that he did not know who it was?

There are several other paragraphs carefully written to give a vaguely sinister or discreditable impression of me, such as that 'Kevin Taylor's main activity during business hours is that of card playing' and that he 'associates with major criminals known to be active in the Manchester area', without putting this 'association' into the gambling context. He states that the source of the £80,000 used for the purchase of the *Diogenes* was 'unknown', deliberately leaving the judge to speculate that it was obtained by some criminal means, when even a half-decent detective could have easily established it was paid for by a loan from Barclay's Bank.

In paragraph ten, Stephenson reports that there were firearms aboard when the *Diogenes* put into Liverpool for a refit but omits to mention that the police had taken a statement from Colin William Faulkner, skipper of the *Diogenes*, who reported it was recommended practice to carry guns on a boat in the Caribbean area because of pirates and that the guns were kept under lock and key.

Here in this paragraph he makes another false statement under oath, stating that, 'Sometime during the summer of 1981 firearms were taken aboard at a time when several Manchester criminals were using the boat.' The guns were actually purchased much earlier, as a matter of record. Stephenson goes on to say the guns were discharged into the sea, which is irrelevant and absurd and therefore one can see that it was included only as part of a general mud-slinging. Stephenson omitted to mention that the Customs and Excise officers in Salford knew of the firearms and were not in the least concerned: because that wouldn't suit his purpose. Instead he says, mysteriously, that 'the disposal of those firearms is not known.' It sounds more sinister, doesn't it?

Similarly, he reported that I sold the *Diogenes* to Alan Brooks, who he describes as a 'convicted receiver and known drug-runner', which is unfair to me since Brooks had not been convicted, or even arrested, at the point when I sold him the boat. I don't have access to Interpol files; how could I have known he was a suspected drug-runner? I had never even met the man.

The aura of *Miami Vice* in such remarks has nothing to do with the supposed fraud against the Co-op Bank but everything to do with the unfounded allegations of drug-trafficking and Stephenson's attempt to give Judge Presst a misleading and sinister impression of me.

Only one question remains, and an intriguing one at that: why did Judge Presst ask for the information deposed by Stephenson to be sealed in an envelope and then give instructions that it was never to be opened, except on his direct order? Could it be that he smelled something fishy? Remember, Judge Presst gave consent for the envelope to be opened at once, as soon as he realized that his order was being used to hide the contents from the process of judicial discovery.

On 8 November, after seven weeks, Mr Loy decided that all four defendants were to go forward on all charges, unconditionally. He had accepted that there was a triable case on respect of myself, Britton and McCann. He was doubtful, however, that Bowley should be included.

In the end, Mr Corkery persuaded him that financial gain was not necessary for there to have been an offence. Other motives would qualify, such as furthering of his career or arrogating too much responsibility. I found this an absurd line of reasoning, since none of these motives for Bowley had even been mooted, never mind proved. However, Mr Loy finally agreed that Bowley should go forward also. I have already said that, without him, the prosecution case would collapse.

We had lost again. I could only think of Buckley's favourite saying, throughout all our unsuccessful court battles, taken from Professor Alan Derschovitz's book on the von Bülow case: *to win you have to lose.*

11
The Road to Ruin

In the meantime, my personal financial affairs had fallen steadily deeper into the mire. In real terms, my businesses had made no income for over two years. Because of police interference, it had not been possible to realize the full financial potential of any of my sites. The accumulation of massive interest charges, plus mediocre sales figures achieved by the receiver of land at Trafford, meant that nothing had been released from the sales to allow salary drawings. Furthermore, since late 1985, no British bank had allowed me to run a current account, even on a credit-only basis.

It is proverbial that men with money stack away funds in secret accounts but I had failed to do this. Perhaps it was part of my gambling instinct, but I had risked all, even my house, on the land development projects . . . and lost. The only consolation, if such a term applies, is that it was not through faulty judgement but because of deliberate outside interference. There were no Swiss bank deposits or secret hoards to call on at this time. What I faced at the end of 1986 was nothing less than ruin.

Gradually, as my standing and income were eroded, the painful and embarrassing process of selling off effects began. There was plenty to sell but, as word of our plight got around, bargain hunters began to offer disproportionately low prices, knowing that I had little choice.

I began to borrow heavily from friends to keep going. At first it was with complete optimism that everything would soon come out all right and I would be able to repay the loans and make a generous settlement towards those who had helped me through the crisis. But gradually, as weeks slipped into months and then into years, it became obvious there would be no easy way to pay back all that I owed. Friends, who were willing to support me for a time, faltered and then couldn't keep going. The good will persisted but there was a limit to how long a devoted friend could go on supporting my family, in addition to meeting their own commitments.

In the beginning, there were outstanding acts of charity. Steve Hayes, ex-CID and now running a successful investigation business, was among the first to dig into his resources and he dug deep. The man drained himself to help me. Hayes knew all about suspect police methods. He had been hounded from the force for a crime he says was a frame-up by a man who was later discredited. Unfortunately, Hayes feels it is now too late to re-open his own case.

Jimmy Rowe, also an ex-policeman, who now runs a major wine retailer in Manchester and who had hardly met me more than a handful of times, wanted to help. Without being asked, he sent an envelope containing £5,000 cash, an extraordinary and unselfish gesture.

Could it be significant that these men were willing to help me because I was under pressure from their erstwhile colleagues, whose methods they could well understand? Time and time again throughout the years of this investigation I was heartened by the way the 'average' coppers stood up to be counted and make it known they did not like what was being done to me and my family.

The unencumbered loan of £70,000 by a businessman has already been referred to in Chapter 7. Another donation of £5,000 came from two businessmen when I needed money to pay the lawyers to bring the summons against Anderton in October 1986. The benefactors made it clear there was more available for the same purpose, if needed. Ralph Stross gave £20,000. There are many others who gave varying amounts, great and small in relation to their total assets, without any real certainty of getting it back. Remember this was at a time when people in general were saying, 'Taylor must be guilty,' on the no-smoke-without-a-fire principle. It must have taken a considerable amount of personal conviction to help out a man in my precarious position and I will always be grateful for these moving acts of kindness and sympathy.

The sad thing is that I used the many donations for the purpose of shoring up my ailing companies. I did not have the prescience to realize they were doomed to failure, because the police wanted them put down and had the means to achieve that end. Ultimately, of course, they were all to go into liquidation and my struggle would have been less harrowing if I had kept the money to provide for my family.

Some respite from the problems came when BBC2 asked to use Wood Mill as part of the set for the series *Truckers*, about the road haulage industry. The house was to represent the luxury home of one of the bosses who was refusing to pay his men and, as part of the action, one of the drivers deliberately crashed his truck into the garden in revenge, creating a great deal of damage. To achieve this effect, the props men created an entire artificial garden on the banks of the Irwell, using their own shrubs and plantings. A special ramp had to be laid, to get the truck back up again. Finally, when the filming was over, everything had to be restored to how it had been. For this I received £5,000. Probably few people who watched the series, perhaps envious of the owner of that particularly beautiful house, realized the pain he and his family were going through.

Some of the stories of help are particularly touching. Once, in my more affluent days, I had assisted an ex-fairground boxer called Joe Plant. He'd needed money and I had lent it to him, no strings attached. It was never repaid. Shortly before the Stalker Affair broke, Plant had died suddenly. But clearly he had kept it within family lore that I had once helped him.

When the second BBC *Panorama* programme ('Stalker and Co.') had gone out in August 1986, Plant's eldest son had seen my financial plight. With no more than the clues contained in the programme to go on, he had left Blackpool and tracked me down. He arrived at Wood Mill at midnight one night, having wandered all over Summerseat trying to find me.

I asked him in for a drink. Somewhat embarassed, the man explained that he had saved £400 and it would have been his father's certain wish that he come and return the favour that I had shown to Joe all those years ago. I was so overcome I could hardly find the words to answer.

It was obvious the lad didn't have much money but I could ill-afford to decline this wonderful deeply felt gesture. Gratefully, I therefore accepted £200 and stated that it cleaned the slate with Joe Plant, for good. It was one of a number of warm and comforting gestures that counter-balanced the vileness of those who were plotting against me, and made our hardship a little easier to bear.

Pressure from the Trustee Savings Bank, mortgagees of the house, began as early as late 1985. Clearly they too had been visited by the police and were alarmed by the imputation that I was a drug-trafficker.

The trouble was that, as matters deteriorated, I became unable to pay the considerable mortgage. What had been easy payments in affluent days were now crippling monthly sums and, with interest piling on remorselessly, the balance due spiralled upwards rapidly.

Inevitably, the bank took legal action to foreclose on the security of the property. I fought back confidently, knowing that the TSB, along with others, had co-operated illegally with the police and were guilty of inappropriate actions that had placed me in the predicament of being unable to pay. Unfortunately, as I was to soon find out, in law the mortgagee's rights supercede all other claims for damages or compensation and it was a no-contest from the start. Nevertheless, repeated rear-guard action through several courts staved off the evil day and held out that all important wisp of hope that made the injustice seem more endurable.

In reality the bank's legal costs were simply added to the mortgage balance and what could have been a small return became a loss situation. But when you are threatened with the loss of your family home, it isn't possible to think these things through in the most calculating and objective manner. Actually, I wasn't so much bothered for myself, but I had to fight for my wife's sake. She loved that house and to lose it broke her heart, though she was very forbearing and valiantly tried to hide her hurt, in order not to put me under more pressure.

Eventually, of course, the TSB won their action and the position became irretrievable. Having taken over, the bank then allowed us to stay on for several more months. This wasn't so much out of compassion or guilt but simply, I suppose, because it is easier to sell a house which is bright and full of people than one which is cold, empty and forbidding. It was galling, however, to have a succession of viewers who had been told the price was in the region of £250,000 looking over the premises. I knew the real value was almost double that amount but there was no chance of getting it, given the circumstances. A few good offers were received but, as soon as the truth about me came out, the buyer withdrew, presumably to wait in the hope of picking it up more cheaply.

One buyer from the Midlands seemed very keen. He was wealthy and could afford £350,000 but when he approached a High Street bank for a home loan he was refused on the grounds that the bank had run a check and didn't like the man he was buying from. It was an absurd and distressing decision that made no commercial sense. It was typical of so many aspects of the nightmare we found ourselves in.

Pressure came from other, quite surprising, directions. In August 1987 Bury magistrates tried to jail me summarily for non-payment of my rates. This astonishing hostility was clearly an orchestrated manoeuvre; the bench had carefully prepared documentary ammunition which was certainly not of a routine sort, according to Buckley. The degree of aggression and lack of sympathy seemed quite out of keeping with the situation. There seemed little doubt that they had been coached by someone higher up and had their cards marked. It took a great deal of diplomatic tact by Neville Heginbotham to talk them out of their extraordinarily savage intention.

By the end of the summer of 1987, my financial demise was so complete I had no choice but to apply for assistance from the Department of Health and Social Security. The dole. It had a gloomy depressing ring to it and was a considerable stigma for a man who had once known what it was like to be independent and secure.

The application took a considerable time and was dogged by questions and objections that would tax any man's patience. Clearly help in keeping off the bread-line was not going to be dispensed without a fight, whether because of bureaucratic disbelief in my circumstances or because of secret interference from the police. But rules are rules and I qualified for relief. They were even obliged to pay my mortgage interest, though it was too late to prevent the ultimate foreclosure by the TSB.

The important point about dole was that it qualified me automatically for Legal Aid. In the times to come the burden of defending myself was to amount to a cost well into six figures. It would have been quite beyond my means to pay such costs myself and would have simply resulted in me being denied the much-vaunted benefits of British justice, even if such a commodity had in fact existed, which I was beginning seriously to doubt.

Finally, in October 1988, we were evicted from Wood Mill. We put most of our furniture in store, against the day when we might need it again, packed our clothes and said goodbye to the happiest home we had ever known. In every sense it had been a very personal house, one that had been sweated over and suffered for. Even my wife and children had helped to mix cement and move stones and timber as the conversions were being carried out. That made it all the more painful to us eventually to lose it for reasons beyond our control. We moved to a small rented house west of Bolton, just off the M61. All we have left to show for our years at Wood Mill is a photograph album showing each stage of the work, up until completion. It is a curious testament – our happy grimy faces smiling from the pages, posed cheerfully among heaps of stones, mud and long grass – a poignant reminder of once carefree days.

*

On the positive side, I still had a great many friends, even in such difficult times. People would often stop me on the street and wish me well. Even policemen; I soon lost count of the number of occasions a friendly bobby on the beat recognized me and smiled or said 'Hello Kevin' and 'Good luck.' Many was the time I was stopped late at night in my car and, as soon as I was recognized, told to drive on with a nod or a wink. 'You've enough problems already,' was the usual comment.

One incident that I recall particularly took place shortly before Christmas 1986. This was after we had indicted Anderton, Topping and Stephenson for the conspiracy to pervert the course of justice but the case had not yet been heard. I had witnessed a crash along Deansgate in which a stolen car had collided with another vehicle. Two public-spirited men had leapt out and performed a 'citizens' arrest' on the occupants of the stolen car. From nowhere, two bobbies on motorcycles had appeared and one of them, who saw I had been watching came up to me. 'Excuse me sir, are you a witness to what took place?' he asked.

'Just watching a couple of honest coppers doing an honest day's work,' I told him.

'You're Kevin Taylor, aren't you?' he said, having recognized me.

I nodded.

'Pleased to meet you,' he said and took off his gauntlets to shake hands. He called his colleague over and he too shook hands. 'We hope you win!' they both said and then got on with their job, leaving me somewhat bemused.

The other side to this coin, however, was not so pleasant. My eldest daughter Kate, who had just started a job which involved her driving, was stopped in her vehicle many times. On a number of these occasions she was breathalyzed (she cannot drink because of her asthma). More than once she was greeted with the comment: 'We know who you are, Miss Taylor.'

Well-wishers were everywhere. Whenever I took Beryl out to dine, someone would invite us to join them or a bottle of champagne would arrive from another table. Often we would eat 'on the house'. Restaurateurs continued to treat me with the same respect and kindness they reserved for their best customers, despite our financial embarrassment. It was as if there was an unwritten conviction that some day the troubles would all be over, the money would return and I would resume where I had left off. It was an eclipse, that's all, not a sunset.

*

I still attended charity functions and helped to raise money for many good causes but, of course, I was able to give nothing. One of the many events I went to in 1988 was organized by the Charity Commandos, of which I was still a member, to raise money for a heart transplant unit in Wythenshawe Hospital, Manchester. It could easily have been embarrassing and painful. Instead, everyone who knew the story came over and offered their sincere good wishes. Drinks were pressed on me and I ached from the number of handshakes and slaps on the back. Someone wrote my name on a £10 note and put it into a draw for a free holiday in Spain but it didn't win. The MC even made a reference to 'One we all know who has given so magnificently in the past who is here with us tonight and we know would give unstintingly now, if only he had the money.' It brought a round of applause and quite a lump to my throat.

But charity, they say, begins at home. I was beset with problems providing for the family. So much so that in a desperate attempt to take care of Beryl and the girls, I turned once more to cards. In an extraordinary act of generosity, Sid Otty, one of the well-known figures in Manchester's club and gaming world, had made me a proposition: he would put up the money to allow me to play cards and then share the winnings. Since he was to stand all losses that might occur, it was in reality no deal at all for him. It was a considerate act of kindness in an unusual disguise.

So, after more than twenty years, I was back at the card table, battling with my wits. But this time it was a very different story. I was fighting for my life and, far from being on top of things, I had plenty of worries to distract me from the cards. The carefree heady days were long past and, as every gambler knows, when you have to win is precisely the time when you don't get the breaks. It was a disaster. I would sit at the tables for twelve to fourteen hours at a time and come away with a few pounds, or nothing at all.

After several weeks of trying, missing sleep and wearing myself out, friends in alarm prevailed on me to stop, before it killed me. Sadly, I had to admit I was now yesterday's man. Once king of the baize, I had finally been out-trumped.

My health continued to deteriorate markedly and people kept commenting that the strain was showing. Others, looking at the 1986 videos of myself talking at the time of the Stalker Affair, can see that I have aged fifteen years in just over thirty-six months. My diabetes was out of control, my blood pressure had soared and there were signs of an old ulcer returning. Acutely perceptive friends even told me that my speech had begun to deteriorate, with a distinct slur developing, yet my alcohol consumption was minimal, compared to what it had been in my days as the town's top host.

Eventually, in October 1988, I was certified permanently sick and on the advice of Harold Cohen, my consultant physician, I applied to be registered as a disabled person. It was a sore blow to someone like me. Of all the things that I have lost in the last few years, the one I feel most bitter about is my health. It is unlikely I will ever be a well man again. The only compensation was that sickness benefit was more than dole money and we now had £78 per week to live on.

But it was the effect of this whole affair on my wife that concerned me most. I could always go back to the streets of Salford, where I began; *Clogs to Clogs in One Generation* could be the title of the Kevin Taylor story. Beryl is incredibly tough, yet, like many women, inside she has a soft and vulnerable aspect. I could see her being eaten up by her outrage at what was happening. It was especially unfair on her, since she too was being destroyed and yet had never done anything wrong. My life-style and political associations, whatever problems they had brought me, were not her fault. I wonder if the perpetrators of this conspiracy ever stopped to think of the way other people not directly involved were being badly affected, or whether they actually cared.

Only a successful conclusion to the trial could now save us from our plight. If, somehow, I could successfully fight the charges being brought, I might then be in a position to claim damages for what was done to me and my companies. Who knows, I thought, we might one day return to our comfortable life.

12
A Plot Within a Plot

Meanwhile, Buckley continued patiently to gather any scraps of data that would help the defence. It meant interviewing dozens of potential witnesses, taking statements, cross-checking facts and other complex time-consuming research. His hat at times was more akin to that of a private investigator than a solicitor at law. Over three years, he covered many miles on foot in search of the truth. He jokes that he has worn out his expensive white kangaroo leather shoes made by Vahe Manoukian, but is so attached to them, he refuses to change them for an ordinary pair. 'I dare not tell you how much they cost,' he smiles sheepishly, 'but when my bankruptcy has been discharged I have promised myself two new pairs.'

Among his many sleuthing triumphs is the exposure of Sir John Hermon's probable dissembling about the meeting in Scarborough on 19 May 1986, at which the decision was taken to get rid of Stalker. Hermon always maintained that he had nothing to do with the events of that day and denied being in Scarborough at all. Asked specifically on this point, the then Home Secretary Douglas Hurd told parliament that he understood Hermon to have been in Belfast on the day in question. This sidesteps the possibility that Hermon could have been in Belfast and Scarborough on the same day. It isn't difficult with modern commuter air-travel.

Buckley got on the trail early in 1988 while watching a video-recording of Peter Taylor, of the BBC *Panorama* team, interviewing Hermon at the end of a programme about Stalker ('Conspiracy or Coincidence', 16 June 1986). Hermon seemed especially tense and uncomfortable, ducking and weaving with his answers. At times he evaded unpleasant questions altogether and proceeded to answer on a different topic, more to his liking. Asked directly by Peter Taylor: 'Sir John, is Mr Stalker the victim of a conspiracy?', Hermon replied, 'Mr Taylor, you are aware that I haven't seen this programme until this minute . . . and I say that I have been categorically reassured that the reasons for Mr Stalker's removal from duty in Greater Manchester have nothing whatsoever to do with his enquiry in Northern Ireland. I only knew a few days before his removal from duty that it was to occur or was likely to occur. It had not even then been confirmed.'

'I realized, as soon as I heard the last two sentences, that he was likely to have been present at the meeting in Scarborough,' says Buckley. He set out to uncover the truth. A visit to the Royal Hotel Scarborough, once owned by the film actor Charles Laughton, failed to gain access to the registration cards for the period. However, a bugged interview with Geoffrey Carr, secretary of the Police Federation, confirmed that Hermon was indeed present and gave details. Hermon had made a flying visit; according to Carr, he did not go to the conference, which was scheduled for the next day; but he did 'meet with executive officers whilst there'. According to Carr, Hermon was there 'for some other reason' (not stated).

All that remained was a little ruse finally to implicate Hermon by his own tacit admission. He had already sued *Private Eye* once, for getting its facts wrong. Why not leak the story about his presence at Scarborough and see if he sued again? If not, he was as good as admitting his own guilt. Accordingly, Buckley caused the information to appear in an editorial leader in *Private Eye* in March 1988. There was no response.

It could be seen as very prejudicial to Hermon, that he may have been part of a decision to get rid of Stalker from the RUC enquiry only days before he and his deputy, Micheal McAtamny, were due to be interviewed under caution concerning what may well have turned out to be a conspiracy to murder. However, as Buckley says, his involvement in Scarborough could be less sinister than it first appears. It may simply be that, having knowledge of Stalker's imminent removal, Hermon must have been conscious of the fact that he would almost certainly be blamed for bringing it about. He would have found himself in a 'no win' situation, unable to explain and unable to complain. A desire to be one jump ahead of his critics may have been why he was there, rather than a wish to influence the decision against Stalker.

This RUC connection in the plot was what we all suspected in 1986 and, other than the revelation about Hermon's hotly denied presence, there was nothing new here. As a matter of record, also implicated in the decision to remove Stalker were Sir Philip Myers and Sir Lawrence Byford, who were known to be present, along with Colin Sampson.

Byford later tried to make it quite plain to Peter Murtagh of *The Guardian*, that he was there for largely cosmetic reasons and that all the talking was done between Myers, Anderton and Sampson. The instrument of this scheme was Chief Constable James Anderton, a willing participant who took it upon himself to report Stalker for supposed misconduct and have him suspended. This much at least is a matter of record.

But notwithstanding this 'official' plot, there had also emerged the apparent existence of a stand-alone conspiracy operated within Manchester's police headquarters at Chester House. Almost certainly this was a push against Stalker himself, based on jealousy and personal attitudes. It is widely known that Anderton is an extremely ambitious man. He made no secret of the fact that he wanted to be Commissioner of the Metropolitan Police. Chief Constable of the RUC was a good stepping stone to that appointment and an almost certain route to a knighthood. One can imagine his feelings at the point when Stalker suddenly looked as if he was going to leap-frog over his former boss and land one or both of the plum jobs.

The fact is that Stalker was a better investigative cop than his own chief. Anderton lacked CID experience, and not only was he a leader missing vital skills, but it appeared that he had developed a huge chip on his shoulder about this point. He became sensitive on the issue and tended to over-react to criticism, real or imagined, because of this weakness in his background. In fact he may have surrounded himself with non-CID men as a snub to his critics, and doubtless he would feel less threatened working with men who did not surpass him in their knowledge of criminal investigation work.

Thus Ralph Lees, Assistant Chief Constable, in charge of CID was a uniformed man who had never, at any stage in his police career, worked as a detective. He knew even less about criminal investigation than Anderton and yet he was in control of a force of several thousand detectives. He was known to be a weak man and broke down into tears when confronted with the wrong done to Stalker by his men. Lees was chosen to be Stalker's successor as deputy chief constable. Could he have known he would be ensuring his own promotion in allowing the actions taken against Stalker via me? Whether it was a conscious act or not, he cannot escape the blame for much of what happened, if only as the executive officer of a force run amok.

The inner plot within the GMP had begun moving towards its ultimate climax from as early as summer 1983, with the Bertlestein matter, and was certainly accelerated by the McGourlay conversation in July 1984. It could not have taken place without the knowledge of the Chief Constable but the instigator was almost certainly Topping. If the Masonic plot theory fits, this is where it came into play (Orange Order in Ulster). It seems improbable that Whitehall would be gunning for Stalker in mid-1984, otherwise why give him the job? But there is no question that Stalker was unwelcome and bitterly resented by RUC officers, from day one. Did they have friends and contacts within the GMP capable of bringing Stalker down?

At least one possibility comes to mind. Simons' role as a close friend of Topping and also as Stalker's Number Three on the RUC enquiry has already been pointed out. He was allegedly a practising Mason and there is no doubt that Topping was 'on the square'. It is no leap of the imagination to suppose one was feeding the other data. Simons, later head of the Commercial Fraud Squad, is a shadowy figure but is clearly implicated in the plot against me. His name turns up several times, including an attendance upon Guy Robson in late 1985, long before the Stalker Affair broke, and in a letter to A J Adler of 27 May 1986, concerning the return of my effects after the searches that month. This last letter, it should be remembered, had the letters DIU/DI Stephenson at the top. Remember, too, Simons was the man who had allowed himself to be interviewed by Robson in January 1986, when I had secretly recorded the conversation. If 'Brethren' wanted action, all the links existed secretly to arrange for an attack on Stalker. We know that Anderton is certainly not a Mason but possible motivation existed.

What seems to have happened is that this second, more hidden, conspiracy came to the notice of the Whitehall bosses at a very timely moment, probably occasioned by reports from Anderton, which were furnished without giving Stalker a chance to defend himself against what was being said. What better opportunity could there be for MI5, the Home Office and other interested parties than to move in on top of the existing plot and encourage it to the full? It would then be possible to withdraw quietly to the background and loudly proclaim that Stalker's removal was a local phenomenon, entirely unconnected with the Northern Ireland enquiry. The MI5 'dirty tricks' tactics are known to include building on an existing partial truth in this way, since the disaffection and lies being spread take far more hold if there is an element of credibility in what is being alleged.

Usually such fortuitous coincidences are hard to swallow and more often than not are contrived explanations, designed to obscure the truth. They make poor reading. Here, however, there was plenty of circumstantial evidence to support such a theory. Put into this double-layer perspective, the Stalker Affair becomes easier to comprehend and the narrative events start to gel together in a way that is attractive.

The twin-conspiracy idea makes particular sense when trying to fit the 1984 events into the jigsaw. As Peter Taylor says in his book, 'The precise mechanisms and details of events between June 1984 and March 1985 have been extremely difficult to establish' (*Stalker: The Search for the Truth*, Faber and Faber 1987).

We now know from statements made by a retired detective, with twenty years' standing in the Commercial Fraud Squad, that the association between myself and Stalker, bringing in the so-called Quality Street Gang connection, had been reported in 1983 but was not being acted on by the end of 1984.

Then something happened in January 1985 that had caused it all to be resurrected and brought about 'an almighty hue and cry' and, as he described it, the mobilization of massive resources under the auspices of high-ranking officers. His statement even tells us what that something must have been: that in January 1985, Stalker met MI5 in London, who agreed to release the tape-recording of the hayshed tape.

In very telling comments, he then goes on to point out that, although Topping had beaten a path to his door in January 1985, followed by the Sampson team in 1986, not one word of his formal memorandum is mentioned in the Sampson Report. It was, he said, the single most significant omission from the report. He suggests a most compelling reason for its omission, which is that it would 'rubbish' the 'apparent spontaneity and revelation' that the disclosure of Stalker's connections had in the events which led up to his suspension in 1986. If Sampson had published earlier appreciations of this material, the immediacy of the 'discovery' of the information used against Stalker would have been seen as a contrivance, bringing back discredited intelligence to justify removing him from office.

This detective informant, incidentally, was a man who had personally handled Bertlestein alias Burton; in fact he'd gone to grammar school with him and the two seemed to understand each other.

One man who fell foul of the central power group at GMP was DCS John Thorburn, Stalker's Number Two on the RUC enquiry. He was a first-rate detective and one of GMP's most liked officers, a man of outstanding integrity. He had been appointed administrative head of CID. Almost immediately Topping, as operational head, began to erode his authority while he was absent in Northern Ireland. Many unwritten tensions and quarrels must have ensued. Ultimately,

Thorburn's job was to be made so untenable by Topping that he saw no other course but to resign.

The cavalier treatment Thorburn received at the hands of Anderton and the others is well illustrated by the example of the memorandum he wrote to the Chief Constable in February 1986, outlining matters about which he was very unhappy in relation to the CID and asking for an interview. This was entirely proper on his part and for someone with his seniority he should have been granted the audience promptly. In fact Anderton didn't bother to speak to him about it at all, so Thorburn quit, angered and disillusioned by what he called the web of deceit at Chester House.

Shortly before leaving the force, nine months after writing the memorandum, he was asked if he wanted to speak with Anderton, as part of a normal leaving routine and said 'No.' However, he was called in to see the Chief Constable anyway, whose only concern it seemed was the self-interest of asking Thorburn to withdraw the memorandum, which he was finding embarrassing. Thorburn refused and there the matter ended. Several retired senior officers we have spoken to have pointed out that Anderton was grossly out of order in ignoring this communication from such an important administrative section head. It says a lot for Anderton's lack of real involvement with his force that he would react this way to Thorburn's memorandum.

The 'Gang of Four' in Manchester, then, would seem to be Anderton, Topping, Simons and, later, Stephenson, though Buckley at that time likened Stephenson to the honest, plodding foot-soldier, rather than a conspirator (later, we were to discover that this was a naïve underestimate of the commitment of Stephenson). Buckley had managed to piece together a fairly convincing body of evidence about the involvement of these four men in the scheme against Stalker and myself.

The man whose role is hard to define is ACC Ralph Lees. Certainly, as the man in charge of the CID, he must accept some of the blame for what was done to Stalker and me by men under his command. But it does seem possible that his guilt is more a moral one than an actual involvement. We now know, for example, that he was kept very much in the dark about the function and activity of the DIU.

The Drugs Intelligence Unit itself was difficult to probe. We know it was set up under the authority of the Chief Constable. Topping was responsible for its day-to-day running. At the end of 1988, the only names we knew were Ware, Hogg, Corfield, Murray, Waterworth, Richardson and Born (operational head), later joined by Stephenson,

Caldwell and Knowles. But how many other figures could be hidden in the background, lurking behind the fanatical secrecy?

There was evidently a paranoid anxiety at Chester House that no one should discover what the DIU was up to, except those directly involved, and this apparently extended even to officers as high as ACC. There were separate quarters in a Portakabin, barred to the average officer, and meetings were intense, secretive and select. It was, in every sense, a 'force within a force'.

Ostensibly, the DIU's purpose was supposed to be investigating drug-trafficking in Manchester. It operated for three years, from February 1985 to February 1988, at a cost of millions; in that time it charged no one. Instead it was a secret weapon, whose target was the Deputy Chief Constable. Its sole task was to 'investigate' me, despite the fact that I was not and never have been connected with drugs.

In the end, of course, I was charged with commercial fraud. Such a flagrant and phenomenal abuse of public funds is almost impossible to believe and must have taken place with the full consent of the Chief Constable. I can only speculate that it must have been fully sanctioned from London. Indeed, we have evidence that, in order to cover up the inordinate expense of the DIU, funds were 'officially' diverted, to hide the real cost. The obvious question is: why? If this enquiry had been completely bona fide, it shouldn't have mattered what the costs were.

David Hood, my barrister at committal, suggests the possibility of a 'dirty' team and a clean team. One would carry out its investigations in an apparently bona fide manner, but using material obtained illicitly by the 'dirty' team. The inexplicable appearance of documents used in this case, which had no prior legitimate history, was to be one of the features which emerged in the trial. Remember, too, the police burglaries which probably took place on my home and office between February and May 1986. Also, of course, there was nothing to stop the 'dirty' team from ringing up potential buyers and spreading disinformation which could never be traced. Again, something we know must have been taking place. It all lends weight to this very plausible theory.

In outline, by midsummer 1989, Buckley was able to lay out the whole plot. If a novelist had offered this story seriously to a publisher, he would probably have been laughed at and told to come up with something more 'realistic' instead of an absurd and impossible fantasy. Yet this is no novel and the characters depicted in it are real people; the truth, which emerged in the trial, only added to this lurid melodrama and did not diminish it in any way.

More evidence was needed to back up our scenario. Key people were interviewed and statements taken. Some witnesses gave valuable information but didn't want to appear themselves for various reasons. Threats of retaliation to those officers who publicly supported the cause of Kevin Taylor possessed unmistakable meaning. That's the kind of evil we were up against.

Among the many people Buckley spoke to was retired CS Charles Abrahams. He was outspoken in his criticism of Anderton, Lees and Topping and their attempt to carry out a secret investigation into the DCC. It violated the correct established procedure, he said, which was that Anderton should have called Stalker before him, to answer the allegations being made; if he wasn't satisfied, he should then have brought in an outside force to look into matters. Yet without giving Stalker any possibility of defending himself against the malicious rumours, Anderton was busy passing prejudicial 'information' to Sir Philip Myers.

Interestingly, Abrahams too had known Bertlestein, though he never handled him, and described him as a 'Walter Mitty' character. He told Buckley that he had heard rumours that Bertlestein was supposed to be an informant for the newly formed 'Drugs Squad' in 1985 but, of course, hadn't realized the significance of what this meant at the time.

Abrahams was enlightening about the allegation of my associating with known criminals. 'Certain police officers would play the name game,' he told Buckley. 'To justify their observation hours they would sometimes file reports to say that certain people had been seen associating with others.'

He described Topping as a humourless and dogmatic individual. His nickname within the GMP, apparently, was 'The Butler' because of his bent and obsequious posture with his seniors. Abrahams was caustic about his lack of experience as a detective. In regard to my case specifically, it was 'unbelievable', Abrahams said, that the head of CID would personally involve himself in any enquiry because (a) this would usurp the authority of the Fraud Squad officers; (b) he would not have the expertise; and (c) any involvement in a prolonged enquiry would take him away from his primary responsibilities, i.e. overall command of the CID. Also drawing on his commercial fraud experience, he remarked, 'The fewer the men you had on the case, the easier it was to work on.'

Stalker himself was interviewed in August 1989. Roger Rees, solicitor to the police authority, in my opinion acting quite outrageously, had forbidden him to speak to the defence in late 1986, while we were compiling our case against Anderton, Topping and Stephenson. At that time, he was still employed as a policeman, of course. Now Stalker was his own man and free to give a lengthy statement, though it contained nothing new and helpful. One interesting titbit concerned a remark made by head of surveillance, DCI Christopher Baythorpe. At his suggestion, Stalker had had a burglar alarm fitted. While in conversation at the time, Baythorpe had apparently said to Stalker, 'Don't think those who you believe are your friends necessarily are,' or words to that effect. It was the gypsy's warning.

Another of Buckley's remarkable successes concerned the location of the lengthy 'book' of Bertlestein's confessions from the Pricerite fraud case. Buckley made a great many efforts to get this document. It seemed to have simply vanished off the face of the earth. The tempting conclusion was that someone had deliberately destroyed it, perhaps concerned about their own position. We were very suspicious, to say the least.

The truth was actually less sinister. By a stroke of good fortune, Buckley discovered it in the vaults at Manchester Crown Court. It had become snagged on the binding of one of the Pricerite creditor files and might have remained there indefinitely, if fate hadn't taken a hand, since repeated searches of these files had failed to reveal it.

The way Bertlestein's evidence was used leaves no doubt that there were corrupt intentions concerning Stalker at this stage. Topping made a lot of mileage out of the fact that Bertlestein had identified me with the Quality Street Gang. This was mentioned in the Sampson Report. In fact my name appears only once, on page 168 of a statement 206 pages long. Nothing was said to tie me in with any crime; it was simply a who's who from Bertlestein's fertile imagination.

What was much more significant, from my point of view, is that mentioned in this document were several prominent Manchester businessmen who had provided false references, necessary to get the long-firm fraud running. Their part in the crime was clear; they had committed an arrestable offence. Yet nothing had been done even to interview these men, never mind arrest them. Instead, Mr Topping saw fit to concentrate all his efforts towards me. Either he was a very bad detective indeed; or, as the reader may suspect, this was further proof that the real target was Stalker.

Then, with six months to go to the trial, disaster struck. Tony Adler, principal of the firm of lawyers handling my case, was arrested and charged with a part in a mortgage fraud. I should point out that first Ian Burton and then Charles Buckley had also been heavily and prejudicially investigated by the police, hoping to find something significant to pin on them, so either getting these men off my case or at the very least frightening them into taking a meeker path than we had followed hitherto.

The legal community was shocked by the news about Adler and, frankly, disbelieving. He was noted as a man of unimpeachable integrity and he seemed a most unlikely man to get involved in something like a mortgage fraud. Was it just more harassment? Understandably, Adler felt he must withdraw. [During production of this book, this matter came to a happy ending when the prosecution decided to offer no evidence against him.] We had been friends as well as business colleagues for twenty years and I was deeply saddened. Though still pressed by the utmost anxieties about my position, I had to accept Adler's decision and suddenly found myself isolated and exposed. Buckley was still unable to exercise his independent practice licence until fully discharged from his bankruptcy; this wasn't due to occur until January 1990. How was it going to be possible to find another practising solicitor to take over the case at such short notice? All our careful preparation could be lost. With so few weeks remaining, it seemed an almost impossible position to retrieve. If it was deliberate police sabotage, it was highly effective.

But, once again, luck favoured me. When all seemed lost, the exact man for the job stepped into view. His name was Richard Cornthwaite, a partner at Betesh, Fox and Co. in Bolton. First, numerous bureaucratic channels had to be negotiated in order to transfer the Legal Aid. It was Friday, 26 May when he was finally cleared to take the case. That left only ninety working days before the trial.

While the rest of the country was relaxing in the record sunshine of the finest Whitsun weekend in decades, Cornthwaite settled down to a mountain of paper and started to read. 'What I read that weekend and what I learned about the case's progress so far from Buckley, soon convinced me that there was something radically wrong with the prosecution's case,' he announced. 'The evidence that Buckley had gathered so patiently over three years painted an irrefutable picture of a conspiracy to frame Taylor for a crime which he hadn't committed.'

'Besides,' Cornthwaite was to say, 'there was one other factor which convinced me Taylor was innocent. The more I talked to him, the more I grew to like him. I didn't believe he was guilty.'

As the weeks went by and Cornthwaite became increasingly convinced that the case was a complete charade, the weight of his responsibility grew proportionately. 'It was one of those rare instances where you felt a conviction would be a complete travesty of justice. Sometimes you get a wrong decision and you are upset because the decision went against you. But if, as in this case, it seemed that Taylor was merely an innocent pawn in a deadly game to discredit John Stalker's RUC enquiry, that sort of practice is anathema in any civilization.'

Unfortunately, I was the one on trial, not the police. Cornthwaite's task was therefore to construct a tenable defence. Here, the approach to the problem bifurcated. Buckley, who had immersed himself totally in the police bona fides and 'mal fides', continued his efforts in this direction. Cornthwaite went to work on the need to answer the actual charges. He explained to me that we might have great difficulty bringing the Stalker connection into court. Even if we succeeded, the judge might direct the jury to ignore the circumstances surrounding the case, and concentrate only on whether there might have been an attempt to get money from the Co-op Bank by deception.

The pressure became too much. With only a few weeks to go, Cornthwaite made an application to have the case adjourned, to allow more time for preparation. The request was refused. Bowley was anxious to get on with the proceedings and his counsel had objected to any further delay. So, as originally envisaged, the trial was set to begin on 2 October 1989.

The difficulty for Cornthwaite was that the police had retained the vast bulk of my business documents. Paperwork which proved we were innocent might well have existed, but who could know after nearly five years?

I had to rely heavily on my memory. We went at it day after day until I was weary and my brain couldn't take any more. It was an impossible task. How was I supposed to remember things that had happened so many years before? Yet one tiny detail could be crucial in turning the evidence used against me. Some of the transactions were so complicated that I couldn't grasp what had actually happened. It began to get so that I started to believe there was something in the prosecution case. Maybe I *had* done what they were alleging. That's how bad it became.

Worst of all was the ever present dread that to fail would mean the loss of everything I had earned in life and, possibly, if the worst came to the worst, a free fitting session for a new and unattractive suit of clothes in Strangeways Prison. Not a circumstance in which one can give one's best mentally.

*

In September a side issue emerged, like a tumour growing on the side of an already diseased body. Peter Topping, who by this time had retired, published his memoirs covering the Moors' Murders. In fact he had very little to do with the infamous murders, which were a *cause célèbre* in 1967. He had become involved only in 1986 when he hit the headlines by starting to dig for the as yet undiscovered bodies of Pauline Reade and Keith Bennet. The reader will no doubt recall that by a remarkable coincidence this was just the time Topping had been indicted on a charge of conspiracy to pervert the course of justice, along with Anderton and Stephenson. Arguably, the cavalcade on Saddleworth Moor was part of an attempt to divert attention from his awkward position at headquarters.

Evidently it worked too. With an army of police on the moors digging in the frozen soil and helicopters ferrying in Myra Hindley to do a bit of grave-spotting, the media had a field day. The whole episode was ghoulish and disturbing, for the public as well as for the families concerned. It cost the long-suffering tax-payer a fortune and did nothing to better GMP's crime detection statistics which, according to a *Manchester Evening News* article on 6 February 1990 entitled 'The Capital of Crime', are the worst outside the Metropolitan area.

In fact the body of Pauline Reade was recovered on 1 July 1987, but no charges were brought against Hindley and Brady in respect of her murder. The question remains, therefore: was there any worthwhile policing motive for such a costly operation?

On 31 July 1988 Topping retired from active service on health grounds. Apparently he had neck problems. Acid wits said it was due to digging in the frost-bound soil. Then he shocked the country and outraged his colleagues by publishing a book concerning the Moors' Murders. It was called simply *Topping*, echoing Stalker's eponym chosen for his own book. Perhaps Topping thought his name too was a household word, and that he was as famous as Stalker. It was serialized in *The Sun* and the whole grubby transaction was rumoured to have brought him a six figure sum. The newspaper deal begged the whole question of whether or not Topping's retirement was a contrivance to allow him to cash in on his Moors' exploits.

The important point is that Topping saw fit to include a chapter on the Stalker Affair. Obviously he was smarting from the Stalker book and the less-than-sweet-smelling image it gave him, and wanted to hit back with 'his side' of the case. It was a very big mistake. Despite heavy 'legalling', his rabid hatred and jealousy of Stalker shows through clearly, and puts Topping in a very bad light.

He also shows himself as a poor detective when he claims to have 'discovered' (his word) that there was indeed a friendship between John Stalker and myself. In fact it had been well known for the best part of seventeen years, and I had been a guest of Stalker's at police headquarters for mess dinners on a number of occasions.

Even more stupidly, Topping has the effrontery to comment on the case, which at the time of publication was still very much *sub judice*. In describing his investigations, he confirmed that I was a businessman with no criminal convictions but then he goes on to say, on the next page, that '. . . good professional criminals often have no, or very few, convictions. The man with a long criminal record is the habitually unsuccessful criminal, as experienced detectives like Mr Stalker know. It is naïve to think that all criminals have criminal records.' Speaking in these terms of a matter still to be tried is, of course, a flagrant contempt of court. It was also a preposterous libel.

Topping tried to hype the case further by describing the detective in charge of operations, DI Anthony Stephenson, as 'a devoutly religious man, known by all his colleagues to be of the highest integrity'. In fact, as has been revealed, the man swore false evidence and was a disgrace to the police force, never mind his Christian ethics. However, it is convenient that Topping takes this stand in print, since he draws himself ever closer into the mesh of intrigue and leaves no doubt that he was both a part of it and was defending it.

These comments about Stephenson, of course, amount to further contempt of court, since such remarks would prejudice a jury against the defendants. In fact, the whole of the close of Topping's book is an attempt to justify himself and his immediate colleagues to the public, since obviously by this stage he was feeling highly nervous about his exposure on the Stalker/Taylor case.

He lets slip that the enquiry into John Stalker was asked for by Anderton and that Anderton had consulted 'high level Home Office officials' who had authorized the enquiry. This is at complete variance with the official story, which has repeatedly asserted that the Stalker case was merely a local affair. Is this why Anderton was said to be furious at Topping and his book?

I was much discouraged. It seemed yet further proof of an Establishment smear campaign which was operating 'above the law', and as the trial approached the opposition seemed to be growing arrogant and almost mocking their victim. Consider that Topping was an experienced policeman and must have been aware of the law concerning matters that are *sub judice*. Even if he wasn't, the lawyers for his publishers (Angus and Robertson, an imprint owned by the Sun

Group of News International Ltd) certainly would be. Yet it was allowed to happen anyway.

In this instance what mattered was not a further assault on my already damaged reputation but the effect on a potential jury. Here was the man in charge of the case saying, in print, that one of the defendants was guilty as charged. The average reader would assume it must be true: there it was in a book and they wouldn't allow them to print it if it was wrong, would they?

Urgent consultations were held with lawyers. They were in no doubt that Topping had committed a contempt of court, but what could be done? Perhaps the damage was already beyond repair? Perhaps Legal Aid, already strained by this case, wouldn't allow any more detours and side issues? So far, the Legal Aid board in Manchester had been very supportive of me. But how long could this be expected to go on? Suddenly, the power of an individual taking on the might of the Establishment seemed frail and insignificant.

Buckley telephoned the Attorney General's office. After some delay in deciding what to do, he took the stance that it would be 'inappropriate' for him to pursue the matter. He appeared to be hostile to the idea that we should take independent action. We decided to take our case before the judge presiding over the trial; it would be up to him to decide if any action was to be brought. His Honour Judge Michael Sachs had by this time been appointed. Rumour had it that he was a fair-minded man and definitely not pro-Establishment but, in a case where so much skullduggery and intrigue had surfaced, who could tell: maybe he had been 'got at'? It seems laughable, in hindsight, but for me it was a very real nightmare. In fact, Judge Sachs gave me leave to proceed with the contempt matter and the summons was issued. It would be several months before this side-issue came to court.

Perhaps the reader has thought of another possibility, which also occurred to me at the time: that Topping was being set up deliberately as a target. We knew that he had been given the nod to write the book though, as I have already said, his seniors were less than pleased with the final publication. Was it possible that by retiring he had isolated himself from the protection of his former fellow-conspirators? It would be ironic indeed if cashing in on the book meant that he was to become the fall guy in the event of a police débâcle.

But as the day of the trial drew nearer, the prospects of a police débâcle seemed unnervingly remote. I was in a very dangerous position, with the whole might of the Establishment legal machinery set against me. I might be entering the last few weeks of my freedom. I hadn't given much thought to what I would do in the event of being sent down but, considering the bad state of my health, I might well have been doomed to end my days in prison. It was a grim prospect.

13

The Battle in Court Four

The trial started, as scheduled, on 2 October 1989. Not all the drama of the first day was confined to the court room. In 1987, on his way to the committal hearing in Manchester, Terence Bowley had knocked a woman down with his car and unfortunately she was killed. It meant a deeply distressing death weighing on his mind, as well as all the other pressures. Not surprisingly, the South Yorkshire Police charged him with dangerous driving, though arguably that death could be laid directly at the door of Anderton, Topping, Stephenson and anyone else who subsequently turns out to be involved in the plot against me, depending on how you view the evidence in this book. The summons was sworn out in January 1989, in connection with the offence. But that summons was not served immediately. Instead, it was held back for nine months and served on the day the trial started. Not only that but some sick-minded person had given specific instructions that it was to be served in person, an act which is almost without precedent, given the offence and the circumstances.

The trial was held in court four of the Manchester Crown Court, with Judge Michael Sachs presiding. It was scheduled to last until February. Entering the courtroom was the first time that all four defendants had met together.

Michael Corkery QC, prosecuting, was assisted by Michael Shorrock QC, a senior barrister on the Manchester circuit. The defence line up was as follows: Richard Ferguson QC and David Hood for myself, Rhys Davis QC and Martin Steiger for Britton, Peter Birkett QC and William Morris for Bowley and Jack Price QC and Anthony Gee for McCann. Richard Ferguson was a Northern Ireland Protestant lawyer, though he had represented families of the IRA on occasion, and I felt this political aspect might give him an interesting edge in the case.

The first morning was taken up with arguing about what charges were to be tried. This in turn affected the evidence that could be introduced. I was surprised to hear that, at the last minute, Corkery agreed to drop the conspiracy charges, leaving only the substantive charges of obtaining money by deception, etc. Instead two new charges of fraudulent trading were brought in against Britton and me. These I understand would enable the prosecution to bring in a wide variety of evidence, in the hope of persuading the jury that some of it was attractive.

The fact that Corkery was so confident of success that he could afford to take this bold step was no comfort for us. It was actually strengthening the prosecution to narrow its target down to a few areas and concentrate all the fire-power on those. Remember, it was only necessary to succeed in obtaining a guilty verdict on even one small aspect of the indictment and my chance to vindicate myself and collect appropriate damages would be completely destroyed. The police would crow that all their efforts had been justified.

The defence case, on the other hand, was very tenuous indeed, unless some of the missing papers could be subpoenaed, which was by no means an automatic right. Few witnesses could be called; the men who could best prove I was innocent were sitting beside me in the dock. If the case was to be won at all, it would be by destroying the credibility of the prosecution. The main hope of success was to get it over to the jury that this trial was an extension of the Stalker Affair and that the motives for bringing the prosecution were corrupt. However, there are accepted legal protocols covering what may be put before a jury and insisting the case was a 'fix' wasn't one of them. The prosecution would be sure to try and block any attempt to broaden the issues sufficiently to include the full background of the case.

The jury were chosen and sworn in and we tried to form an impression of the men and women who were to decide our fate. It was generally agreed that the average juror could not reasonably be expected to understand the very complex issues involved. Not that the facts themselves were hard to grasp but they were being obscured and distorted by the interpretation the prosecution was putting on them. In the event, we were totally wrong on this point; the jury came to understand this case backwards and obtained a thorough grasp of all the issues.

Mountains of papers were brought into court, which made conditions rather cramped. The benches were stacked with box after box of documents, ledgers and files, all cross-referenced, made into packs and labelled. The jury, prosecution, defence and judge all had to have copies and every sheet had to be kept track of. This aspect of the case must have been a monumental task in itself. To accumulate this library of information, the prosecution had utilized a formidable team of men working on the case, some of them full-time for nearly four years. The defence could only operate singly or in pairs. Legal Aid did not run to the expense of allowing sufficient man-power to cope with the demands of the situation.

Corkery's opening speech was expected to take two days but it lasted almost a week. From the first, he referred to me and my fellow defendants as 'criminals' and accused us of 'the utmost dishonesty', presumably intending to establish in the jury's minds that we were guilty men and anything we might say was already, *ipso facto*, a lie.

It was part of Corkery's undoubtedly successful technique to hold the floor as long as possible and drum into the jury the so-called facts of the prosecution as if they had already been proved. Some of the allegations had been robustly demolished at the committal stage but this didn't stop Mr Corkery from bringing them up all over again, as fresh and incontestable 'facts'. One of our barristers was heard to remark: 'It was as if Mr Corkery hadn't been at the committal!'

He even tried to argue that rises in property prices should not be taken into account at valuation, which would make a mockery of the whole business of land speculation and property development. No sensible person could accept the argument that acquiring land and obtaining planning permission for better use would not enhance its value. We were left wondering just how much the court was influenced by these misleading remarks.

In the guise of helping the jury, Corkery had them mark various exhibits with a highlighter pen, to support his line of argument. This was entirely contrary to the clear directions of Judge Sachs, who said there were to be no markings, because the opening comments were not evidence – the jury, later in their deliberations, might take these marks as gospel and be misled in forming an opinion.

One's whole impression of Corkery in the opening was that of a man who, as Buckley said pithily, 'felt that the world owed him a conviction'.

First came the bank witnesses, leading with David Davenport, Bowley's assistant. The defence barristers raised strenuous objection to the fact that he had been kept waiting outside for three full days before taking the stand. We felt this was 'third degree pressure'. The barristers were also shocked by the fact that Davenport was given his witness statement but not shown a copy of his deposition at the committal.

This was subsequently true for all the Crown witnesses and showed the lengths that the prosecution were prepared to go to avoid the full truth and only tell a convenient part of the whole. In fact the committal deposition should really be seen as the balance of the witness's evidence, the clarification and ratification of what was being laid in evidence in front of the examining magistrate, not just incidental comments. I understand it might be possible to argue that it was not improper for the prosecution to do this but there could be no doubt that it was a failure to be totally frank.

Originally, Davenport had been intended as the Crown's star witness, but before introducing him at the trial, Corkery hinted that his testimony should be viewed as less than reliable: 'Make of it what you will,' he told the jury. The reason was clear: at the committal, Davenport had testified to the effect that Bowley cut corners with numerous clients and had given me no preferential treatment. This came out again in the trial and of course was very damaging to the prosecution argument. Eventually, he refuted almost everything the prosecution was trying to prove and made it quite clear that the few irregularities which could not be contested should be seen, not as misdemeanours or criminal acts, but simply as mistakes.

His cross-examination must have been very difficult for Davenport. On the one hand he clearly wanted to tell the truth as it was, but risked further censure within the bank. He had already been told he could never rise above his present staff grade because of his part in the alleged misconduct of the Rangelark account. On the other hand, he was trying to play down the implication of the bank's errors in my predicament, to minimize the bank's liabilities in any possible future action. He looked overwrought with anxiety while giving his evidence.

Davenport caused something of a sensation by actually admitting he had been pressured by the police when making his statement. Fortunately, he had the courage to tell the truth on the stand and, once again, his evidence was often at marked variance to what he was supposed to have said. So damaging was his testimony, that in the re-examination Corkery was eager to destroy Davenport's credibility and had to be admonished for cross-examining his own witness. He was to do this many times with other witnesses too and clawed back many points by doing so.

Next came Stephen Wood, another member of Bowley's team in the Corporate Lending Department. As at the committal, he too was helpful to the defence, though supposedly a prosecution witness. He reinforced a lot of what Davenport had said. His own statement, Wood said, contained several inaccuracies but he had been coerced by police officers into signing it, despite protests. Wood seemed most unhappy with the treatment he had received from the police.

What was disturbing in the parade of witnesses which followed is that more than half hinted they had been intimidated or directly threatened into making a statement they were not happy with. None of this seemed to embarrass the prosecution, however. I naïvely assumed when this sort of police behaviour came out in court, the trial would be stopped automatically. It soon became clear that this was not to be the case.

I complained to my counsel that he was not on his feet enough, putting a stop to some of the prosecution tricks. Corkery was a master at do-you-still-beat-your-wife tactics, such as 'Were any other clients involved in improperly representing the value of securities?' I felt Ferguson should be harrying the prosecution, who were having it far too much their own way; however he constantly advocated a 'wait and see' approach. This passive stance, coupled with his too aggressive cross-examination of friendly witnesses like Davenport, which was really just playing into the prosecution's hands, became such a major cause of concern to me that we had a meeting of lawyers on Sunday, 22 October. I told Ferguson my views. It was agreed amicably that he would withdraw from the case.

This left David Hood, a junior barrister, not yet a QC, to handle all of this immensely complicated, indeed almost overwhelming trial, at first without even a junior to assist him. Fellow defendants were very antagonized by this turn of events, feeling that I had disastrously weakened my case and that this in turn would damage their chances. The judge too seemed to take offence and appeared to pointedly slap down Hood for the least little indiscretion, in sharp contrast to the way he handled Corkery. My absolute confidence in Hood, stemming from his marvellous performance at the committal stage, was in no way diminished by the fact that he started out hesitantly.

The problem, I later learned, was that the prosecution were playing tricks, unpredictably altering the order of appearance of their witnesses. This, too, I'm sure, was a deliberate tactic, to make it harder for the defence. Only after a meeting at which Corkery had been pressed to agree a definite sequence of witnesses could Hood begin to organize his thoughts and introduce a cohesive approach to exposing the weaknesses and contradictions of the prosecution evidence. From then on, it was marvellous to watch the way he gradually took over the reins and began to stamp his mark on the trial until, eventually, he dominated it.

The fact remains that during those early weeks it was very uphill for us. There were 175 interruptions by Judge Sachs, on behalf of the prosecution, recorded in only the first seven weeks. That seemed to reflect his view of our probable guilt, though I am told it is wrong to make such obvious inferences. No matter how many times an allegation was rebutted, another witness would follow on who brought it all up again. The same topics recurred over and over: inflated valuations, lack of a valid charge on the Tottington land, cross-firing and the false claim that the bank ended up being owed substantial sums of money. The reader is referred again to Chapter 4 for the facts.

One willing, indeed enthusiastic, prosecution witness was Lewis Chadwick from the advances department of the Co-op Bank. He was so eager that he would race ahead and answer questions that weren't even being asked, flicking through papers and calling attention to documents that were not immediately in question. 'He couldn't get it out fast enough,' recalls Britton. Chadwick appeared to have an encyclopedic memory for details. He was able to quote dates and paragraphs in memoranda from four years earlier.

Yet even this glittery-eyed beaver let the prosecution down. On one occasion he admitted never having seen the Thomas Holt valuation, which rested on incorrect estimates of the available shale at the Poynton site. It was important to the prosecution case, especially in respect of McCann, that the bank had been misled by this valuation. Yet here he was saying that it had probably never even been submitted to the advances department. By the end of his first day he was thoroughly flustered and seemed to have 'forgotten' remarkably important details. So it was clear that his memory feats were, after all, nothing more than police rehearsing.

Next day, a remarkable thing happened. On returning to court, Chadwick suddenly remembered numerous facts that he'd forgotten the day before; he now recalled that he *had* in fact seen the Holt valuation. Significantly perhaps, Chadwick was seen arriving in the court that morning in the company of DI Anthony Stephenson. Even the judge, whom we felt was not being sympathetic up to this point, seemed to turn a little incredulous and made a remark about the sudden cure of amnesia. Chadwick, unabashed, stuck to his assertion that he'd remembered it all in the car on the way home.

The defence, of course, wanted to know if Chadwick had been party to the illegal access to bank information instigated by Topping and Stephenson beginning in December 1985. But Chadwick stuck to the story that he knew nothing of the investigation into me until 16 July 1986, a day he remembered with punctilious and convenient accuracy.

Bowley's successor as corporate business manager, John Cowburn, was another witness who seemed to want to make things tough for us. He was noticeably loquacious and detailed when it came to something which implicated Bowley and myself, yet became extraordinarily vague and non-committal with his answers when it could have helped the defence. The most kindly explanation of this behaviour is to suppose that he too was under pressure from the police and, possibly, faced loss of status within the bank.

Against most other testimonials, including that of his senior, Cowburn insisted that the Rangelark account was the only one which was irregular. Yet he had said to me, when he took over in 1985, that the Rangelark account was in satisfactory order after a routine inspection, which normally takes place when a manager is replaced.

It was Cowburn, remember, who at the committal insisted there had been cross-firing. This was demolished once and for all by deposit records produced by Britton showing that the credit to Propwise had been lodged on the same day as the deposit to Rangelark from the Lacerta account. There was no question of trying to float one credit against the other and the pathetic assertion by the police that there had been a crime was shown to be nothing more than an internal delay within the bank in crediting one of the accounts.

Unquestionably, however, the most important bank witness for us was Roger Gorvin. As a director at the Co-op Bank, he was a man of considerable authority. Gorvin repeated the fact that the Rangelark account was never in jeopardy and that it was his opinion that there had never been any risk to the Bank and that Bowley's judgement had been sound. In contrast to Cowburn he seemed to take the trouble to add a rider to anything that might appear damaging to Bowley, thus limiting its adverse impact. 'We miss his talents,' he admitted, at one point. Even more remarkably, he told the court he had been sympathetic enough to Bowley to telephone him after his dismissal: hardly what one would expect a director to do with an employee guilty of a conspiracy to defraud the bank.

Concerning the cross-firing, he said, 'It was possible to have that chain of events take place perfectly innocently.' On valuations, his comment was: 'You can run through until you find one you like.' As to Bowley's failure to observe all the rules, 'Conditions have to be practical within the real world,' he stated. These were important words, coming from a man who sounded mature and experienced, with expertise in banking. He must have given the court confidence in what he had to say.

At Gorvin's appearance, it was decided to subpoena the Co-op Bank for all the files relevant to the case. Being cautious of overplaying his

175

hand, Buckley succeeded instead in engineering that Judge Sachs should direct the issue of the subpoenas personally, which he did. Corkery, predictably, wanted this material to come to court via the police, but the defence insisted that bank officials bring the documents directly to court and, fortunately, we won our point.

From here it became easier. Big cracks began appearing in the police 'evidence'. For example, Britton had submitted to the Co-op Bank a 'Heads of Agreement' document for a suggested Trafford scheme involving Arnmark Ltd (which never materialized). The police had used the original as evidence, taken from our files at St John's Street, which was no more than a draft document. It reputedly showed an attempt to defraud the creditors of Rangelark (it actually omitted to mention provision for payment, that's all). But when the bank version of the document came to light, overwritten by Britton and initialled by Gorvin, it revealed a completely different story and showed that a payment to Rangelark was very much part of the proposals. This of course was the final or 'legal' agreement.

On Monday, 13 December, there was an interesting development. The jury sent a note to the judge's bench, asking why Bowley had been dismissed, when Davenport and Wood, who had carried out most of the 'nuts and bolts' work on the Rangelark account, had simply been demoted. This question was put to Gorvin without the jury being present to make sure the defence were happy with his reply. In fact we were delighted to hear him testify that he had nothing to do with Bowley's dismissal and, since no financial gain was involved, he would not have sanctioned it personally if he had.

As a further coup, it allowed Peter Birkett, cross-examining, to elicit the fact that Bowley had taken the bank to a tribunal for unfair dismissal and they had settled out of court for a figure substantially in excess of their legal obligation, which seemed to sum up the bank's overall view of Bowley's supposed crime and, by inference, my role also.

After the bank witnesses came the valuers and surveyors. Here the elaborate charade of trying to prove that we over-valued land began to crumble under the strain of close scrutiny, exactly as it had at the committal.

Again, the shale on the ex-brickworks site at Poynton seemed to be a source of endless ferment. David Appleton was the supposed 'expert' brought on to say that the maximum shale on the Poynton site was 30,000 cubic metres, no more. In fact, he stated emphatically that he had never tried to calculate the maximum amount of shale. He was a landscape architect and not a chartered surveyor. His brief had merely been to put together a package for planning permission as a tip and his principal interest was in the air space. He had made the shale calculations from an aerial photograph and missed a number of outlying heaps. Without belittling Mr Appleton's abilities, I say it was absurd to use such a man as the definitive opinion on the quantity of shale.

Appleton can't have helped the prosecution by testifying that Poynton was a 'potentially very valuable site', because of its double value, first from the tipping rights and then the later sale for developmental use. He also told the court that the local council wanted something done about the site. In its existing condition it was an eye-sore, sitting, as it did, right on the edge of the Peak District National Park. So, far from being a poor buy, over-valued, it showed all the promise that I had foreseen. Coincident with the early weeks of the trial, it was granted planning permission for a forty-bedroom motel and the site is probably now worth well over £1 million.

A completely different shale estimate was given by Peter Harrison, an ex-manager at the original brick-works. He thought it might be as high as 200,000 cubic metres, in some places up to a depth of 20 feet. Shale had been imported to the site for over two decades. He also said that there had been back-filling of the site with reject brick materials for several decades, in fact since the brick-works were founded in the 1920s. This would be far superior to the shale itself and could only add to the value.

I have already mentioned that Dr Varey was the man with the most expertise in matters to do with tipping sites and his offer of £265,000 (which I turned down) is probably the best estimate of the real value of the site at that time. His figure for the air-space was 400,000–500,000 cubic metres, whereas Appleton had said 150,000. The shale, he said as an expert, could not be measured accurately without bore holes and that is probably the most sensible comment. So how could we be shown to have over-estimated it?

What makes it all so ridiculous is that Raymond Glyn-Owen, the official valuer for the Co-op Bank, made it quite clear that the bank did not take the shale into account for valuation purposes. This folly seemed to me to happen many times; that the prosecution would put forward witnesses who contradicted their own case. Some experts estimated low, some high; one valued the land at one figure, another would value it much higher or lower and so on. It was hard to see where it was all leading. At one point, one of the barristers, I think it was Jack Price, stood up and asked, 'What are you trying to prove?'

I believe, as I had suspected all along, that there was no real issue. It was simply the desperate hope of the prosecution to make it all seem so utterly confusing that, somehow, the mud would stick.

There was a light-hearted turn of events while Glyn-Owen was on the stand. We had heard from Appleton that conservationists had fought any development at Poynton on the grounds it was the habitat of the greater crested newt. I already knew from my property dealings that this animal comes up everywhere as 'an endangered species'. When Jack Price drew Glyn-Owen's attention to the fact that Holt's first statement had given the shale as 300,000 cubic metres, yet the second statement said 85,000 cubic metres, and asked him what could have happened to the missing shale, it was Judge Sachs who answered, 'The newts ate it.' The court erupted into laughter and from then on the newts became a running joke, to ease the tension of what had hitherto been a very tough battle. Thus, Jack Price, when the court had been told that the Poynton site had been granted planning permission for a motel with a restaurant and pool, christened it the Newt Motel. Looking back, I think that Judge Sachs had grown thoroughly bored of the dross of evidence and this was his answer.

Of course we were careful not to draw the conclusion that the judge was now favourable to our cause, simply because some of the humour happened to fall at the prosecution's expense. But Britton was particularly heartened. All through the months leading up to the trial and during the opening stages, he had suffered the most acute anxieties. Several times he had groaned and the judge had remonstrated with him, via counsel, that he must not show his disagreement with the evidence being given.

Corkery, naturally, tried to discredit the all-important Bernard Thorpe valuation of the Trafford site at £1.5 million. The planning permission for DIY retail, it was said, was 'restrictive' under section 52. But it was only outline planning, we knew, and that could easily be changed. Rangelark had taken advice from counsel on this point and, besides, after years of experience in the property game, we were well aware that Trafford Council had no grounds on which to refuse further reasonable uses.

The inconsistencies in the valuation evidence amounted to yawning chasms in places. Stuart Emerson, a valuer with McDonald Hogg, testified that he had valued my home, Wood Mill, at £225,000, which was very low. The prosecution were making much of the fact that Bowley had ignored this valuation (without telling me, incidentally) and had relied instead on earlier far higher valuations. However, it emerged under cross-examination that Emerson was not a qualified valuer at the time of the valuation and that he had only done two houses before Wood Mill, which would hardly give him the experience to put a price on such a unique property. Also, it was learned he had made a mistake with his measurements and was 2,000 square feet out. At the market rate of £45 a square foot, that was a considerable error, which discredited him as a witness and went a long way to vindicating my estimates of the house's worth.

The absurdity of most of this evidence is that a valuation is merely somebody's opinion. It is not possible legally to argue that a valuation figure is 'wrong', only that it is not consistent with what other experts say. The inconsistencies were made worse by the prosecution's trick of showing the witness only what they wanted him to know, at times suppressing additional vital information. Thus Scanlon Provis valued the Poynton site at £20,000 but this was without knowing the land had the benefit of planning permission. Their estimated value was not unreasonable, based on the information they had been given by the police; it was 'correct'. But with knowledge of all the facts, their valuation was £165,000; a very different 'truth'.

One of the key surveyors was Thomas Holt of Peter O'Hare Associates. It was his valuations on Trafford, Tottington and Poynton that had been supplied to Judge Presst as *prima facie* evidence of over-valuing sites. However, we were more interested in his experience at the hands of the police than on his testimony concerning the properties. He was interviewed three times; the first lasted most of the day. He was allowed to go to the toilet but could not remember having had a break for a meal and was certainly not told he was free to leave the police station at any stage. The general atmosphere of the interview made him feel 'implicated', he said. On the second occasion he was told he was 'no longer under suspicion'. Suspicion of what? he was asked in court. He couldn't say. Asked if he had been cautioned while making his statement, he said, 'Those words might have been spoken,' but he couldn't remember with certainty.

Some of this was demolished by Corkery, as with many other witnesses who felt they had been somehow threatened or bullied. 'Did the police do anything improper?' was his line of question. Of course, the witnesses all backed off and said 'no'. Holt was no exception. But how is the average individual supposed to know what the police are allowed and not allowed to do? I say the important thing is how the witness felt, not the actions of the police. If he or she felt threatened, that means the statement was taken under duress.

There were scores of other witnesses, mostly minor, who contributed very little. The bulk of their evidence was pointless or self-defeating for the prosecution. For example, a friend of mine, Derek Rothwell, was brought on to testify I still owed him money. I think it was merely to put me in a bad light. Under cross-examination, he was forced to admit that he had never asked for the money back. The important part of his evidence concerned the fact that he stated clearly that, although he realized the police had visited him because 'they were after Taylor', he said the impression at first was that they were 'after Stalker'. This was the first time that the Stalker connection was put over unequivocally to the jury.

The pace hotted up with interesting disclosures from Keith George, of Wimpey Homes Holdings Ltd. He was brought along to testify that Wimpey were not interested in the Tottington site, though we had supposedly said they were going to buy. It was another example of the way idle chatter with the bank manager was translated into 'fact'. As I have already said, no bank would dream of taking such information as evidence of worth, until it was put into writing. Nevertheless, the police clung to this flotsam as evidence that we had misled the bank.

However, George's evidence became of enormous interest to us, because his files contained a contemporaneous attendance note dated May/June 1986, about a visit by two police officers, claiming to be Special Branch, who, he said, had told him that I was under suspicion of drugs dealing and organized crime. If proof were still lacking (hardly the case), here was all we needed to show that the police were using this elaborate fiction to discredit me. It will become clear to the reader in the following chapter that, by this time, the police already knew that I had no involvement in drugs and had agreed this among themselves. Yet they still used it as a ploy, cynically and calculatingly.

One of two important revelations before Christmas was nothing to do with the police conspiracy but concerned another startling plot altogether. The facts came from Mr Colin Wicks, district valuer for Trafford Borough Council. He had valued my Trafford site in 1987 for the Trafford Urban Development Council and had come up with a figure of £1.2 million. TUDC wanted a valuation of £1.7 million, to allow financing to top all other bids, and he admitted there was some pressure. Note that this business of over-valuing securities was a crime I was accused of committing, yet here were local government officials wanting to conspire to do exactly the same thing.

Mr Wicks, sticking pedantically to his opinion, had refused to change his valuation. This left the TUDC needing to make up the short-fall of £500,000. An application was made to the Department of the Environment but they refused. So Michael Shields, chairman of the TUDC, using his other hat as the chief executive of Trafford Borough Council, tried a manoeuvre of his own. He revoked the planning permission extant on my Trafford development site, which effectively crashed the value. Nor was that all; he was in a position to exclude other potential purchasers by refusing any further worthwhile planning permission for the site. To make doubly sure of destroying potential competition, he let it be known to anyone interested that if they tried to buy, a compulsory purchase order would follow. At that point, it seems hardly surprising that Cyril Neild, the receiver of land appointed by the Co-op Bank, should have given up attempting to market the site properly and this was probably the origin of the strange conditions he imposed at sale (see Chapter 4).

Ultimately, the Trafford site was sold to the TUDC for £1.2 million, which is precisely the figure they wanted it for. After many years in the property game, one is used to the cut and thrust of commercial tactics, but it was disconcerting to hear of a public servant mixed up in dirty dealings of this sort. We wanted to see Wicks' files on these matters, naturally. At first he insisted they were protected by the Official Secrets Act but, luckily, that assertion failed and we obtained the vital evidence we needed which backed up his amazing disclosures.

But undoubtedly the most sensational development before Christmas emerged under the cross-examination of Mr Leonard Fenton, an Examiner at the official Receiver's office in Manchester. The defence was staggered that the prosecution should call him as a witness, to bring evidence gathered while Britton and I were being examined in respect of the liquidation of my companies in 1986. Apparently, I should have been advised at the time that I had a right to remain silent in front of the official Receiver, pending the conclusion of the trial. Instead, in response to my insistence that I couldn't give much valid information without my company records (the police had taken the lot), I had been threatened that if I didn't answer questions informally I would be forced to do so in a court hearing (for which there is no right to silence). Buckley's formal request for an adjournment, pointing out the many ramifications of the case, including the Stalker connection, was also abruptly rejected in a letter which 'reeked of overkill', to use Buckley's expression.

Fenton told the court that he had been instructed by his seniors to co-operate with the police and ask me certain questions that they wanted answering. This, effectively, gave the police more information, to which they were not legally entitled. Not that there was anything incriminating to learn. But it showed clearly that the Department of

Industry had been subverted and that there was more to this enquiry than just Machiavellian police tactics. I don't believe this widespread corruption could have happened, except at the instigation of the government or, at the very least, MI5.

Uncovering this connivance also raised more than a suspicion that the police themselves had put down my companies. We had heard rumours that in the months ensuing after the house and office raids that they had gone to the Inland Revenue with our files. It seems more than probable that the police had hatched a plot to persuade the Inland Revenue to put the companies into liquidation, then get information by the back door from the official Receiver.

Thankfully, Judge Sachs directed that the 'evidence' was inadmissible and it was thrown out. He accused the police of being in 'cahoots' with the official Receiver's staff and his use of this pejorative term was enormously encouraging to the defence. It must also have done the credibility of the police little good in the eyes of the jury. Trying not to be over-optimistic, I began to feel that, surely, no jury was going to convict us in the face of such a blatant affront to common justice.

By Christmas it was obvious that the judge didn't like what he was hearing. He must be given all credit for a sea change, brought about by his responsiveness to where the truth lay. A formidable figure from the point of view of discipline, he nevertheless was no shirk when it came to grasping the nail firmly. He began, I think I'm right in saying, by being fairly sure of our guilt. This was probably due to the fact that he was greatly impressed by the witness statements he had read before the trial (they were designed to have just that effect, of course, and included hearsay, innuendo and all kinds of prejudicial and pejorative phrases, as well as 'facts'). Sachs probably thought he was dealing with a true bill of indictment. The Crown had an elaborate and sophisticated story, of that there is no doubt. But after three months of hard grind in court, there was 'not a single pea left on the stick', as Buckley put it. Every issue raised by over ninety prosecution witnesses had been demolished or modified in such a way that it bore no recognizable relation to the case summary by the Crown.

It was time to face the police as witnesses. Judge Sachs allowed us to defer this until after the Christmas recess, in order to take it straight through, without interruption.

14
The Abscess Bursts

If the parade of witnesses leading up to Christmas could be said to have damaged the prosecution case, there was no question that when the police officers involved in the enquiry took the stand, they destroyed its credibility totally.

As a result of taking each officer, page by page, through his official notebook, establishing what he had been doing, when and where, it became possible at last to build up a detailed picture of the character and momentum of the investigation. It was no longer a matter of mere speculation. Here at last, in our hands, was the proof we needed that the whole charade of an enquiry had been carried out in a corrupt, sinister and wholly improper manner.

Irksomely, some pages of the notebooks were found to be stapled down. The judge was allowed to see what was written there, but not the defence. The police, predictably, insisted that these sections had nothing to do with my case. Given that the men were supposed to be full-time investigators, this seemed unlikely to say the least. The irony is that even without these pages, the notebooks were extremely damaging to the Crown.

We found out that the codename for the enquiry into Stalker and myself was 'Operation Kalooki'. No prizes for guessing where that came from. My codename was 'K1'. Stalker, apparently, was known as 'FEB' but we never found out why. The important point is that all officers, without exception, vehemently denied being involved in investigating Stalker. Why then give him a code designation? It wouldn't make sense unless it was expected to refer to him frequently.

The hierarchy and members of the DIU showed up, including Born (operational head, in charge), Caldwell, Knowles, Murray, Ware, Hogg, Corfield, Richardson, Waterworth and Stephenson. All communications went from Born, to Topping and then direct to the Chief Constable, locking Anderton into the plot once and for all. This routing by-passed ACC Lees and, of course, Stalker himself. What was revealed for the first time was the fanatically covert nature of the activities of the unit. All officers were sworn to vigorous secrecy and apparently there had been uproar at one point when it was discovered that one of the statements taken by the unit had gone missing. Given the appalling standards of behaviour by this group of men, the desire for secrecy doesn't seem surprising. But it begged the question whether or not the initiating order for this confidentiality came from far higher up, to try and protect some important people, perhaps not even policemen, with dirty fingers in the pie.

Topping's obvious involvement with the whole charade was confirmed, but on a scale beyond even what we had expected. It was evident from the notebooks that there had been frequent conferences and briefings by Topping, sometimes lasting several hours, making his disavowals of any unusual emphasis on this enquiry totally disingenuous. He had even briefed the team before the arrest and it is now my belief that it was his idea to send his men to the office, in violation of the agreement we had made to go to the police station voluntarily.

We also learned more about Corkery's role. In just the notebooks we were able to see (not all, by any means), we found references to several conferences at which he had met, and apparently instructed, the police on behalf of the DPP's office. We knew about the meeting on 24 July 1986, when no less a person than Anderton had been present, though we had no confirmation until this point that Corkery had been involved so early in this very obvious Stalker connection. But there was also a meeting on 16 October 1986, involving Topping, Stephenson and Corkery; another on 20 May; one on 19 June, again with Topping present, in London; one on 27 August and finally, with Topping and Stephenson, in Manchester, in counsel chambers on 19 January 1988.

Then there was the matter of the visits to the Co-op Bank. From various entries, Hood was able to trace at least eleven visits, totalling over seventeen hours, that had taken place between 26 November 1985 and 19 February 1986, before the Access Orders had been granted. We wanted to establish what had taken place at these meetings. It became a major issue with each and every officer giving evidence. Despite intense pressure from our barristers, not one of them would answer the simple question: what was said on these visits? Clearly they had been briefed that the consequences of revealing what had illegally taken place would mean catastrophe. Fear of the repercussions had evidently caused them all to close ranks and, rather than answer, every officer resorted to saying, 'I don't know', 'I can't remember', 'Just general enquiries', 'Updating', 'I've forgotten' and so on. They were obviously lying and from this point it seemed to me unlikely the prosecution was going to be believed. Even the judge became frustrated by the obvious evasion and joined in, unsuccessfully, in trying to get candid answers. It was a farce: each man was fighting to save his hide, rather than tell the truth as a policeman should.

Appalled? There is more. We also learned details about the bullying of witnesses. From police notebooks we learned that Bowley's assistants, Davenport and Wood, had been interviewed on a total of over thirty occasions between them and many of these interviews had been at different police stations. This was harassment, not to say intimidation, since it would frighten the witness by implying that he too was a suspect. One officer, asked why the police hadn't gone instead to the witness, said cutely, 'Mr Wood was quite happy to come and see us.' In fact Mr Wood had testified to the court before Christmas that he was very unhappy indeed about it.

The notebooks also revealed that several intended witnesses had been extensively investigated themselves, including looking at their mortgages, banking and other affairs and even the affairs of immediate family to key witnesses. The significance of this is quite clear: there could be no possible association between a witness's private life and the alleged fraud, therefore the police were trying to get dirt with which to frighten or blackmail the witnesses into co-operating and signing statements which discredited me.

It even emerged that at the time of my arrest they had given consideration to who might be willing to stand bail for me and had gone to one man's home, surveyed it from the exterior and taken the registration number of his car. Mild though it may seem, this in itself was a serious invasion of privacy and Judge Sachs was rightly indignant. But by this time it was obvious he had little sympathy with the way the police had carried out their enquiry.

First on the stand was D Sgt Kenneth Caldwell. He was one of two men who were brought in towards the end of the enquiry, to get some action. He had been present for sixteen months and in that time knew of nine other officers, full-time, involved in investigating me. Hood worked out for the court's benefit that that came to a conservative ten years of police time (actually nearer twelve). Considering that there were several men on the case years before that, and making allowance for surveillance teams and other part-time back-up groups, not to mention police lawyers, accountants, drivers and other personnel, we worked out for ourselves that between fifty and sixty man-years of police time had been expended on this (ultimately) abortive attempt to get me convicted.

Like all his colleagues, Caldwell denied over and over being involved with the Stalker enquiry. Among the many contradictions to this claim revealed by his notebook was the fact that a Trafford nightwatchman had been visited several times, because it was believed that Stalker had been seen in a car close to one of my property sites. The report was clearly nonsense (what would it prove, even if he was?) but the surprising number of interviews show little less than an obsession with Stalker and his possible whereabouts.

On 15 July 1986 Caldwell was liaising with the West Yorkshire Police 're DB/JS statement'. Somewhat later, on 9 March 1987, he's at West Yorkshire HQ and engaged with DCI Robinson (Sampson's Number Two) 're current enquiry'.

He repeated time and again that enquiries in the business context had been carried out 'discreetly' (this was the man who had told Keith George, from Wimpey Homes Ltd, that I was guilty of drug-running and involvement of organized crime). When shown George's contemporaneous note to this effect, his comment was, 'There is little in that with which I disagree.'

I was also surprised to learn via Caldwell's testimony that my friend Angelo Dundee had at one time been a target. There was an attempt to assert that he was involved in drugs. Two detectives had gone to the USA to check out this angle though, predictably, it was claimed they had 'other business' and Dundee was a side enquiry. Apparently, members of the DIU also met with detectives from New York, at a hotel in Stockport, to try to get a lead on this matter. The reader can imagine the embarrassment caused when I prompted Hood to ask Caldwell if he knew that Dundee had been a guest of honour at a dinner at Chester House in 1984. Caldwell evidently was unaware of this.

We also had an opportunity to look more fully into alarming reports that police had been reputedly coercing or bribing criminals with their freedom, if they would put something damaging on paper concerning Stalker and myself. In Caldwell's notebook we found an entry for 26 November 1986, during the time he was investigating me, showing that he had visited a man called Francis Patrick Crawford in the central detention centre of the magistrates court. A second meeting had taken place on 28 November in Strangeways Prison. Crawford had just been arrested on fraud charges and was remanded in custody. He was obviously at his most vulnerable. Hood accused Caldwell of offering Crawford inducements if he would make up lies about me. Caldwell denied this and stuck to his story, unconvincingly. However, the wording in the notebook is quite clear: 're intelligence and current enquiries'. The reader is left to make up his or her own mind.

Tackled about the Co-op Bank, Caldwell lost his jokey arrogant manner and entered the amnesia zone at once. He had no idea what was said on these occasions; he couldn't remember. Some of the visits were 'updating' the witness Chadwick, he said. Chadwick was the man from the advances department so eager to dish it out to Bowley when giving evidence. There were a dozen visits in all and the judge was clearly perplexed that Caldwell should have gone in person, instead of telephoning. Hood was concerned that giving Chadwick data after taking his statement might influence his evidence. It was 'a common courtesy', claimed Caldwell, which is nonsense. Hood challenged him on the fact that the bank did not believe that the charge over my home, Wood Mill, was invalid, until Chadwick reported this was so to Gorvin, two days after signing his statement. This information must have come from you (the police), asserted Hood. On the face of it, it seemed that Chadwick, in his eager-beaver enthusiasm to get at Bowley, had allowed himself to become a dupe of the enquiry and was manufacturing and firing their bullets.

However, there was a slightly lighter side to this grim parade of mischief, which offered a little welcome relief. Britton was frequently followed, we learned. There were times when two detectives would get on the train with him at Davenport and 'tail' him into the office. Why this should be necessary, God only knows, though it goes some way to explaining where all the man-hours went. We were all amused to hear that, on one occasion, Britton went in the opposite direction, to visit another client, and the detectives, ending up on the wrong platform, missed Britton's train altogether.

The next man was D Sgt David Knowles, an obviously cold tough Special Branch character. Notebooks revealed he had visited Trafford town hall and the day after his visit Rangelark had been sent a letter from the town clerk with a fourteen-day warning that planning permission would be revoked on the Trafford site, unless replied to forthwith. Nothing had progressed in respect of the site for twelve months, no pressure or warnings; now this, all of a sudden. The inference is unavoidable. Knowles denied it and said his visit to the planning officer 'may have caused him to look again at the file and prompted the letter'.

Harder to talk his way out of was an entry concerning two men who had visited the Trafford planning office, expressing an interest in my land. Knowles, who by a remarkable coincidence was present at the same time (or was he tipped off by a 'mole'?), had taken their car registration number. As Hood asked, 'What possible honest motive could there be for that?' At first he claimed it was because he thought he was being followed but later admitted this had been a lie (on oath). Knowles had restricted the men's access to the file on the site but allowed them only 'the minimum amount that was required by law'. He justified this by saying he thought they were going to steal the documents. One was reminded of the lying fantasies that schoolboys get into, once they have started on a train of falsehoods, talking themselves deeper and deeper into the mire. I doubt if there was an individual in the courtroom that didn't realize this was an example of the interference with potential customers for our properties that we always knew had taken place but were now seeing proved.

Probably the worst evidence I had to face came from this man. In October 1988, his entries showed that he had gone home to change, collect a pair of binoculars, and motored to Wood Mill. There he had hidden in the bushes, to watch me and my family being evicted from our home. He had scribbled it all down, even a note about Beryl carrying out towels to the car. It was shocking, to think of police in the bushes, gloating at our misery. The excuse was that they needed to know where I was but it rang hollow and insincere: I was in Court at the committal hearing. Up to this point I had felt somewhat sorry for these men, seeing them being torn to shreds by the defence barristers and made to look stupid and shady. Not after that. Of all the emotional experiences in the five years I suffered, nothing came close to the impact of this revelation. I was gutted.

One very important entry concerned both Knowles and Caldwell. On 5 March 1987, there was another note concerning Lewis Chadwick, who eagerly reported to the police that he had been threatened by his then senior (head of the advances department) Henry Colyer. Apparently Colyer had said to Chadwick words to the effect that: 'You had better be right with what you said to the police because if Bowley gets off he'd be sure to sue the bank for a lot of money and that means you will get your arse kicked.' Furthermore, Colyer had stated that he didn't trust the police, neither did anyone else in the bank and Chadwick would be wise to do likewise. These were shrewd words by Colyer. Knowles had written them down eagerly, perhaps hoping for action against Colyer. The result was disastrous. It was quite clear from his expressions that Judge Sachs didn't like what he heard and Hood dates the start of the collapse of the police case from here. After all, the bank were supposed to be the injured party and yet their officers were saying they didn't trust the police.

Incidentally, this recorded exchange explains why Chadwick would
be an exceptionally willing prosecution witness. Also why Colyer was
never called, despite his crucial position.

D Sgt Keith Ware is another man I wouldn't like to be left alone in a
cell with. By another of the many curious coincidences in this story,
he had been involved in investigating the Pricerite long-firm fraud in
1983, along with DS Derek Burgess. He must have been present when
Bertlestein first alleged I was associated with the Quality Street Gang
and that a senior GMP officer was 'on a pension' which, in a way, is
where it all began.

Ware was the officer who dealt with my former manager at the
Moulton Street Precinct, Victor Roberts. According to him, Roberts
needed little questioning: he sat willingly and gave copious 'information' to the investigation in 1986. Remember, Roberts was the man
I once helped by paying for his engagement ring, wedding and
honeymoon and put a deposit on his first home, as a gift.

Ware himself had been present when Topping entered the bank in
December 1985. Asked what the visit was about, he 'couldn't remember'. It was incredible: he had been accompanied by his own supremo,
probably the only time in his career that head of CID would take such
a remarkable step, and yet his memory was blank.

At this point, he said that he had 'never been involved in investigating a deputy chief constable before'. Here, for the first time, a police
officer was saying that the Taylor enquiry was a Stalker enquiry. Ware
was a cold, hard man and not the kind to get flustered. Why had he
made this remark?

Subsequently, we learned a lot from Ware and his testimony. Hood
felt he may have been trying to give us something without jeopardizing
his career. I found this hard to believe from a man who had spent the
best part of five years trying to destroy me and put me in jail, despite
knowing – as he must have done – that I had committed no crime.
More likely, he was trying for a soft landing after the trial, in the event
that the police lost.

Ware dropped several bombshells. One was that there had been a
secret visit from an RUC high-up on 26 March 1986. Ware had been
detailed to drive him back to the airport, which in itself was unusual.
There were police chauffeurs. Presumably, it was all to keep it tight
within the small group who were in the know about Stalker. Coincident
with this visit had been a flurry of intensified activity within the DIU,
he said. Asked how senior the man was he wouldn't be specific, but
said 'above the rank of chief superintendent'. The obvious question

is: 'Could it have been Hermon?' In any case, it seemed to me, here at last, was valuable proof that my case was really about Northern Ireland.

Ware also told the court that on 26 September 1985, there had been an urgent call from the Chief Constable for progress reports from the DIU. This wasn't hard to explain; it was on 18 September that Stalker delivered his interim report to RUC headquarters in Belfast. The general thrust of Stalker's enquiry and its unrelieved criticism of policing in Northern Ireland would have become clear as it was read over the next few days. By 26 September, someone would be thirsting for action against Stalker. Once again, chronological details lead one to the inevitable conclusion that I was being targetted because of Stalker and his RUC enquiry.

In fact it was obvious by this time that it was never really an enquiry into myself about Stalker. It was an enquiry into us both, simultaneously. The search warrants and Access Orders had all been about digging for dirt on Stalker, exactly as Buckley had said. Thus, on the day that the urgent update had been called for, Ware's notebook says he made an enquiry at a travel agents 're: Taylor and Stalker'.

Ware, remember, had been present at the bogus search on my home. Significantly, he said he had not been asked to look for drugs. He had chosen to remove certain photos of the fiftieth birthday party because, they 'disturbed' him. He repeated this word several times. He denied having been instructed to look for photographs but, as Hood pointed out, those removed were very blurred and hardly a good likeness of Stalker. Ware also claimed to be 'concerned' when I had said (at the time) that Stalker was present until 3.00 am. 'So what?' said Hood. 'Mr Anderton is well known for attending parties.'

Hood called Ware's attention to the fact that, within weeks, the photographs had ended up in the hands of the West Yorkshire police and were the instrument of removing Stalker. Asked if he had known all along that the sham enquiry into me was really about Stalker, he said, 'I don't think when I arrived [in the DIU] anybody said we were there to investigate Stalker.'

'But it was obvious that was what was happening?' demanded Hood.

'Yes.'

Judge Sachs came in on this too: 'Did you feel uncomfortable in this enquiry?'

'Yes, many times.'

'Did you feel you were being used in any way?'

'Not at first. But in the end, yes.'

There were other admissions, such as an entry in the notebook for 16 June 1986, 'Britannia Building Society, enquiry for W Yorks'. Are we to ignore the coincidence that the Britannia was Stalker's building society? In fact it could be seen that much of Sampson's 'independent' enquiry into Stalker had actually been carried out by junior officers within the GMP, so incestuously linked were these two investigations.

Yet another notebook entry concerned following up the names of people who had been present at a Swinton Rugby Club social I had attended. Asked if it was an attempt to link Taylor in with some members of the criminal fraternity, Ware replied: 'You put it rather strongly, but yes.' The rottenness of the prosecution was now so evident there was almost a palpable odour in the court.

Ware gave us our most sensational day out of the whole sixteen weeks. We were wrung dry with emotion at the end of it and even hardened barristers were admitting they had never seen or heard anything like it.

Yet even with Ware, there was a light-hearted moment. Peter Birkett, cross-examining for Bowley, asked Ware if he had heard of Menorca, which he had, and the Hotel Castel Playa Fiesta, which of course he hadn't. Birkett then asked Ware what were the chances that a CID officer from GMP would '. . . just happen to be on holiday at the same time as Mr and Mrs Bowley, at the very same hotel?'

'Remote,' replied Ware, looking puzzled.

'Would it surprise you to know that Mr Topping was there?'

'I faint,' grinned Ware and threw his arms high in the air with a theatrical sweep.

Last in this quartet was DC Peter Hogg, the man Buckley describes as the most offensive and belligerent policeman he had ever had to deal with. His opinion of the majority of the men on my case is unflattering: heavy and unsubtle men, put on the case to crash through some kind of a result.

Asked by Hood if he knew that his nickname was 'Hotty Hogg' because of his reputation for intimidating witnesses, the man said, 'It's news to me.' But I doubt it.

Corkery tried to salvage this point by asking: 'Does it say anything in your notebook about threats?' Hogg's reply, 'I wouldn't write threats in the notebook,' was hardly a reassuring denial.

Five entries, in July 1986, concerned interviews with Angela Simpson, the fraud investigation officer of Amex. Hogg and another officer, Corfield, seemed to be the two men chiefly involved with Amex, though we know Stephenson had visited Angela Simpson, because of the telling entry in her diary, saying: 'Stephenson Manchester 10.30 re drugs Kevin Taylor'. The reader may recall my comment that her two statements, taken under the aegis of the Access Orders into my alleged involvement in a fraud, concerned only the details of my expenditures on the holiday with Stalker in Miami.

But, as at the committal, the man we all wanted on the stand was DI Stephenson. Even before he made his appearance, the court was aware that the main bricks in the police case were collapsing. Hood's ploy up to this point had been to go through each of the notebooks, pounding home the same points incessantly until the jury got indigestion: the Stalker connection, the heavy-handed prejudicial enquiries, the illegal entry at the bank and threatening of witnesses.

From here on, he had to adopt a different approach, or risk alienating everyone through sheer boredom. The resulting performance was later described by Buckley as 'an art form'. The sequence of questioning was quite deadly. Bear in mind that Stephenson had had forewarning of what was to come but it didn't help him. Hood came at him from the sun and, once he had started his man rolling, it went faster and faster.

Stephenson had to answer Hood's questions and yet, at all costs, stay away from any admission as to what was done at the Co-op Bank and other sensitive areas. His only weapon, of course, was to say 'I can't remember' and he used this over and over until the court were sick of it and I doubt one person in the room believed he really had such a bad memory.

Like the others, Stephenson wanted to dissociate himself from any Stalker connection. Yet entries from other notebooks had already shown him with dirty fingers, despite his ardent denials of this. What was particularly surprising was to read that he and Caldwell were at the West Yorkshire Police headquarters on 9 March 1987. We do not know what this visit was about but, on the face of it, Stalker was still being investigated seven months after his re-instatement.

His notebook contained an entry for 13 June 1986, saying: 'Research re current enquiry and liaison with W Yorks officers'. I have already remarked that it was obvious, by this time, that the DIU, along with the West Yorkshire police, were employed in investigating Stalker, and the denials that the target was Stalker were disingenuous.

We learned from Stephenson's evidence that, at the point when he was brought in (late 1985), all lines of enquiry had drawn a blank. His bosses wanted a 'result'. The drugs line had failed, so had organized crime, he admitted to Hood. Stephenson had to break through at the bank. In this perspective, the Access Orders assume enormous importance. It was truly a 'last ditch' attempt to get some dirt on Stalker and me, otherwise the case would have died then and there. Judge Sachs himself was very interested in this point: 'You are saying there was no evidence of a crime until the Access Orders were obtained?' Stephenson confirmed this was correct.

As a result of this remark and the fact that it became obvious that the case hinged around the dishonest obtaining of the Access Orders, Judge Sachs was to refer to 'the fruits of this poisoned tree', which gave me the title for this book. Stephenson admitted he was under pressure from his seniors to get a result 'one way or another' (one can imagine that the emphasis wasn't really as even-handed as this). He had a few documents from the bank which, in isolation, might be used to put together a shaky case. But he needed legitimate material and hadn't got any. So he chose to lie to a judge under oath, to obtain the all-important Access Orders, and for that reason, I have no sympathy with him or the fact that, in doing so, he wrecked his career. Even if one allows him this one crime, there was the fact that he had repeatedly used the 'drugs' lie to cheat his way into places where he would not otherwise have been allowed access, long after he knew that I was not guilty of any drugs dealing.

The Co-op Bank itself is a perfect example of this. By the end of 1985 Bowley had been transferred and the bank were hardening their attitude towards the enquiry. Bank inspectors had repeatedly told the police they had examined my accounts themselves and could find nothing wrong. Stephenson was desperate for them to make a formal complaint, even though they were unwilling, and tried to persuade them.

'It was difficult to get the bank inspectors to believe there was a fraud,' he said in evidence.

Hood: 'You worked on them?'

'Yes.'

We know that Topping had been present on at least one occasion. It turned out to be more than once. Asked why he had been present, Stephenson was vague and said he had wanted to 'introduce himself' to the bank. It was preposterous that the head of CID should be involved in a matter this trivial or need to visit the bank personally. He was obviously trying to put pressure on the bank, by virtue of his rank.

'Whose idea was it for Topping to go?'

'His own.'

'What sort of things did he say while he was there for two and a half hours?'

'I can't remember.'

'Was this a show of strength so that Mr Shepherd would give you the information?'

'No.'

'Did you mention drugs on your visit to the bank?'

'As an aspect, yes.'

'You implied Mr Taylor was laundering drugs money through the Co-op Bank?'

'It was one aspect.'

'But people laundering drugs money are trying to get rid of money, not borrow £60,000?'

'Yes.'

'Was organized crime mentioned?'

'It may well have been.'

'So you've visited the Co-op Bank three times thus far, the DIU four times, and now with the head of CID – to confirm that Mr Taylor is guilty of criminal deception and link him with drugs and organized crime?'

'Yes.'

All without a shred of evidence! Probably nothing shows the corruptness and evil intention of the enquiry better than the bloody-minded stubbornness with which Topping and his men had kept at it beyond this point. There was no case extant and no legitimate evidence, no complaint from the bank and they could not be persuaded that a crime had been committed.

But press ahead they did. In collusion with the bank's own officers, they obtained illicit documents with which to try and construct a story which would successfully get an innocent man in jail. To succeed, they themselves had to break the law, which they did with cavalier wilfulness.

A decisive question, which David Hood pressed relentlessly with Stephenson, was: what was the source of the valuations included as evidence in the submissions to Judge Presst for the purpose of gaining the Access Orders? These were by Thomas Holt, of Peter O'Hare Associates, and concerned the Poynton, Trafford and Tottington sites. If he confessed to having obtained them by some illicit means, then the prosecution case would be in deep trouble.

In fact these valuations could only have come illegally from the Co-op Bank or as a result of the burglary in my office in February 1985 (Chapter 5) but Stephenson referred constantly to his 'informant'.

When pressed by Hood, he kept saying feebly that it came from sources 'within the DIU'. This couldn't possibly be the case and Hood took him through each of the individuals in turn and Stephenson had to admit that it wasn't possible for any of his fellow officers to have come by the information in any legitimate way.

He then claimed it came from Peter O'Hare himself but detailed revelations from his notebook showed that, in fact, he didn't see Peter O'Hare until some months after this time. Another lie. Remember Stephenson was on oath. Hood kept bringing him back to the fact that he had got it from the Co-op Bank, but Stephenson adamantly stuck to his story that this wasn't the case, although at one point he did admit that it was 'a possibility'.

The man was clearly dissembling. Even the judge, cynically, suggested that perhaps the valuations had been picked up from the dustbin.

Victor Roberts was another suggestion. Whereas it was clear from the notebooks that Roberts had spent many hours with the police doing his best to destroy me with malicious accusations, by the end of 1985 he had not spoken to me for several years. He could not possibly be the source of information regarding transactions in the Co-op Bank and, in any case, would not have been in a position to supply valuations. Again, grudgingly, Stephenson was brought to admit that this was not possible.

Hood became very caustic about the mystery informant: 'Was it a male or a female?'

'Presumably male,' replied Stephenson.

'How is this "person" connected with the commercial world?' asked Hood.

'We were investigating commercial possibilities,' was his apology for an answer.

And so the questioning went on and on, and the replies took on this Alice in Wonderland quality. Eventually Stephenson lapsed into saying: 'I'm not certain where it came from. Nobody in the unit can remember where it came from.'

'They all seem to have had a memory lapse,' said Hood.

'Apparently so,' replied Stephenson.

Judge Sachs joined in: 'Have you ever seen this person?' he asked and Stephenson naturally said he hadn't.

Hood asked him: 'Did you tell the Recorder of Manchester, Judge Presst, you couldn't verify the documents?'

'No, I didn't.'

It hardly needs to be said that the wording of the Police and

Criminal Evidence Act demands a high degree of candour and truth in applying to a circuit judge for Access Orders. All 'relevant' information must be supplied.

The questioning then moved on. Stephenson's initial case was fabricated around the fact that the Tottington site was bought by Lacerta and not Rangelark. The bank had supposedly lent money to Rangelark for this sale (not true, see Chapter 4). Hood tackled him on how he came by this information. Stephenson claimed it was from enquiries at the planning department in Bury Council, but as Hood said, Bury Council could not possibly have led him to the Co-op Bank; although it would show that Lacerta had bought the land, it could not show that the Co-op Bank was financing it.

In any case, his notebook revealed that Stephenson's visit to Bury had taken place fourteen days after he had been to the Co-op Bank, so he had again deliberately misled the court.

By this time, it could hardly be said these lies were to try and make the indictment against me stick, since the case had collapsed. By now he was fighting for his own freedom, trying to avoid admitting anything incriminating, knowing well he could ultimately be indicted for his part in this shoddy conspiracy.

Asked whether he had told the Recorder of Manchester, Judge Presst, that the bank had made no formal complaint, Stephenson said he had told the judge verbally that this was the case.

Hood: 'You were asked at committal, and you said "I failed to tell the Recorder of Manchester the Bank had made no complaint."'

'I don't recall that.'

'You have just told this court that you did tell him.'

That afternoon Stephenson turned up with someone we had never seen before. Hood asked him: 'You have a gentleman in court; what is his role or function?'

'He's my son-in-law.'

'Does he have a profession?'

'He's a solicitor.'

Clearly Stephenson was a very frightened man at this stage.

Hood on the attack again: 'The Presst information says, in paragraph 23, there was an £820,000 indebtedness. Where did you get that information?'

'Dun and Bradstreet.'

Hood took him through this possibility step by step and it had to be eliminated. The judge then cleverly picked out that on 6 December 1985 there was an overdraft of £819,000; on 21 February, it was up to £840,000 and by 6 September, it was £820,000, 'the day after you visited the Co-op Bank'. The suggestion is clear that Stephenson was made privy to those figures by someone at the bank.

'I have no recollection of that.' (Hood felt phrasing it that way instead of a plain 'No' was significant.)

Then Sachs came on again: 'This isn't your first fraud enquiry. Where did you get that figure from? It must have been a source close to or at the bank. Well, where did it come from?'

'It sounds like the bank.'

'How did it come into your hands?'

'I don't know.'

'It must have come from the bank?'

'Yes.'

'And it came to you. Of that there is no doubt. How could it have come from within the bank to you?'

'I have no knowledge.'

Judge: 'You didn't carry it in your head. Are the papers destroyed? You only saw Mr Shepherd?'

'Yes.'

'It must have come from Mr Shepherd?'

'That is the inference, yes.'

'There is no other possible deduction.'

'No.'

'It must have been said prior to 27 February.'

'That's possible.'

'There is no other deduction.'

'No. But to my knowledge Mr Shepherd said nothing to me.'

Judge: 'Did you give Mr Shepherd assurances?'

'No Your Honour.'

Hood: 'There might be severe financial consequences for the Co-op Bank.'

'Yes, I am aware of that.'

Then, on Wednesday, 15 January, Stephenson turned up with a document about the Salford Aluminium Company which, he said, 'reflects on matters before the court'. By this stage, the strain must have induced in him a state of temporary madness, because by no stretch of the imagination was it relevant. Yet to bring it into court was to evaporate the last droplets of integrity he might have as an officer of the Crown, anger the judge implacably and hasten the collapse of the case. Once more one is reminded of Buckley's aphorism: guilty men make mistakes.

What transpired was that he had got this document by asking Ware something about the records available and they had had a conversation about it the night before, which was not allowed while evidence was being given (contempt of court).

Judge Sachs was shocked. He adjourned proceedings and recalled Ware. Ware said he couldn't remember any such conversation, but said he had learned about the case 'from the early evening newspapers' and had mentioned it to Stephenson. Questioned repeatedly, he was evasive and again fell into amnesia about events less than twenty-four hours before. No, there hadn't been any conversation, he said emphatically.

Judge: 'Sergeant, are you telling me that you pulled out papers and handed them to Mr Stephenson without any prior conversation with him, indeed, no conversation at all?'

'I'm sorry Sir, it was this morning. I showed them to Mr Stephenson knowing he had been to the liquidator.'

After more evasive replies, the judge snapped: 'This is a very serious matter Sergeant. Be frank and tell me everything that passed between you today and yesterday. Tell me.' These last repeated words contained more than a hint of exasperation, indicating Sachs was getting to the end of his patience with this dissembling.

'I didn't speak to him,' insisted Ware.

Eventually the judge gave up and rebuked him saying: 'You are an experienced officer and what you have done amounts to contempt.'

'I can only apologize.'

'I will consider what must be done about conduct which is wholly unacceptable. There must be no further repetition of conduct of this kind.'

'I was trying to jog my memory.'

'That is very, very unpersuasive.'

'I put myself in Your Honour's hands.'

'You can leave this court but may be required to return,' the judge told Ware and then, turning to leading counsel for the prosecution, he said angrily, 'Mr Corkery, I find all that very alarming.'

'No doubt my learned friends will use it as ammunition at the appropriate time,' replied Corkery, dismayed.

At this moment the judge sank back into his leather armchair, turned to Hood and uttered the words which I think I will remember best from the whole sixteen-week trial: 'Start shooting, Mr Hood!' This just about summed up the mood of the court at this point.

Hood resumed his cross-examination and this time, when asked if there had been any conversation with Ware, Stephenson came clean and admitted there had been an exchange both the night before and that morning, knowing it was contempt. This made a liar out of Ware and pointed up his own perjury of the night before.

We were now in the dying stages of the trial but, before events ran their full course, there were still more sinister happenings to come to light. Information sheets had apparently been used at the office of the DIU but these had been destroyed 'when the prosecution file was completed' (which of course it wasn't). It also transpired that notes from witness interviews had been destroyed. This is contrary to the attorney-general's guidelines and very suspicious conduct on the part of the police, to say the least. Other documents, he told us, had been incinerated. The similarity to the cover-ups of the Watergate Affair seemed too obvious to ignore and the defence was very disturbed by all this.

Asked if this was normal practice, Stephenson said: 'It was in this case, yes.'

I repeat the question, said Hood, 'Is this normal practice?'

'No it's abnormal practice.'

Stephenson then blundered into another quagmire. He claimed that he had been seeking additional information in files at the DIU headquarters.

'What files?' demanded Hood. 'You never mentioned any files over the last two days. You referred to general knowledge within the unit. There was no reason not to mention files.'

Judge: 'Why on earth didn't you tell us of their existence?'

Stephenson really squirmed and said: 'Because I can't find them!' It seemed there were supposed to be files in the office and files even in the corridor outside. All had inexplicably gone missing. Somebody was very frightened indeed.

The judge pointed out that documents should be kept until the case is concluded and said, completely amazed at what he was being told, 'I find it quite extraordinary. Some officer should be called from the DIU. I am very concerned.'

Stephenson ended the day, miserably and uncomfortably, still unable to explain the origin of the valuations used in connection with the deposition for Judge Presst. No one else in the unit could help him. White as a sheet, he said he'd been 'left holding the baby', a remark which found its way into the papers the next day.

That night, a few friends and I went to dinner in a restaurant in Westhaughton. Six men, including some we knew to be Special Branch, followed us there. Evidently there was desperation to try and keep alive the flagging trial, by finding some indiscretion on my part.

Next morning on 18 January, according to Judge Sachs' instructions, the senior officers of the DIU – Born, Waterworth, Murray and Richardson – were brought to court. Hood asked for their notebooks to be produced and it was clear that none of them wished to have them read. Born was particularly unwilling. The notebooks were heavily stapled.

Questioned first, Born and Murray denied any knowledge of the source of the Presst documents. But before this line of questioning progressed very far, the judge ruled that the cross-examination must be confined to the subject of the missing files and their whereabouts.

Each in turn denied knowing where the files were but said they hadn't been destroyed. Stephenson had been emphatic; there had been an incineration of 'unwanted' material. Born was the only one who said that information not relevant may have been disposed of but denied that anything had been burned. No one was willing to back up Stephenson's testimony.

When the senior officers had gone and Stephenson had returned to the stand, Hood asked him more explicitly what he had meant by saying he was left holding the baby. Stephenson had no answer.

'You are at variance from the testimony of so many senior officers,' Hood pointed out.

'I can't explain and I'm not going to try,' said a dejected Stephenson. By this time, he must have realized that he would be the target for all the censure and blame and that his seniors had cleverly manoeuvred him into the firing line. They had effectively distanced themselves from all that had been done.

The final run-up to the finishing line came, appropriately enough, in regard to the Presst deposition. It is fitting to recall that this is exactly as Buckley had predicted in 1986 and why he had fought so hard for so long to get sight of that document.

Hood first led Stephenson, line by line, through the Robson correspondence, piling on the agony excruciatingly, hammering home the fact that I had repeatedly offered to co-operate with the police. His victim wilted lower and lower, each word cutting him down like a dagger thrust. After this onslaught, Hood then returned Stephenson to the Presst deposition and the fact that in paragraph 27, he had sworn under oath that there was no likelihood of getting my co-operation.

By this time, Judge Sachs was ready to do battle and joined in the cross-examination. 'That was untrue, wasn't it?' he asked Stephenson.

'I believed it at the time,' replied Stephenson, white as a sheet.

'What was the basis for your belief?'

'It was not in Mr Taylor's authority to give permission.'

'But it wasn't true.'

'It was inaccurate.'

And with those words, the entire £10 million edifice of lies, bullying, corruption, innuendo, deceit, perjury, contempt of court, coercion, malice and subterfuge collapsed in total ruins. As Stephenson had admitted earlier to the judge in person, without the Access Orders there was no case. The Access Orders had been obtained by deceit. There was no case.

Hood here tactfully passed the mantle of honour on to Peter Birkett, who used the authority of his newly acquired silk gown to make a formal submission to the judge, that under his common law jurisdiction – not even his statutory powers under Section 78 of the Police and Criminal Evidence Act – the case against us be dismissed. Corkery was on his feet and made a desperate final effort to save the case and divert from the common law prerogative, by telling the judge that Section 78 of the PACE Act 1984 was full of complexities and not as simple as it looked. The final joke was on Corkery. As I afterwards found out from my barristers, Judge Sachs had sat on the committee which had drafted the PACE legislation. He was the most inappropriate man imaginable to complain to about the shortcomings of the Act.

Judge Sachs, who by now understood all the issues completely and had no illusions, stopped the trial 'to allow the prosecution time to consider their position'.

It was lunchtime. In a fever of anxiety we had no choice but to wait until the court re-sat at 2.00 pm. The rumour quickly spread that Corkery was telephoning the Attorney General for advice. Would they withdraw?

No one dared hope too strongly that, after five long years, the agony might be at an end. Nevertheless, a justifiable optimism allowed me to phone Beryl, who dashed to the court in time for the reconvening at 2.00.

Word seemed to have travelled like lightning on other channels: Granada TV cameras were standing by and reporters arrived in droves, including Mike Unger, editor of the *Manchester Evening News*, in person. Outside court four there was an air of electric expectancy.

Tension was heightened by a delay in re-starting. Apparently, Corkery's call was taking an inordinate length of time. Eventually, we all filed in and, as soon as the jury were reseated, Corkery took to his feet and told the court that, 'It would no longer be right to ask the jury for an adverse verdict against any of the defendants.' Sachs beamed and indicated he thought this was 'quite proper'. The indictments in respect of each defendant were read out and, as instructed by the judge, the jury foreman returned a verdict of 'not guilty' on all counts. The benches erupted with emotion. Beryl burst into tears and friends comforted her. Indeed, several sobbed with her. It was all over.

Judge Sachs thanked the jury and said a few flattering words to them, referring especially to their diligence and cheerfulness. Contrary to the defence's expectation, they had surprised us all by grasping every nettle and thorn of the case. Frequent notes to the judge asking sensible and searching questions had shown us just how perceptive they had been. Sachs excused them from further jury service for life.

Claims for costs were settled, particularly welcome in McCann's case. Finally, His Honour rose and took his leave of the Court. He was visibly moved and seemed almost to want to wave goodbye to his loyal jurors.

For me, Britton, Bowley and McCann, it was the end of a nightmare. We walked from the dock – free men.

15
The Aftermath

Outside, the TV cameras were waiting and I was asked for an impromptu interview. I could only think of saying, 'It just goes to prove it was a malicious prosecution from start to finish.'

In the meantime, the jury had gathered on the concourse in Crown Square and, unbelievably, they applauded as I emerged. A policeman was heard to comment that in all his years of service he had never seen a demonstration like it.

Inevitably, a party followed and the champagne flowed freely at nearby Drummond's Club. As word got around, we were joined by countless friends as they flocked in to wish us well. Imagine the surprise when several of the female jurors turned up, asking for 'poor Mr Britton'. Over a glass of bubbly, they explained they had felt especially sorry for him in his predicament. He was the only one of the defendants who didn't miss a day of the trial, but sat and listened to every single malicious word.

That evening TV news networks erupted once more with the Stalker case, and the whole issue, with its festering wounds, reopened as if it had been only yesterday. Stalker himself had plenty to say; as far as he was concerned, the collapse of my trial vindicated him.

On *Newsnight*, Sir John Hermon shocked us all again by saying that the police had withdrawn 'on a technicality' and that I hadn't been proved innocent. I've heard some hypocrisy in my time, but that just about took the biscuit, coming from a man himself so involved in Stalker's removal. Peter Snow had to remind him that I had been found not guilty by a British court of law and that what he was saying was totally insupportable on a public platform.

Next day, friends called me from far and wide, to say they had seen syndicated TV reports of the collapse of the case, broadcast as far afield as the USA, Australia and Switzerland. I even heard from friends in Zimbabwe that the front page of the *Harare Gazette* had carried the story of how I had defeated the British Establishment. That's how significant the Stalker case had been, internationally-speaking, and I only wish those who were guilty of its instigation and orchestration could understand just how much they have damaged this nation's reputation for justice and probity.

Topping was inevitably asked to comment for the media and, on 19 January, he was quoted in the *Manchester Evening News* as saying, 'the case had nothing at all to do with bringing Stalker out of Ireland. The investigation into Taylor was proper and correct and had to do with him alone. I have nothing for or against Taylor or his colleagues. I don't know Mr Taylor and have never even spoken to him.'

He added that the enquiry had started for 'the proper reasons. Information had come into our possession about Mr Stalker which was passed to higher authorities. There was an investigation into a number of matters concerning people in Manchester and out of that emerged issues about Mr Taylor's affairs which had warranted further enquiries. It is wrong and misleading to connect these matters with the Northern Ireland enquiry.'

He claimed they 'regularly assessed the evidence with great care because of the sensitivity of the connection – I stress, through friendship – between Mr Stalker and Mr Taylor.'

'It was decided by leading counsel to proceed with the prosecution of Mr Taylor. I have never judged if he is innocent or guilty. It was only for me to investigate.'

More humbug and propaganda.

Probably the most sensational new development after the trial ended was Stalker's claim that he had a document which he said proved there had been collusion among 'senior civil servants' to remove him. There was much speculation in the media what this might be. He was challenged by the Home Secretary, David Waddington, to produce his evidence. But Stalker seemed reluctant and said he wasn't willing to divulge his secret, unless to someone in 'proper' authority.

Eventually, he was given the audience he wanted with Waddington and it was revealed that someone had supplied him with a copy of the 18 May page from Hermon's diary for 1986, on which was scrawled 'A CC seeing BS, RA and TK and that DH was au fait with developments'. This was the day before the Scarborough meeting. TK is widely assumed to be Tom King, Secretary of State for Northern Ireland at that time; DH, Douglas Hurd, then Home Secretary. But who was BS? Barry Shaw was then DPP for Northern Ireland and many people jumped to the conclusion that it was him. But Hermon elsewhere refers to the 'DPP' by his office and not by name. Instead, *Private Eye* suggested that it might be Bernard Sheldon, then legal director of MI5 and now retired. If that was so, the impact is devastating. Might it not mean, as I have suspected all along, that the MI5 'dirty tricks' department was behind what was done to Stalker and me? This would explain the involvement of Special Branch in a very inconsequential minor fraud in a provincial city far removed from the events in Ulster. The utilization of MI5 services might also go some way to giving an understanding of the sheer magnitude of the onslaught against me and the prodigious use of resources, all to get a conviction on a trivial, supposedly unrelated matter.

Finally, who was RA? Everyone seems to think it was Robert Andrew, permanent secretary at the Northern Ireland Office, which is perfectly plausible. But it could have been Sir Robert Armstrong, then the Cabinet Secretary and head of the Official Committee on Intelligence. This body is made up of the most senior civil servants in the Home Office, the Ministry of Defence and the Foreign Office. At the time of Stalker's RUC enquiry this man was Britain's most senior civil servant. Even more significantly, he was one of the key architects of the Anglo-Irish Agreement, signed on 15 November 1985.

The important point, surely, is that Stalker's document doesn't really prove anything, except that there was a meeting. Beyond that, everything is pure conjecture.

An enormous anticlimax set in a few days after the initial fuss had settled down. For several weeks the thing I wanted to do most was sleep, which I did, deep and long. As the stress and pain eased, my thoughts underwent a profound change. Far from being jubilant at the collapse of the trial, I began to feel resentful that it had come to an end too soon.

It had been my goal to get the senior officers of the DIU onto the stand and make them accountable for their actions. I knew that what was in their notebooks would have devastating consequences for certain important people, if it ever saw the light of day. Obviously, this danger was recognized by the prosecution and I have little doubt that they were willing to withdraw their case rather than risk any further revelations. There were clearly some very frightened people and I've become increasingly bitter about the possibility that they might escape retribution.

Also, there was the matter of missing files and documents. It seems unlikely we shall find much incriminating material in the end; it will have been 'lost' or destroyed by the time I have my day in court. Accordingly, one of the first actions I needed to do was issue written warnings of our intent to pursue the matter and instruct the police not to destroy any documents or files relating to the case. After watching these men at work for many years, I have little doubt that they will seek to avoid or divert the process of the law and any just retribution it may bring. Certainly, they would not stop at further destruction of papers and notebooks and any other elaborate cover-up they thought they could get away with. If this happens, I can only hope that destroying the evidence will, itself, be seen by a fair-minded court as an admission of guilt. We shall see.

On Tuesday night, 23 January, I was guest of honour at the '400 Club' dinner, at the Midland Hotel. I found it very moving to be given a standing ovation. I only mention this event because it was at this dinner I learned from a serving police officer – who I'm sure would have had access to the truth and had no reason to lie – that I'd been chosen as a target to use against Stalker almost by chance. Senior officers had apparently considered possible action against two Irish businessmen in the city, also associates of Stalker. It had been decided not to attack these men, because their nationality would create an unwanted political dimension and, in addition, they were far stronger than me financially. So I was chosen. That's how brutally cynical the origin of my five-year ordeal had been.

On 29 January, Stephenson and Ware had to re-appear before Judge Sachs on the matter of their contempt. His Honour decided that they had been punished sufficiently by their public humiliation and they were let off with a reprimand. Outside the TV cameras asked me for comment and I said, 'I am satisfied with the verdict', but I was raging within. These men had been guilty of cheating and conniving to get me in jail and they were let off with nothing more than a slap on the wrist. I felt they should have been charged with perjury, at the very least.

But there was more to this. During the closing stages of the trial we had subpoenaed the notebooks of eleven officers. These were not used. We had also asked for the return of my photograph albums. John Bonney, defending Stephenson and Ware, appended a request to this contempt hearing, that we should be made to pay costs in respect of this subpoena action. It was outrageous and Judge Sachs, thankfully, refused. But the interesting point in all this was that, in the course of his submission, Bonney came to make a remark in which he found himself saying '. . . in the interests of national security, and Ireland . . .' He fell silent suddenly, when he realized the implications of his words.

A week later, Topping's contempt case came up in the High Court in London. Mr Justice Henry Brooke, brother of the Secretary of State for Northern Ireland and former Standing Counsel to the Attorney and Solicitor General's office, composed the panel with Lord Justice Mann, who I had faced before. Mann had refused leave for a judicial review of the Presst documents in July 1987.

In a curious turn of logic, their Lordships decided that the matter of contempt was academic, since I had been acquitted. This entirely overlooked the fact that, as it was explained to me, once a contempt action is begun, it must proceed perforce, otherwise the plaintiffs are liable for the costs. Imagine my shock, therefore, when the barrister for Topping successfully pressed for costs which were awarded against me, for which they could return if I ever earned money in the future.

It was little more than a heavy punitive fine for having the temerity to fight for my rights and it was particularly galling, since I believe the Attorney General was wrong not to take action himself against Topping and his publishers. I was, in effect, doing the Crown's housekeeping. The only consolation was that their Lordships did not find that there had been no contempt, which would have been too much to bear.

Within days of the end of the trial, an interesting rumour began spreading in the city: that the senior members of the DIU, all Masons, had put up only non-Masons as police witnesses, knowing that they would take the blame, if the case was lost. It may never be possible to prove this is true but it must be obvious by now that the Masonic influence has been endemic all through the enquiry.

At the end of it all, I suppose the reader will be looking to me for my views and some comments to summarize the outcome. I can only say I am at something of a loss in attempting to do this. In the end, it is not possible to comprehend what is incomprehensible and, to me at least, it defies any logic that an elected government of a free people should go about its affairs in such an outrageous and undemocratic manner.

Saddest of all, perhaps, is the way the Stalker Affair has corrupted so many police officers. Some of the men involved in what was done had been perfectly decent, until their involvement with the DIU.

Several of them, I know from comments made by lawyers with years' experience at the Manchester Bar, had once enjoyed the reputation of being upright and honest coppers, yet they had been drawn into the web of deceit and irretrievably corrupted.

Jim Anderton is a case in point: a man I had once admired unreservedly and considered a friend. I was very sorry indeed to learn of his part in the Affair. I began by assuming that what was happening within the GMP was a mark of bad leadership, that he was letting his men get out of control. It was only with all the facts on view that it became clear that he was more involved.

Yet, I find I have no axe to grind. Most policemen do a terrific job. I'm a very firm believer that most youngsters who go into the police do so with a real sense of vocation. Unfortunately, what happens is that the job corrupts, especially middle-ranking officers. They get to see only the worst side of life and some of them get tainted by it and they start to act like criminals, instead of officers of the law.

But of course this goes far beyond the police. There can be no doubt that those in Whitehall played their part. The unmistakable stamp of power is there in the profligate excesses of the enquiry. Yes, I believe that MI5 was involved but, in that sense, they too were probably no more than tools. What happened to Stalker and myself was nothing less than oppressive government; a gross abuse of the power invested in our leaders, for the furtherance of their own ends.

Nothing new in that, of course, but it's depressing to know that we now have it here, in Britain. Once we were the civilizing influence in the world and now we are little better than a dictatorship, despite all the cant about democracy. I've often heard it said that it doesn't matter which political party is in power, that this country is run for the benefit of about eighty families. Today, I believe that to be truer than ever.

During the five years of what must be the most expensive attempt at a frame-up of all time, I had become something of a 'part-time lawyer'. At least, I had in the sense of becoming aware of many issues and the way in which there had been a serious erosion of the rights and freedoms of the individual under the present government.

I have learned enough to be very concerned about the state of the law. There is no reason to suppose that what happened to me won't happen again, or go on happening. I only hope my fight may become a blueprint for those who, in the future, may find themselves faced with apparently insuperable persecution.

I think what this country needs is a major shake-up at the highest levels of the judiciary. There is a growing disquiet, reflected more and more frequently in the media, that so much authority should be vested in our Law Lords, many of whom are, to put it politely, ancient. Some are frankly senile. The time may have come to see them replaced by younger men, who are free of the 'ivory tower' mentality and more in touch with the realities of the everyday world. One man I would particularly like to see go is Lord Donaldson, the judge who put the Guildford Four behind bars. He implied I was a criminal in May 1989, when I had turned to him for relief from my troubles, and I have lived to see him proved wrong.

There was still one tantalizing question which remained unanswered to taunt us, as there is at the end of all good detective stories: why had Judge Presst asked for Stephenson's information to be sealed in an envelope? In the weeks subsequent to the trial, we learned the truth.

We were stunned to discover that the ubiquitous Mr Topping had been present at the application, along with Stephenson, and he had stated to the judge that the matter was one of 'national interest'. Topping had even directed the judge that no notes were to be made. A quite proper concern for security had been the reason that Judge Presst had wished to keep the papers confidential and, in this light, his actions seem entirely defensible. There was no national issue, of course. He wasn't to know at the time. It was simply a case of certain odious police officers lying to cover their tracks and prevent disclosure of their endemic role in a particularly nasty intrigue. Judge Presst must have realized he had been lied to as soon as the Stalker scandal became public.

The story began with Topping and now, it seems, it ended with Topping. In between was a plot of such sinister means and motives that it struck at the very foundations of the role of the police in our society. I am glad to have survived it but I am very sorry to have witnessed it.

Chronology

1932   2 January
                Taylor born in Salford.

1951/52   Serves in Korea.

1954   Discharge from army.

1954/1962   Various jobs, leading on to selling.

1962/66   Professional gambler in London.

1965   Marries Beryl Rooney.

1966   Taylor returns to Manchester and sets up Vanland.

1971   Taylor meets Stalker at PTA meeting.

1972   Taylor purchases the first plot of land at Moulton Street
                near Strangeways Prison.

1974   Purchase of his house, Wood Mill.

1975   Taylor visits Malawi, Kenya, Zambia, Botswana and
                Sudan.

1979   Taylor stands as Conservative in local elections.

1981   February
                Taylor buys *Diogenes* in Miami.

                June
                Taylor entertains four members of 'Quality Street Gang'
                on board *Diogenes* in Miami.

                December

Taylor and Stalker holiday on *Diogenes*.

1982   2 January
Taylor's fiftieth birthday party attended by Stalker and a number of men with former convictions.

6 August
Diogenes arrives in Puerto Banus having crossed the Atlantic via Salford.

27 October
Kinnego IRA landmine kills three RUC officers.

11 November
Thomond, Burns and McKerr shot dead by HMSU.

24 November
Tighe killed and McCauley wounded at hayshed by HMSU.

12 December
Grew and Carroll shot dead by HMSU.

1983   Stalker on Royal College of Defence Studies course.

22 August
David Bertlestein, alias Burton, makes a 206-page statement which associates Taylor with 'Quality Street Gang'. No crime is imputed.

1984   11 January
First meeting between Kevin Taylor, Britton and Terence Bowley of the Co-op Bank.

1 March
Stalker appointed Deputy Chief Constable of Greater Manchester Police.

21 March
Contracts exchanged re sale of Moulton Street Precinct to Viranis.

24 May
Stalker appointed to head of Northern Ireland enquiry.

9 June
Golf course conversation with McGourlay.

17 July
CS Topping submits confidential report to Assistant Chief Constable, Ralph Lees, concerning relationship between Stalker and Taylor. Report received by Anderton.

4 September
David Bertlestein sentenced to two years for Pricerite
fraud.

28 September
Completion of first stage of Trafford development.

20 December
Completion of Poynton sale.

1985   2 February
Diogenes into Dartmouth.

February/March
GMP interview Bertlestein in Preston Prison.
Special unit set up to investigate Taylor and his affairs
(Drugs Intelligence Unit), nicknamed Operation Ka-
looki.

March
Bertlestein dies in prison of natural causes. Anderton
informs Sir Philip Myers about the allegations relating
to Stalker/Taylor. Stalker requests access to tape and
transcripts.

1 April
Bill of sale of *Diogenes*.

2 April
Contracts exchanged on part of Tottington site.

9 and 10 April
Cheques drawn from Lacerta to Rangelark, Rangelark
to Propwise, and Propwise to Lacerta, after telegraphic
transfer of £85,000 from Barclay's Bank, Gibraltar.

22 April
Stalker writes again to Sir John Hermon, requesting the
suspension of two police officers.

29 April
Contracts exchanged on remainder of Tottington site.

7 May
Bowley effected draw-down of £240,000 to Rangelark
current account.

June
Stalker meets MI5 in London with Sir John Hermon.
DS Ware interviews Taylor's sister, Margaret Water-
house.

7 August
Taylor's twentieth wedding anniversary dinner at the
Mason's Arms, Nangreave.

9 August
Guy Robson writes to Chief Constable James Anderton
and tells him what is happening.

15 August
Superintendent Ryan replies saying more information
needed.

5 September
Guinness Peat offer £1.6 million for Trafford site.

6 September
Ryan writes again saying he can't help but the correspondence has been passed to CID command at force
headquarters.

8 September
DS Ware and DI Richardson attend the Co-op Bank
where they meet Hylie Shepherd.

11 September
Superintendent Machent writes to Robson saying it is
not possible to identify the officer involved.

18 September
Stalker delivers an interim report to Sir John Hermon.

26 September
Anderton calls for urgent progress reports on the DIU
enquiries.

15 November
Anglo-Irish Agreement signed in Hillsborough Castle,
Belfast.

24 November
Stalker attends Conservative Autumn Ball at the Piccadilly Hotel.

26 November
DI Stephenson first visits the Co-op Bank and speaks
to Hylie Shepherd.

3 December
Letter from Messrs Travers, Smith and Braithwaite,
solicitors representing the First Interstate Bank, reports
contact from DI Anthony Stephenson.

6 December
Robson spoke to DS Simons of the Commercial Fraud Squad on the telephone. Simons refused to reveal the exact nature of the enquiries but says they were now 'past tense'.

9 December
Guinness Peat deal falls through but Mayfair and City Properties now want to buy for £1.6 million.

16 December
Guy Robson writes to John Simons and is told the enquiry has passed by Kevin Taylor.

1986   6 January
Meeting with DS Simons and Guy Robson, secretly tape-recorded. Taylor first offered for interview.

13 January
Guy Robson writes to Anderton to complain.

15 January
Stalker reads Guy Robson's letter addressed to Anderton marked Private and Confidential. Stalker tells Anderton he is distancing himself from Taylor.

17 January
Reply received from Anderton supposedly dated 3 January. A second letter received dated one day later: Anderton will neither confirm nor deny that enquiries are being undertaken.

3 February
Robson writes back demanding an answer.

3 February
Anderton's reply to Robson's letter of 13 January promises if any interview is necessary Robson will be contacted.

7 February
Co-op Bank receives the Bernard Thorpe valuation, at £1.5m.

13 February
Hermon submits Stalker's Interim Report to DPP.

27 February
Stephenson applies for the Access Orders. Stephenson's affidavit stated inter alia Kevin Taylor involved in drugs.

28 February
Taylor encounter with Anderton at Variety Club of Ireland social at Piccadilly Hotel. Anderton claims Taylor made the first approach.

12 March
DI Anthony Stephenson obtains Access Orders to Co-op Bank, Access etc by swearing his Information in front of the Recorder of Manchester, Judge Arthur Presst.

24 March
Guy Robson writes again to Anderton concerned about the fact that the application was *Ex Parte*.

2 April
Anderton replies, finally admitting that there is an enquiry.

25 April
Robson writes back pointing out the help and co-operation offered on several occasions.

28 April
Anderton replies complaining about Guy Robson's letters, saying he is 'satisfied as to the propriety and necessity' of the investigations.

9 May
Search warrants executed on Taylor's home and offices, accountants' offices, solicitors' offices and elsewhere. Taylor retains Ian Burton, a solicitor.

15 May
CS Roberts reports conversation with Burton to Topping.
Topping writes a three-point minute which is later hotly contested by Roberts.

19 May
Scarborough meeting.

27 May
'The Last Supper'.

28 May
Stalker phoned by Robert Rees, Clerk to the Police Authority.

29 May
Stalker sees Colin Sampson who tells him he is removed from the Northern Ireland Enquiry 'for ever'.

30 May
Police Authority announces Stalker on extended leave pending investigation of alleged disciplinary offences.

16 June
BBC TV *Panorama* on Stalker: 'Conspiracy or Coincidence?'

30 June
Receiver appointed to manage Trafford site.

6 August
Sampson Report completed.

22 August
Meeting of Police Authority to discuss Sampson Report. Stalker reinstated.

23 August
Stalker resumes work.

12 September
Anderton appointed president of ACPO.

23 September
Taylor issues summons for disclosure against Anderton and GMP Authority.

10 October
Conference in Birmingham between Taylor and his lawyers. Leading Counsel advised there was sufficient evidence against Anderton, Topping and Stephenson to justify a charge of 'conspiracy to pervert the course of justice'.

14 October
Beryl Taylor acting for Rangelark successfully applies for a summons against Anderton, Topping and Stephenson on the charge of conspiracy to pervert the course of justice.

15 October
Application for disclosure of the documents used in obtaining search warrants heard by Mr Justice Scott. Application refused.

24 November
Anderton granted application for Judicial Review of summons brought by Beryl Taylor and Rangelark Ltd.

11 December
Anderton makes his controversial AIDs 'cesspit' speech.

16 December
Moors Murders re-opened.

18 December
Stalker resigns.

1987   January
Anderton gives his 'Prophet of God' speech.

4 February
Spanish police announce breaking of 'Octopus', drug smuggling ring, involving Alan Brooks, who bought *Diogenes*.

27 February
Hearing of Judicial Review (JR One) in front of Lord Justice May and Mr Justice Nolan.

13 March
Stalker finally leaves GMP.

3 April
Summons brought by Beryl Taylor quashed by Judicial Review.

13 July
Leave to appeal to the House of Lords against quashing of Bury Magistrates summonses refused.

13 July
Application for judicial review of Presst Information refused by Mr Justice Mann.

15 September
Bowley is arrested.

30 September
Taylor and Britton arrested on conspiracy charge.

5 October
Vincent McCann also charged with conspiracy.

4 November
Leave for judicial review of Presst Information granted by Lord Justice Parker and Mr Justice (Paul) Kennedy (JR Two).

1988   9 February
JR Two heard by Lord Justice Glidewell and Mr Justice French. Glidewell describes it as a 'breathalyzer attack' on the PACE Act 1984.

7 April
Application to European Commission on Human Rights.

18 September
Start of the committal proceedings.

October
Evicted from Wood Mill.

8 November
Committal concluded; all defendants go forward on all charges, without conditions.

1989   2 October
Trial of Taylor, Britton, Bowley and McCann begins.

December
European Commission on Human Rights rejects application.

1990   18 January
Sensational collapse of sixteen-week trial